P9-CDW-130

Praise for Jacobs' & Kelly's *Smogtown*

"Remarkably entertaining and informative...this book is just amazing, a gripping story well told." — *Booklist* starred review

"Historical heft [and] style delivers substance in true Hollywood fashion, with character-driven plots draped in glamour and sensation... the history of smog has never been so sexy." — *Los Angeles Times*

"In this tale of underhanded deals, gritty politics, community organizing and burgeoning environmentalism, the corruption is plentiful and the subplots replete with intrigue...the authors offer a zany and provocative cultural history." — *Kirkus*

"Finished with a particularly powerful, forward-looking epilogue, this friendly, accessible history should appeal to any American environmentalist." — *Publishers Weekly*

"A meticulous chronicle of the city's signature airborne grime and the civic and social forces that emerged to stop it." — *Bookforum*

"The narrative that emerges is more than a tale of a region and a populace besieged by smog; it is also a parable for a nation beset by environmental and social problems. Among the pleasures of this well-researched cultural history is revisiting the past." — *Slate*

"Well-documented, highly engaging and widely relevant... *Smogtown* is not your typical 'greens' diatribe against big business and weak government. No, Jacobs and Kelly are much smarter and fairer than that." — *Sustainablog*

One of Booklist's *top ten environmental books of the year; silver medal, Independent Publishers Book Awards and Green Book Festival; recipient of the Green Prize for Sustainable Literature; featured in* The New York Times, Author@Google, C-SPAN, *and elsewhere;* Sacramento Bee *bestseller.*

Praise for Jacobs' *The Ascension of Jerry*

"This is not just another Hollywood Whodunit. In the end we find it is really about one man's search and struggle to find his own personal truths and redemption. Well written and highly recommended."

—Steve Hodel, LAPD Hollywood Homicide
detective (ret.) and bestselling author,
Black Dahlia Avenger: A Genius for Murder

"Jacobs delivers a seductive tour of an LA rife with murder-for-hire plots, political corruption and sociopathic schemes. Against this backdrop the young Schneiderman comes of age, to ultimately emerge as the last man standing. A terrific book—I couldn't put it down!"

—Stephen Jay Schwartz, *Los Angeles Times*
bestselling author of *Boulevard* and *Beat*

"Chip Jacobs' chops as an accomplished newspaperman are on brilliant display in [this] delightfully off-kilter true-crime tale… Jacobs' prose is intimate, darkly funny, and crisp as he follows the twisted path…But here's the thing: Jacobs' ear for a good story is pitch perfect…*The Ascension of Jerry* isn't an old song in a new key, but an entirely new song about crime, fear, and a weird kind of redemption that could only happen in the general vicinity of Hollywood. Jacobs is a genuine writer, not a wannabe scribbler. He knows what makes us keep turning pages…"

—Ron Franscell, celebrated true-crime author

"Jacobs uses his boundless reporter's energy and well-honed sense of Southern California to tell a gripping tale of serial mayhem and the curious life of Jerry Schneiderman. It's reassuring to see the right writer was paying attention."

—David Willman, *Los Angeles Times* Pulitzer-winning investigative reporter and author of *The Mirage Man: Bruce Irvins, the Anthrax Attacks, and America's Rush to War*

"Chip Jacobs explores the underbelly of an LA murder-for-hire ring that leaves many dead and a successful space planner, Jerry Schneiderman, so affected by PTSD that he embarks on a widespread muckraking campaign that targets major political forces in Los Angeles and beyond. Pitched as a 'roots of Occupy story' (aside from Mark Twain's, of course)...*Ascension of Jerry*... will leave you closing your blinds and forever looking behind your back for the crazed psycho-killer disguised as an ordinary blue collar guy."

—*ForeWord Reviews* staff pick

"The pay for some deals is wonderful, but the drawbacks that can come along with it may be too much to swallow...*The Ascension of Jerry* is an enticing true tale of getting one's life back in the midst of...skullduggery, highly recommended."

—*Midwest Book Review*

Bookforum *title to watch; bronze medal, Southern California Book Festival; silver medal, Hollywood Book Festival; author highlighted on true-crime featurette on Lionsgate DVD for the movie* Sinister.

Praise for Jacobs' *Wheeler-Dealer*

"...With both dramatic flair and detached fairness, Jacobs eloquently reveals the soul of a charismatic and courageous character. Had Gordon's career taken place on the screen instead of behind it, he would have been the Christopher Reeve of his day."

—*ForeWord Reviews*

"...a brilliant and uplifting true story...highly recommended for anyone in a similar position or [who] has a relative there—to open their eyes to the possibilities."

—*Midwest Book Review*

"This amazing book is all heart...Jacobs blends the skills of an investigative journalist, the glitz of Hollywood, and the smooth storytelling of fiction to weave a profile of his larger-than-life uncle that will leave you crying, laughing and gasping in wonder, often on the same page. Bravo!"

—Denise Hamilton, bestselling author of
Los Angeles Noir and *Savage Garden*

"Readers looking for a glamorous Hollywood story or a tale of gentle uplift should be warned: This is not that book. Instead, Chip Jacobs has written something far better—a witty, clear-eyed account of a charming and utterly impossible man whose ferocious willpower transformed his personal nightmare into a lifelong Technicolor hallucination."

—A. J. Langguth, bestselling author of *After Lincoln*

"FDR's body and Sammy Glick's brain? No, but close—and better. *Mon Oncle d'Amerique* has nothing on Chip Jacobs' Mon Oncle d'Hollywood, the picaresque, quadriplegic Gordon, who is at least as good a story as anything he helped to put on film... Gordon is a premiere citizen of Hollywood As She is Spoken—unsentimental but believing utterly in the art of the possible."
—Patt Morrison, award-winning columnist

"...Jacobs has documented a marvelous life, and done so without the sentimentality that ruins so many life stories of people with disabilities ..."
—*The Internet Review of Books*

"It will make you laugh, it will make you cry, and it will make you want to turn your dreams of the impossible into a reality..."
—Andrea Dimech, *Action Online*

Bronze medal, Hollywood Book Festival

THE PEOPLE'S REPUBLIC of ~~CHINA~~ CHEMICALS

THE PEOPLE'S REPUBLIC

of ~~CHINA~~

CHEMICALS

by William J. Kelly and Chip Jacobs
A Genuine Vireo/Rare Bird Book

This is a Genuine Vireo Book

A Vireo Book | Rare Bird Books
453 South Spring Street, Suite 531
Los Angeles, CA 90013
rarebirdbooks.com

Set in Minion Pro
Printed in the United States of America.
Distributed in the US by Publishers Group West.

10 9 8 7 6 5 4 3 2 1

Publisher's Cataloging-in-Publication data

Kelly, William J., 1953–
    The People's republic of chemicals / by William J. Kelly and Chip Jacobs.
    p. cm.
    ISBN 9781940207254
    Includes bibliographical references.

1. Air—Pollution—China. 2. Air quality—China. 3. Environmental policy—China.
4. Environmental management—China. 5. Economic development—Environmental aspects—China. 6. Climatic changes—China. 7. China—Environmental
conditions. I. Jacobs, Chip. II. Title.

TD883.7.C6 K45 2014
363.739/20951 —dc23

Also by William J. Kelly

Smogtown
Home Safe Home

Also by Chip Jacobs

The Vicodin Thieves
The Ascension of Jerry
Smogtown
Wheeler-Dealer

This book was composed through secondary sources (books, journal reports, newspapers, magazine articles, blog posts, etc.), direct interviews with people listed in the reference section and William's trip to China in Summer 2013. Monetary values listed in material from secondary sources have not been updated to current values. In a quick note about names, the Chinese, as do many other Asian cultures, list their family names first and given names last.

CONTENTS

PREFACE:

CHINA OR CHOKE

SOMETIMES IN LIFE YOU pick the job, other times—as in this story of treacherous air that didn't need to be—the job picks you. We'll be blunt here. As much as we enjoyed sitting down with you before, we never imagined narrating another murky yarn of atmospheric pain and karma. Please don't be irked. Nothing personal. It's just that we'd believed, as self-deputized gumshoes covering this beat, that we'd said enough. In *Smogtown: the Lung-Burning History of Pollution in Los Angeles*, we'd figured that the vaporous scourge predating Shakespeare's era was creeping toward worldwide extinction early in the twenty-first century. Sure that nauseating, grey-brown cloud from an oversaturated sky would loom occasionally, particularly in third world countries boot-strapping their way to a brighter day, but nothing endemic. Today's unlucky victims, gaunt faces often sputtering for breath in morphine fogs, would be the last shoveled into graves needlessly. In our minds, the beast lacked the staying power for reincarnation across the Pacific Ocean, positioned sweetly to stalk millions. Not after a half-century of excruciating learning in our own boyhood town.

But stay it has. And it's deadlier than ever.

Let there be no doubt, all the same, that California had begun smog's obituary. As our book recounted, the marauding fumebanks that smothered whole communities in perpetual exhaust particles and industrial flotsam from the forties on—that grimy smudge that rendered Los Angeles at once national laughingstock and giant medical experiment—were mainly nostalgia by 2008. Ambitious regulation wed with public insistence on a healthy airshed had licked the worst of it. Newspapers had long stopped publishing front-page smog forecasts. Harebrained citizen's schemes to pipe face-stinging air through astronomically expensive smog sewers, or vent holes dynamited through the peaks of the San Gabriel Mountains, could be lithographs for an offbeat museum. Even the unlikely crusaders we'd sketched—the twinkle-eyed, university biochemist who proved Southern California's beloved cars, not industry, were primarily responsible for chunking the atmosphere; the bouffant-haired mother activists who needled the male establishment with skull-and-crossbones cakes and political ingenuity into accelerating the cleanup—had faded to something less than wax figure status themselves. In short, the trauma inflicted by decades living under the chemical dome of our own suburban, freeway-centric indulgences was on the skids. The paramount word in our title, as such, was *history*. As in done.

The hot mess of global warming evident in ferocious weather and disappearing shorelines commanded the nail biting when *Smogtown* appeared, and rightly so. What more was there to unpack about its photochemically charged ancestor? Los Angeles' expertise, be it with rulebook-savvy or chemical inventories, was there for everyone to adapt. No magic attached to the science. The phlegmy past did not have to be prologue.

Now we realize that we must've had hydrocarbons on the brain. The aerial misery that globalized manufacturing grafted onto Asia since the nineties, with sieges of barreling smog often laced with exotic toxins, was a drone strike on our hopefulness. *Poof. Dead.* With it went the exhilarating notion, ours alone maybe, that developing nations could sidestep decades of assault by unpocked air, water and soil. Money debunked all of that. Air pollution, turns out, wasn't an environmental Aristotle there to arm us against climate change. It was collateral damage to be finessed until the carousel of profits from dirty manufacturing was no longer worth the blowback for the pinstriped men in charge. In China's case, low-wage production and feeble workplace and environmental regulations became industrial Viagra that foreign manufacturers could not stop popping. US-Sino trade relations, long so chilly, thickened into codependency, and the millions of American blue-collar jobs transplanted to the Far East may be lost for good. But examine what constitutes "good." While a green spirit infuses much of everyday life in the first world, the People's Republic has descended into a toxic state unparalleled in recorded history, partly just to stock Targets and other retailers with all the iPhones, hoodies, and bedazzled St. Patrick's Day hats they can sell.

Remember the cheeky humor and whirlwind cleanup preceding the Beijing Summer Olympics? We do. *Smogtown* had just gone to the presses as China's jubilant, one hundred million dollar Opening Ceremony electrified a worldwide audience with its buffet for the senses. Against a packed house winking with camera flashes, 15,000 performers banged drums with Day-Glo sticks, metamorphosed amoeba-like into a calligraphy scroll, recreating the country's past with militaristic precision and gravity-taunting acrobatics whimsical to behold. Only a few decades after baptizing itself in a state-capitalist economy that must've had Marx and Lenin twitching in their crypts, China was never cooler as an international destination, never more neon, nor more primed to exploit it. The Games were its platform to rebrand itself as something nobler than a GDP wonder-machine. The Asian Tiger, strutting like a superpower, had put a little Las Vegas into its soul for a coming out bash centuries in the making. Goose bumps abounded.

By effectively spending roughly one billion dollars per Olympic day on a catchall regimen torn from a tree hugger's manual—new rail lines, factory mothballing, tree planting, no-drive-days, *et al*—the capital achieved decent enough air during the Games to inoculate itself from foreign ridicule. Michael Phelps, Usain Bolt, and the other athletes lucked out. Generally. It was in the years afterward as the data piled up with the casualty count that *we* took stock of what we'd underestimated. China's Olympic razzle-dazzle had zoomed past Potemkin village metaphors and right into soupy catastrophe.

One day in winter 2011, as the US economy circled the drain and Occupy Movement tents flapped, we crinkled our brows and searched our green souls. Whatever divergent paths we'd taken since our book *Smogtown,* the horror-show contamination in which Asian cities dripped in a witch's brew of poisons from a supposedly bygone menace infiltrated us, too. Didn't we owe our audience a dot-connecting explanation? Was the West Coast's marathon arm wrestle with its troposphere merely a table-setter for this assignment? Rising juggernauts like China and India were asphyxiating their populations in starbursts of industrialization and urbanization at levels that practically shattered their air-monitoring devices. To exhume the plenty we didn't know about smog's second act there, we did what came naturally. We harvested archives. We consulted PhDs. We Googled until our fingers tingled.

Then we gasped

The number of Chinese succumbing annually to preventable smog deaths effectively matched the number of people killed in the US on 9-11 *every day of the year*, never mind the masses perishing from indoor air pollution or ingesting water flecked with heavy metals. Full-blown ecological ruin was not just bristling in the so-called "factory of the world." It'd crashed through its tipping point with a macabre thud. Consider this. As the Chinese rooted on their Olympic athletes at the Blue Cube swimming arena and other venues hyped for their eco-bells and whistles, only one out of one hundred of their fellow citizens inhaled air that met international health standards. From costal Guangzhou to inland Lanzhou, millions of people writhed with heart and lung disease or cancers roused by one simple act. They ventured outdoors.

Just like Southern Californians in the fifties, though, average Chinese by the tens of thousands have shrieked no more, defying authorities quick to stomp out dissent with beatings, sham imprisonments, and Web censorship. Create too much fuss and they'll make you disappear. But watching loved ones waste away and local nature crumble awakened something heroic. It tapped into a well of scrappy disenchantment over how the economic revival that lifted some 300 to 400 million out of poverty had exposed far more to boom-time toxins.

Grassroots protests against dirty industry in which villagers battle riot troops armed with tear gas and batons in wild, oft bloody confrontations have skyrocketed since 2000. Whether they're wisps of an Eastern Arab Spring or something sub-revolutionary has yet to crystallize. What has presented itself is the depth of the crisis. One white-hot manifestation is China's nearly 500 cancer villages, manufacturing hamlets where remarkably similar illnesses are felling neighbors in shockingly high proportion. Normally spawned by water contamination in remote towns run by factory bosses, these death zones have sledgehammered families and generational dreams, obliterating along the way any lingering fairytale that all would ride China's rip-roaring GDP to happiness. Cancer for years now has been the number one cause of death in the People's Republic, up immensely since the eighties. "Before the factories were built…we were free of strange diseases," said one man who lost his father and aunt after his village stream was tainted by a nearby paper mill and chemical plant.

In recent years, Apple and other iconic American multinationals that outsourced work there have drawn outrage over their own suppliers' environmental sins. Universal denunciation might've been shriller, but the lower-priced goods their customers depend on have propped up a US middle class hobbled for decades with inert wages. Every minute of every day during the mid-2000s Americans purchased about 460,000 dollars worth of Chinese goods in a cash register reminder of the world's redrawn industrial pyramid. Some of that merchandise was assembled at slapdash facilities perfumed with noxious compounds that we wouldn't let our pets get near. And that isn't the end of it. A third of the country's carbon dioxide emissions belch from factories churning out shippable exports. So there is a thread-line between that microwave oven warming your coffee and the charry vapors that stewed around its creation.

Anyone brushing off China's suffering as somebody else's ecological trouble might want to buttonhole a climatologist. In coming years, the butterfly effect is threatening to feel pterodactyl. Scientists for decades have nervously eyeballed a phenomenon known as the "conveyor belt in the sky," the tropospheric drift across the Pacific Ocean of China's factory pollution as well as Gobi Desert dust in increasing volumes. Asia's vagabond detritus is probably closer than you realize. It's fuzzed visibility in national parks, deposited mercury in US waterways so fish in them are unsafe to eat, tripped West Coast air quality warnings, and upended worldwide weather by turbo charging storms and polar region warming. One Chinese swirl reached the US with a dimension exceeding the Grand Canyon.

Of all these consequences, it's the higher altitude ones that well may be the most terrifying for the planet's future. China's coal-burning gluttony is of such magnitude that it devours nearly as much of the rest of the globe. By banking so heavily on the "black gold" to leapfrog out of its locked history, the country is by far the single biggest emitter of the mainstay greenhouse gas carbon dioxide. Whether global warming sails past the disastrous precipice that gives scientists insomnia could well pivot on the nation's willingness to wean itself quickly from coal—and whether others with economic stakes in the eternal fuel allow it.

In sum, the marvel lionized as "China Inc." has become a toxified netherworld that'd leave Rachel Carson, author of the cautionary *Silent Spring*, tongue-tied. Slice sampled, it's a nation where three of the globe's most air polluted cities once lay on the same list as radioactive Chernobyl; where acid rain gnawing at respiratory tracts, crops, and buildings regularly soaks one-third of the land; where hordes of children are unaware of the sky's organic color or are perpetually ill; where jumbo jet turbines wear out freakishly fast from corrosive particles; where a new coal plant large enough to electrify Dallas once debuted every ten days and where, without far-reaching change, some economists project the smog calamity could escalate an inconceivable seventy percent by 2025.

Given the hazy brotherhood between Los Angeles and Beijing, it was only a matter of time before their ironic rendezvous. April 2013 found Jerry Brown, in his second stint as California governor, in China selling a picnic basket of the state's environmental know-how. "We're not interested in politics," Brown, the Q-tip-bald maverick, said at a swanky restaurant that four centuries earlier was the redoubt of a Qing Dynasty prince. "We're interested in business." Less harmful gasoline, cleaner power plants, trash-to-energy technologies, and such could be California's export to a faraway land gagging on its own prosperity.

But what about us? The Great Smog Sequel, was hardly writing itself. Al Gore, eco-demigod, wasn't volunteering. Academics hunker down on technical angles that social historians like us weave into fabric. So, psychically, we wrestled with dilemmas that begged reconciliation. With *Smogtown,* we'd danced to the creature's demise, only to appreciate that we'd been carnival barkers of a victory that trillion-dollar free trade blew to smithereens in the mystic empire that had graced civilization with printing, the compass, gunpowder, and other inventions eons before Europe's gilded thrones had begun to rustle. Silence meant surrender. We couldn't, not with our octane personalities. Bloodshot eyes and all, we leapt in. We'd give the People's Republic the LA treatment.

Studying Beijing, our jaws dropped further than anatomically possible. On harsh days there was an inhalation gauntlet to be survived rather than a pageantry of dynastic landmarks to soak up. The ashy overhang in a legendary bicycle mecca was partly due to China's gushy affection for the internal combustion engine, which welcomes more than 1,000 new vehicles each day to the city's gridlocked roads. Pollution attacks resistant to government countermeasures cloaked gaudy high-rises a hundred yards away while routinely sending thousands to emergency rooms in wheezy distress. Public outcry for aggressive cleanup and transparency is mounting despite pervading consumerism and pushback from the masters of resistance—state-controlled utility oligarchies and provinces getting rich off industry. Nonetheless, after years of fudging and deception, the Politburo has vowed it's gotten the message.

Until then, facemasks are often mandatory in the metropolis that cutups tag "Greyjing." Many follow the US Embassy's pollution-index Twitter feed, which briefly soured US-Sino relations, and once read "crazy bad" during a siege. Experts queried whether they'd prefer breathing New York's air after 9-11 seeped it in jet fuel and toxic fragments or Beijing's air chose Manhattan's. Fact is that smokers' lounges at times are less unhealthy than a few gulps of China's finest.

To find out why, Bill touched down in Beijing in summer 2013. He got an immediate whiff of acrid sulfur walking out of the plane before sunrise to wearily walk through the massive airport toward customs. Customs and immigration agents looked stern in pressed uniforms, but interacted with incoming passengers in a hurried, mechanical-like fashion. Finally curbside, China's industrial haze came into full sight as Bill met the driver. They began to creep through a sea of rush hour traffic into central Beijing where people scurried to work on foot and by bicycle. Soon, Bill boarded a bullet train to whir at 200 miles an hour to Qufu, home of Confucius. It was there, gazing into China's past, that he began searching for clues into what arguably is the greatest environmental crime in human history. He went into Anhui and Jiangsu Provinces to the south to meet with provincial and municipal officials and crossed paths with fast-paced businessmen. He sought to gauge their attitudes, which loom so large in this story of ecological plight. Next, he flew west to the heart of China's coal country. Then he traveled by land through smoky Shaanxi and Shanxi Provinces, where coal creates fabulous fortunes. Finally, it was back to Beijing into the fog-like atmosphere of an increasingly common summer pollution episode.

As Bill wandered Tiananmen Square and met with people in this city both ancient and futuristic, he found there's little doubt that the dark, aerial curtain is beginning to get to even those inside the Great Hall of the People. It's there that China must draft a new energy blueprint to not only slash the murk that sometimes canopies over two-thirds of the nation, but also a growing cloud of greenhouse gases. Only those privileged suits with special air purifiers can decide whether to go forward with a Leviathan expansion of the nation's coal production in the shadow of Inner Mongolia, Genghis Khan's old stomping grounds circa 1200. It's here that the future of climate change may hinge. Just as once-restive Californians came to appreciate, Asia's braintrust must recognize that a nation breathes its choices. Except this time we're all going to be living with it, wet or dry.

Again, we bring you this saga because we've lived it in Los Angeles—the dreariness, the silent casualties, the incessant blame-mongering, the madness of a sunless existence. Our hometown lungs remember every painful breath. So, here's our oath. We're following the crud that had no business sticking around to its true green source, the money that makes the smoggy world keep spinning.

CHAPTER 1:

THE EMPIRE CENTER

IN MAY 2007, A frowning Chinese grandmother in black pants clutched a child in her arms against a sheet metal sky, baffled in her grief. The lurking poisons that buzz-sawed Qiao Xiaoling's family far from Beijing were a mystery to her, an unapprehended killer even. Was it the scraping air, the bitter-tasting water, maybe toxic motes hidden in the rice? With so much illness from the clanking wheels of commerce in this energy boomtown of the New China, you'd need a mobile lab packed with epidemiologists to snatch the answer. For the sixtyish woman from Linfen with graying, short, cropped hair, all that painful unknowing framed her face with a kind of granite sorrow. Qiao looked like she'd cried herself dry.

Leukemia had first taken her husband. Lung cancer next grabbed her thirty-four-year-old son, saddling her with his apple-cheeked three-year-old to care for in this valley of chemical hegemony. Salvation would be escape from the pathogens spritzing around her little brick place if only there were a plane ticket. "I'm scared in my heart and worry about this little boy," she confided to NPR. "I think about moving, but I don't have the money." Her dead-end choices, a common dilemma for many in a generation that outlasted war, famine and purges, was the antithesis of some reclining nearby in well-appointed offices. For them, grimy air signaled slag heaps of money inching higher.

People of a certain age remember Linfen wasn't always like this, slicked in coal grease and factory ash. Once it was Valhalla in the outdoors, fragrantly green. The city on the banks of the Fen River Valley 470 miles southeast of Beijing was cherished for its spring water and fecund agriculture. Its moniker was "The Modern Fruit and Flower Town," a place where the cobalt skies stretched forever. Sightseers tromped in to explore the Hukou Waterfall a few hours drive away and, even closer, a historic temple with an exquisitely preserved glazed pagoda. Legend has it that 5,500 years ago, amid the hawthorn trees, a wise, if malnourished man named Yao altered the course of history here. Yao dug a water well that enabled the Han tribe to settle around it, where Linfen eventually became China's first hub. Even today, the hills surrounding the Shanxi province city are finely brushed in green trees and, sometimes, dreamy mist. Their gentle, well-worn peaks are not the soaring, rugged outcroppings characteristic of America's west of the Rockies. They're more comparable to the Appalachian Mountains rippling through the US's own grungy coal country.

China's indefatigable hunger for energy brought a touch of that West Virginia miner ethic to Linfen. Along the way its civic personality coarsened, morphing from tender flowers and crops to extracting what some Chinese cooed was "money in the ground."

A trio of coalfields with tens of billions of tons of reserves hard-packed into the earth was the object of everyone's ambition. All that untapped energy was too tantalizing to resist in a country ravenous for fuel, not just to stuff Tran-Atlantic cargo ships with pallets of manufactured goods, but also to construct pretty much everything for its own citizenry. Before long, inky smoke spiraled over the mountain-encircled basin ideal for trapping pollutants with a meteorology resembling Southern California's. Illegal, private mines were tunneled alongside approved ones. Lusting to make their own money, other heavy manufacturers in the zone treated metals and chemicals.

Coal, however, studded itself as the region's blockbuster product. Unlocking it even commandeered the sky. Between emissions from power plants, industry and heat-shimmering tailpipe exhaust, Linfen, with a 4.4 million population, turned into a smog punch line of the new millennium. "If you have a grudge against someone, let this guy become a permanent citizen of Linfen," an environmental expert once said. "Why? Punishment."

Come the mid-2000s, Linfen's lower atmosphere was downright volcanic in texture, recording only a fraction of days in which air quality attained standards. Morning commuters often needed their headlights to slice through the brume that reddened eyes and scalded throats. Coal trucks rumbled 24-7 down its roads, some of them only recently paved. From their payload bays, dark granules tumbled out, where they were pulverized by traffic at street level and then uplifted with dust into the air. Carbon grit was the municipal cologne. In Beilu Village alone were a coal plant, a coke oven, a power station, and a pharmaceutical factory. Car dealerships on Linfen's outskirts flourished from the action, netting some of the highest sales in a nation that can't get enough cars.

Previously a lightweight in coke production from coal, the People's Republic was racing toward making half the world's supply of it. As the US and Europe weaned themselves from fabricating coke-fired steel, Linfen and similar cities gladly picked up the slack. Leaden skies were tacit in the bargain. For Linfen street sweepers palming tree branches to brush away endless coal dust, all that dirty work was a full employment act.

The thrumming energy industry certainly translated into frenzied schedules for local doctors and morticians. In the city's most polluted districts the fatality rate for people fifty-five and older was ten times China's national average. Cancer sometimes felt infectious in the tropospheric mixology of smoke and vapors, hunting down scads of people aged thirty to forty. Residents complained of retching on what they inhaled, of black film coating their hands and faces. People who avoided lung cancer had to dodge bronchitis and pneumonia, lucky them. Mothers in the coal belt kneaded their hands over what awaited their children. At 8.4 percent, Shanxi suffered the planet's highest birth defect rate. One malformation tripped by in vitro exposure was so gruesome— as in disconnected brains—that some parents must've prayed for the Creator to take their offspring before it suffered a life hardly worth living. Overall, spending a day here, inhaling sci-fi dark air, was equivalent to puffing three packs of cigarettes.

Greetings from China's Chernobyl, a tongue-in-cheek allusion to the catastrophic 1986 nuclear-plant meltdown in the former Soviet Union that released 400 times more radioactive material than the atomic bomb dropped on Hiroshima. The World Bank during the 2000s embedded Linfen along with sixteen Chinese cities on its list of the globe's twenty most contaminated towns. Just by themselves, Linfen's carbon emissions were enough for the Blacksmith Institute, a New York-based environmental group focused on developing nations, to classify it as one of the ten most polluted cities *anywhere*. Besides Chernobyl and Linfen, others in Blacksmith's infamy included Dzerzhinsk, Russia, a former Cold War chemical-weapons manufacturing site; Ranipet, India, the location of a onetime tannery facility; and Haina, Dominican Republic, an old battery recycling center. Summarizing what others wanted to sob, one Linfen resident said, "We ruined Mother Nature."

Roughly 200,000 people closest to industry, according to Blacksmith, were most vulnerable to the downside of the town's manufacturing riches. Hovering above them and in them were hydrocarbons, lead, arsenic, fly ash, carbon monoxide, and particulates. Yet Linfen had national competition in one arena. The World Bank lumped it in with Tianjin, Chongqing, Shenyang, Zhengzhou, Jinan, Lanzhou, Beijing, Chengdu, Ahmedabad, Anshan, and Wuhan in its grouping of the *most* particulate-walloped cities anywhere. Even so, Shanxi province functioned like China's national furnace. And Linfen, where acid rain makes the dissolving walls appear like they're weeping mascara, is its Big Bertha. "Black isn't a shade in Linfen," explained one writer. "It's the entire palette."

As is their duty, the apparatchiks tried putting Linfen's best face forward. Thinking tourism, they built a plaza garlanded with replicas of the Great Wall and Tiananmen Square. In 2005, the Miss Universe bikini pageant was hosted here. The charcoal reality—leafless trees, blaring truck horns, terminal diagnoses—continued unabated, blasé to window dressing. The Linfen that helped kick-start hydro engineering and artisanship all those centuries ago was a sooty fossil.

◘

AROUND THE TIME THAT Linfen could've used its own civic oxygen tent, something extraordinary dawned on an island on China's southern tip not far from Hanoi. The people shrieked a collective "No" on a bandwidth that must've been felt in Beijing, a "No" never really heard before. Hainan, an oval, Belgium-sized territory with a tropical climate, in a previous epoch had been a sanctuary for criminals and shamed public officials. It was the Japanese who occupied it during World War II that started nurturing the region's mineral wealth (rubber, iron ore, bauxite, alluvial tin). Afterward, the Maoists closed some of that mining, jittery about Hainan's strategic vulnerability to invaders. But in 1984, as Los Angeles hosted the Summer Olympics against a tidal wave of apprehension about its gunky air, Hainan hit the jackpot. Under Deng Xiaoping's economic reforms, it was designated a special zone for outside investment. The former oasis for the disgraced was moving on up.

Over the next thirty years, Hainan matured into a Honolulu-meets-Atlantic City destination for the affluent. Investors jetsetted in with bags of cash for deposits on luxury villas or apartments with balcony bathtubs. Developers grinned about a possible casino and racetrack. One five-star hotel charged guests eighty dollars just to sleep in a tent during the Lunar New Year. Thanks to the island's real estate bubble, the stench of inside-deal making wafted with the tangy aroma of freewheeling capitalism.

The pandemonium erupting there in October 2012 wasn't so much about the rich-poor class divide cleaving China today. For the Politburo 1,300 miles away, it was equally sobering. Protestors and activists in years past had rallied against chemical plants, consumer-goods factories, wastewater facilities, and textile makers to register their displeasure with industry corkscrewing up in their backyards. Rarely before, however, had there been a popular backlash over coal—at least not until some 10,000 residents from in and around the small, coastal village of Yinggehai spoke with their feet in a protracted, week-plus-long melee with Hainan authorities. A coal-fired power plant and coal-receiving harbor, whose construction had resumed after a public demonstration in April shut it down, was their target. Officials had tried the musical chair tactic, offering to relocate the roughly 665 million dolar project to another neighborhood. Nobody wanted the plant-harbor there. After an elderly female protestor was hurt by police trying to grab back a sign she'd taken, and thousands gathered to defend her, simmering tension spilled over into civil warfare. "Almost every night," one villager told the *The Washington Post*, "you could hear the glass being broken, the shouting and fighting." Police erected checkpoints as a stranglehold, preventing citizens from entering or leaving. They fired 1,000 tear gas canisters; one during an April skirmish landed in a kindergarten class. Schools and shops were closed, homes searched, most-wanted lists printed. In revenge, some official vehicles were smashed.

Dozens wound up in custody or in need of doctors. Still, townsfolk would not relent. An activist from Jiangsu province to the north explained why outgunned citizens were risking their hides over the sacred fossil fuels, which were formed over millions of years from the altered remains of prehistoric vegetation. "Environmental issues are connected to [economic] targets, and to do with officials wanting to get rich and earn a promotion. Eventually, they always end using military force to suppress them and to cover it all up in the name of progress. This is a system-wide problem."

◘

AN OCEAN AWAY IN Burbank, you'd be surprised by how few degrees of separation there are from the bleakness of Linfen, the coal rebellion in Hainan, and this concrete-laden, suburban city north of downtown Los Angeles. The city where *The Tonight Show* was once broadcast percolated with blue-collars; Beijing back then didn't even make pencils. Down the road, Lockheed Corp. designed and produced sleek fighter jets and spy planes for the Pentagon in an assembly line hard against an aqueduct. Tacked around were smaller defense contractors, plating shops, industrial-lubricant makers, and the like. Nobody bronzed any trophies. Los Angeles County, for all its Hollywood sparkle and luscious real estate, was a citadel of American manufacturing, pumping out paint, beer, sedans, etc. until the free trade movement had its say.

Even in the 2000s, well after Lockheed had relocated along with a caravan of other companies tired of red tape and high costs, the county still employed more people in the field than work-boot Chicago, Houston, and Detroit. Today, none of those statistics can disguise the fact that where 800,000 once drew manufacturing paychecks here only roughly half do now in a 153 billion dollars per year sector. Clubbed hardest between 2006 and 2009 were businesses trafficking in furniture, mineral products, textiles, and metals—all categories in which China excels.

A 200 million dollar-plus outdoor shopping mall called the Burbank Empire Center rests on the land where Lockheed's B-1 plant used to sit, vibrating with classified activity. The irony stretches as wide as asphalt. A paint-fading replica of one of its twin-tailed warplanes crowns the mall's entry signage, pointed north toward the mountains that local smog used to gobble.

Depending on your politics, the hanging mockup is either sentimental eye candy of US supremacy or a reflection of its post-glory stupor. Close by, a federally run Superfund cleanup of soil and water fouled by chromium-6 and other lethal solvents left behind by Lockheed and its old industrial neighbors chugs along. Still, there's only so much waste to eliminate, because not much new gets assembled around these parts anymore. Not unless you count the glazed confections in wax paper from the Krispy Kreme donut franchise.

On a drowsy Sunday in 2014, the palm-tree fringed shopping center, with its colorful, big-box signage cantilevered high overhead, seemed to warble a uniquely American ditty about suburban gratification a galaxy away from third world strife. People were sipping Starbucks lattes, texting, chatting about the upcoming Super Bowl, hunting bargains, and absolutely not pointing at filaments of drifting Chinese smog overhead. You only had to walk thirty yards from the parking lot into three of the stores—Best Buy, T.J. Maxx, and Michael's—for a fluorescent-lit verification about who's in control of *this* empire. Of fifty-one sundry products, some of them major brands, thirty-one, we discovered, were made in China. We're talking ear-buds, coaxial cables, hair dryers, Apple keyboards and mice, toy horses, baby blankets, Tonka trucks, braziers, and flip-flops. (Guitar strings, Duracell batteries, Crayons, and Mason jars were US assembled. Trailing China and the US in our unscientific sampling were India, Germany, Taiwan, Portugal, Vietnam, Mexico, and Malaysia.) It was the same story of red-and-yellow supremacy at big-box Target. Quizzed on how many customers seek out domestically produced merchandise, a husky, indifferent Best Buy salesman was stumped. "Honestly, man, not many," he mumbled. "Maybe one in a hundred."

Not far from here, close to the corporate headquarters of Walt Disney and Warner Bros., is the Golden State Freeway that branches up the spine of California. Night and day, it's chockablock with diesel big rigs, many of them weighted with Asian cargo shipped through the whirring ports of Los Angeles and Long Beach. All these connections are why dense Burbank is way more breathable than Asia's factory hotbeds. Talk about reverse polarity. The Chinese are sucking industrial fumes that used to be billowed stateside, while the West Coast economy whose manufacturing helped defeat the Soviets and computerize the world serves primarily as middle-man/delivery boy for Far Eastern goods fabricated for pennies on the dollar.

Qiao Xiaoling, the grandmother in unisex slacks whose husband and son cancer stole during Linfen's energy get-rich rush, would probably do anything to get herself and the boy to the Empire Center (or anyplace in California, really.) She'd be a sales clerk, a cashier, maybe some customer's nanny. But no genie took pity on her; no winning Lotto ticket slid under her door. For all we know, she's remained in Shanxi province, bound in a vapor lock of dark particles from the crumbly stone that powered America's own high-polluting Industrial Revolution.

You do have to be careful drawing parallels, still, for when it involves the People's Republic and coal, it's more than complicated. It's ancient.

CHAPTER 2:

FIRE & COAL

THE OLD TEACHER SAT under giant cypress trees surrounded by students. In his outdoor classroom, he quietly shared what it meant to live the virtuous life, modest in material possessions and in harmony with other people and nature alike. Long before Christ preached in the streets of Jerusalem, Confucius had returned to his small home city of Qufu on China's coastal plain south of Beijing. The city is flat, walled, filled with low-squatted buildings of stone with red and yellow tiled roofs bedecked by dragons and other figures to ward off evil spirits. In the cold of winter, fires burned inside to keep families warm, filling the cobbled streets with wisps of smoke when the air was still. In the morning, sentries opened the gates and people walked beyond the city's walls into the surrounding farm fields, carrying night soil to fertilize the land and to till, plant, and harvest as the season dictated.

It was here where Confucius, the *éminence gris* of Chinese social philosophy, spent his last days before dying in 479 BC, teaching a handful of loyal students what he had learned through a lifetime of travels, observing and chronicling China's social order, and studying ancient texts that described a harmonious past. In old age, he was revered, a legend in his time like the Greek philosophers Socrates and Plato. Yet respected as he was, he had grown weary of what he had seen traveling China's separate kingdoms. Bearded and rotund in old age, the scraggly teacher mostly found contentment in teaching his most loyal students and wandering the spacious gardens of his home within the walled city.

Throughout his life, the leaders of China's kingdoms sought him out. They wanted his advice on the matters of the day. He preached to them, just like to the common folk, patience, pacifism, compromise, the golden rule, communalism, reverence for ancestors, the aged and learned, the principles of both the good leader and good citizen. If only both the leaders and the people would heed his advice, Confucius believed China could unite for a harmonious future. "The moral character of the ruler is the wind," he said. "The moral character of those beneath him is the grass. When the grass has the wind upon it, it surely bends." At least as long as the ruler is virtuous. Yet, by the end of his life, he was disillusioned. Instead of virtue and modesty, he complained that China's rulers—while paying only lip service to his principles—were mostly busy feathering their own nests with material possessions and chasing the beautiful, young women.

Defeated when he died, his family and loyal students buried him beyond the farm fields outside the walls of Qufu in a forest carpeted with leaves and illuminated by gentle sunlight shining through the rustling trees. Only seventy-two students he had touched ever earned his highest honors. They would carry forth in an effort to propagate his teaching and realize his dream of a communal society, in which people lived in harmony with one another and with nature. Hundreds, perhaps thousands of others had listened, but disregarded his wisdom once they returned to the business at hand. As much as they struggled to propagate his teachings, the disciples of Confucius made only limited headway.

Little more than two hundred years after their teacher died, the Emperor Qin Shi Huang carried out a ruthless military campaign to unify China's seven squabbling kingdoms, ignoring virtually everything Confucius taught. At the age of just thirteen, Qin set out to parlay smoky mastery of fire to create a fearsome army to do the job. Amid smoke and metallic fumes, his blacksmiths labored and sweated to forge weapons and tools for his armies. Once armed, Qin unleashed his warriors from his home in Xi'an. They wielded chrome-plated swords, spears, and bows and arrows as they marched on a merciless campaign to subdue anyone who stood in their way. They travelled with conscripted slaves who swung picks and shoveled dirt to build roads as they progressed, along which common soldiers marched while officers rode small Mongolian horses. Generals and high-ranking officers rode in carriages. Within ten years they conquered all the kingdoms and brought them to heel under a system of centralized government connected by a network of roads and canals. Though targeted by assassins, Qin imposed his will, ordering book burning, downplaying Confucianism, and standardizing measurements. When not barking orders to his command, he swilled elixirs he thought would give him immortality.

The soldiers' shining swords were made by Qin's blacksmiths. They burned huge amounts of wood in hot furnaces to melt copper and other metals to first forge brass swords. Soon Chinese blacksmiths would burn coal instead, as using wood caused rapid deforestation. After fashioning the weapons, the blacksmiths dipped them into a molten mix of chromium and mercury and let them cool. Once cooled, workers reheated the swords to a temperature hot enough to boil off the mercury, but not hot enough to vaporize the chromium. Instead the chrome remained on the surface, giving the swords a polished look that intimidated opponents on the battlefield. One can only imagine how the health of those who worked the crude, smoky furnaces was affected, but it was surely viewed as merely a cost that individuals paid for a greater cause.

At the heart of Qin's success was his ability to harness energy on a scale perhaps never before seen in the world. As a result, vapors of metals, hydrocarbons, carbon monoxide, nitrogen oxides—the stuff of air pollution today—shrouded China's cities on still winter days. They were emitted from home hearths, kilns used to fire clay pots and plates, and furnaces to melt metal. Energy allowed China's inventors and masterminds to make more tools and build great public works that made the nation self-sufficient and wealthy, superior to all surrounding cultures— Japan, Thailand, Mongolia, and Tibet. As the Chinese invented new tools and technologies and increased their mastery over fire, this wealth increased in successive centuries, allowing its population to grow by leaps and bounds.

The young emperor, who'd succeeded his father's short three-year rule, established the first capital of his integrated territory, for every empire needed a showpiece center. It was in Xi'an, which lies in the central part of China at the eastern end of the Silk Road, a 4,000 mile route across Asia to the Mediterranean along which traders brought silk from China westward. To protect the nation from invading Mongol marauders, he organized more than 700,000 slaves to build the Great Wall, moving huge stones into place along China's northern border. It was a feat of human and animal energy.

The ruthless Qin was feared and viewed as an evil emperor. He knew it. So immediately upon assuming the throne, he put what archaeologists believe were hundreds of thousands of slaves to work building a twenty-two square mile tomb in which he would place a replica of his army to protect him in death. The slaves toiled continuously throughout his life, digging to construct the sprawling series of underground chambers on land remote from Qin's palace and the city surrounding it. That's because Qin wanted to keep the project a secret so he could not be attacked in the afterlife. To do so, archaeologists have reasoned from skeletal remains found in the tomb that Qin executed anybody he feared would reveal the location of his tomb. To create the army that would protect him in death, artisans fashioned clay warriors modeled after individual soldiers, so that no two looked alike. They fired and painted the replicas before methodically lining them up in military formation in the pits, which were covered with wooden ceilings supported by posts and beams.

Most kept watch to the East, where the majority of China's people lived in kingdoms that Qin savagely conquered. Consequently, he feared his subjects were most likely to rise up and attack from that direction when he died. And rise they did. Within three years of his death, the same slaves who built the Great Wall invaded the tomb, smashing the Terra Cotta warriors, grabbing their weapons, and lighting the underground structure on fire. They raced out, free at last, sacking the government Qin established in Xi'an. It caused China to fall into disunity, but justice was done. Air pollution, though, remained as China soon regrouped under a new emperor.

China's smog, then as now, was a man-made concoction in which the skies became clouded with impurities. Burning wood and, soon after Qin, coal to manufacture things, heat homes and water, plus an immense population and stagnant air were the causes. The nation, including occupied Tibet, covers a diverse landmass today totaling 3.7 million square miles. Only Russia is larger. China's north is dry and cold. Its south is warm and wet with verdant landscapes. Major mountain ranges traverse the interior of the country, out of which flow some of the world's greatest rivers: the Yellow in the north and the Yangtze farther south. These waterways carry soil distributed over fertile valleys and a productive, coastal plain similar to the Mississippi Valley in the US. Much of the western and northern reaches of China are desert-like, covered with scrub grass that animals still graze today.

Even before Confucius and Emperor Qin, with the advent of farming 5,000 years ago, China became the world's most populous civilization. Until the twentieth century, its economy was based upon holding land in an agrarian, feudal order that cherished political stability. For the most part, the early peoples thrived. There were as many as 80 million during the Song Dynasty between AD 960 and AD 1279. Other civilizations—Babylon, Persia, Greece, Rome, the Aztec, Mayan, and Inca—coalesced and collapsed. China, though punctuated by repeated conflict in which dynasties rose and fell, remained.

After Qin, China reunited and advanced by molding the landscape for intensive agriculture, mostly on the alluvial flood plains of its rivers and coastal flatland. China's interior was too arid or mountainous to farm at levels that could support so many hungry mouths. To keep apace, leaders turned to increasingly elaborate infrastructure and bigger government. By AD 221, the Han Dynasty assembled a sophisticated bureaucracy of scholars. Commonly known as Mandarins, these men were learned in the teachings of Confucius and Chinese classics. Like civil engineers, they supervised construction of an extensive grid of dikes, irrigation ditches, protective walls, palaces, and granaries. Peasant-workers were drafted for the heavy lifting. The government taxed landholders to finance the public works that any caped Roman emperor would've admired.

The Chinese invented and used tools virtually unknown in the West. First century BC Chinese farmers operated winnowing machines that separated grain from chaff. The Europeans would need another 1,400 years to duplicate the technology. In the following century, the Chinese learned how to better maximize their harvest by fitting horses and oxen with breast-strap harnesses that strengthened their pulling power. Only 800 years later would the West swap them for primitive throat-bearing harnesses that choked their draft animals when they strained. Excavation was another advantage for the Chinese in the early centuries. They tapped salt brine, for instance, by turning a borehole drill as deep as 800 feet into the ground. The innovations had no end. China packed gunpowder by the tenth century AD to blast rock for building. By the seventh century AD, wood block printing of books was devised. George Babcock Cressey, a US geographer, observed that China's prolonged success was akin to a climax forest that utilized nature up to her limits.

Was it any surprise, then, that China viewed itself at the pinnacle of humanity? Affluent and well equipped, walled off from invaders and isolated by mountains, deserts, and long stretches of ocean, it was a fortified, contented giant. So much so, in fact, that it had no navy or merchant sailors except for a brief period during the Ming Dynasty from AD 1405 through 1433. For the most part, it was an inward-looking civilization, independent and self-enriching, dependent on no distant resources or trade relationships. Unfortunately, this insulation fostered what the Mandarins saw in neighboring nations: cultural stagnation.

Marco Polo, the Venetian adventurer and trader, failed to realize the stark days ahead during his eventful visit to China in AD 1298. Polo, who chronicled his impressions in his time-honored book, *The Travels of Marco Polo*, was especially entranced with what he termed a mysterious "black stone" dug from "veins" in the mountains—a stone that burned long, hot, and without flame during the night. Families of means throughout Cathay, as northern China was then known in Medieval Europe, combusted the jet black fuel to warm water for baths, enjoyed by the Chinese three times a week. Peasants depended on it to survive cold winters by placing nuggets in their hearths. Marco Polo may not have been a geopolitical expert, but he recognized that China's trees would "soon prove inadequate" as a fuel source given China's population. "These stones," he wrote, "may be had in great abundance, at a cheap rate."

Had Marco Polo traveled to London in his day, he would have found the black stone the fuel of choice, so what he tripped over in Cathay was nothing new. But it was also old. The Chinese had been unlocking the heat properties in coal as early as 206 BC during the Han Dynasty. Around AD 960 in the Song Dynasty, artisans fabricated swords, shields, armor, and spears from coal-fired furnaces for 150,000 troops guarding the capital, then in

Kaifeng in what is now Henan Province. As many as 3,000 men toiled at the iron mill there, the biggest in the land. While Europe languished in the Dark Ages, the fuel lifted Kaifeng into a dynastic stronghold of Asia.

Before Europeans arrived in large numbers, China was already digging deep into the Earth, converting rock to energy. Each year, it excavated millions of tons of coal from pits (also called mines) as deep as 130 yards, more than the length of a football field. Miners had to climb down ladders into the holes to dig out their quarry with pick axes. They'd fill bags with it and carry up the backbreaking loads to the surface. Potentially lethal methane gas, which could asphyxiate workers in the confined space underground or ignite an explosion if an ax caused a big enough spark, was vented through hollow bamboo poles. Handicapping their productivity wasn't so much gas as water. Hard rains were known to inundate the pits. As an engineering remedy, the Chinese sometimes diverted the water by carving tunnels to channel it to downhill areas. Where mines were close to rivers, they transferred the product to boats heading to cities reliant on coal for home heating and cooking. Craft makers and artisans needed it, too. They spun glass and ceramics with coal-burning furnaces. The versatile material was also adopted to make lime for cement and to power stills.

An enormous population in a country with its forests being increasingly leveled to clear land for agriculture and harvest timber for fuel increasingly turned to what Polo found so intriguing as its national lifeblood. Scrambling to meet demand, mine operators beefed up their workforce and invented new devices to lift greater amounts of coal from the pits. They hammered together more ladders and contraptions, including a kind of conveyor-belt with leather buckets cranked by both men and oxen. Nobody had told the emperor's court that China was sitting on one of the Earth's richest coal deposits, and that its ground contained relatively scarce conventional oil and natural gas.

Not surprisingly, even in distant yesteryear, sulfurous fumes and soot danced and hung in the air. Northern cities torching the rock during the freezing winter felt it most severely. Unlike Los Angeles, China's airshed stagnates the most not during the roasting summer, but in winter and spring. It's then when contamination builds up. That's because during winter, air tends to sink over Asia's cold interior landmass, forming persistent high-pressure systems associated with dry weather. Strong winds whip from the interior toward the crowded coastal plain when high-pressure systems form, kicking up dust from farmland lying barren during winter. Throughout much of China's history, the particles from dust clouds have penetrated even the most tightly sealed houses, coating furniture and fabric with fine, yellow silt. Peiping—which was later known as Peking before its name changed to Beijing—was enveloped by them. The silt-laden clouds, which could sweep long distances like a tidal wave, would even strike Shanghai 800 miles to the south periodically. Once the high-pressure winds that propelled the dust died down, more punishment was in store. The air could become almost unnaturally still to such an extent that coal fumes and soot sometimes mixed with fog to tent towns in gray overcast. Between rampant coal use and routine dust attacks, old-fashioned smog was long a fixture of early life.

What was present was the cliff-edge of resource disaster. With China's oversized citizenry exploiting the land to the fullest, it still sometimes netted a deficient yield of food, water, and minerals when it mattered most. During good times, there was usually enough to satiate everyone. In more dire periods, the material deprivations were obvious. Floods, droughts, and pestilence were often around the corner, threatening famine, if not social bedlam. Productivity margins derived from China's innovations no longer sufficed. Hence, many of its denizens lived on the razor's edge of ecological overshoot, prone to natural calamities that no emperor, compassionate or wicked, could solve. Crop failures put the entire country at risk. China's north resembled America's Great Plains in the thirties, vulnerable to the dust bowl syndrome of implantable fields and wind-borne grit flying every which way. The Loess Plateau, a mammoth area roughly 4,000 feet in elevation, once was a fertile grain-growing enclave. But centuries of excessive hoeing and harvesting eroded it something awful. An agricultural breadbasket no longer, the plateau's degradation carried far. It punished Beijing and other cities with gritty, choking dust clouds. The butterfly effect, where one distant action has a multiplying impact elsewhere, was already flapping.

◘

GARBED IN DARK SILK and a velvet bonnet, the old Emperor Qianlong sat on his throne, haughty and wise as the foreign "barbarian" from King George's court approached. Musicians played festive music and special tents flapped in the breeze, just normal trappings for the Imperial Majesty and his court of Mandarin advisers. It was fall 1793 in a colonial world of European barons and conquered peoples. At stake was a trade deal for England that might've been the biggest ever. No nation but China had a population bigger than all of Europe, all potential customers, and not to mention natural resources. A master of ceremonies led British Ambassador Lord George Macartney up to the emperor, who looked at him with saggy, condescending eyes and a pointy moustache, expecting the stranger to kowtow, or prostrate himself, before addressing him. He'd judge later whether the hawk-faced Englishman's proposals were worthy of the Middle Kingdom's attentions. In the emperor's mind, China stood supreme given its grandeur, wealth, and mystic past.

King George III had other ideas. After recovering from defeat by American revolutionaries, Britain's economy needed Macartney to succeed. Its production capacity for finished goods was exceeding domestic demand with coal burning in wide use during the emerging Industrial Revolution. Mechanical spinning-machines and looms in mills and other mechanized factories were rewriting the rules of the world. George III needed China to open to the "fair competition of the market" to keep his nation's economy growing. He'd sent Macartney specifically to cultivate a more supple trading relationship with the Chinese by prying open the nation's entire eastern coast for British trading ships. As it stood, only the port city of Canton (today's Guangzhou) allowed foreign vessels to enter. The King desired a British embassy too, where trade relations could be further broadened.

Appreciative of their challenge 5,000 miles from smoky London, Macartney and his retinue came bearing gifts of magnificent scope. Before leaving England, they loaded onto their warship some 600 presents, among them fancy clocks, telescopes, porcelain vases, howitzer-type cannons, carriages, and even a hot air balloon to dazzle the Chinese with ingenious English novelties. Ninety wagons, 200 horses, and some 3,000 porters carried the gifts from port to Beijing. The Chinese weren't impressed, at least not the emperor's advisers. Privately, they disdained the wares as idle amusements, merely gifts the "red-headed barbarians" had brought to pay tribute to the greatness of China.

After weeks of discussion over whether Mccartney would kowtow before the emperor, he finally agreed to bend one knee. Soon he was escorted to the tent where the emperor sat. Tension was drum-tight. In the interests of diplomacy, Mccartney knelt and the emperor treated him and his party to an opulent banquet.

When the festivities were over, Qianlong gathered his council. Macartney afterwards kept lobbying the emperor's court about broadening trade. Then one day, he was summoned to the palace, where a letter from the emperor to King George sat on a chair. It read, "If you assert that your reverence for Our Celestial Dynasty fills you with a desire to acquire our civilization, our ceremonies and code of laws differ so completely from your own that even if your Envoy were able to acquire the rudiments of our civilization, you could not possibly transplant our manners and customs to your alien soil. Strange and costly objects do not interest me . . . as your ambassador can see for himself, we possess all things." There'd be no additional ports opened to European merchant ships, nor a British embassy in China. Before long, the Chinese recommended that Macartney leave for home as winter approached. The astonishing booty he brought for the emperor would be found sixty-seven years later in disuse in a storehouse.

Mccartney sailed home, but Britain wasn't willing to give up on China's untapped markets or resources. Rather than cramming another vessel with opulent goodies, the trading nation commissioned an armada of warships to achieve what negotiations could not. Gunboat diplomacy would sway the emperor. For decades to come, the British created economic opportunities through superior firepower and technology, which cast a reign of terror over China.

On the offensive, the Western vessels sailed up rivers to reach the interior of the country. Once more, too, they toted along opium to sell the Chinese on the black market. The tarry substance from poppy plants is a potent, addictive drug that when smoked puts the user in a dreamlike state of passivity. The government tried banning the drug, but there was too much profit in the contraband purchased cheap in India and the Middle East and then sold for a big markup. The ban threatened to disrupt an English strategy that traders knew as arbitrage: buy cheap and sell dear. Furious at the ban, England unleashed in 1839 what historians tagged the Opium Wars. British warships blockaded Chinese ports, seizing territory and firing cannonballs that left people cowering in terror. By the time the killing and panic subsided, China threw up its hands in military defeat. Britain got Hong Kong and was no longer expected to subjugate itself to Chinese customs, including kowtowing before the emperor.

The Opium Wars marked the beginning of a slippery slope in which other nations followed England to make similar inroads. The old Middle Kingdom was losing more territory and areas of influence. In the second half of the nineteenth century, it surrendered Vietnam to the French and the Korean peninsula to Japan. Outgunned and outsmarted, China had become an international doormat, picked clean of some resources and belittled as a lost civilization of fools. Poverty spread. So did anxiety that the outsiders would slice and dice the country for their everlasting benefit in the same manner they were in Africa and did later in the dusty Middle East. The land of 400 million survived intact only by the skin of its teeth. It took a series of deft, if slow, concessions to buy time to try to reclaim what they lost before the clock ran out on their fighting spirit.

The Empress Dowager Cixi's Viceroy Li Hongzhang engineered the concessions, while seeing the allure of the West by the late 1800s. The bearded septuagenarian, with a reputation as one of China's most brilliant thinkers, adapted the homey philosophy "If you can't beat 'em join 'em." China, he believed, needed to embrace Western science and technology for itself. So while the Empress preoccupied herself with pageantry and decorating her palaces, Li pursued Western know-how under a two-pronged strategy. First, he arranged for Western companies to make strategic investments in China, which fattened the Mandarin class and ultimately backfired as resentment grew among the peasants. Simultaneously, he began sending Chinese students abroad to study science and engineering. They were meant to return and guide the nation toward modernization. This backfired, too.

Coal exemplified how Westerners used the new investment opportunities to their advantage and it undercut Li's grandest hope. The viceroy dreamed of mining coal at a colossally improved clip as a path toward national strength, particularly at the Kaiping mine in Hebei Province, known for its high-energy content. Li observed that the relatively small country of England became Earth's most powerful empire by successfully exploiting the energy in each handful of the mineral. Why not his homeland, the civilization that may have first enjoyed coal's magic energy? To that end, he persuaded British engineers to integrate the steam engine into moving coal from the Kaiping mine. A steam locomotive soon replaced camels and mules yoked to haul the fuel to cities like Tianjin sixty miles away in the 1880s. The proudly named *Rocket of China* churned out smoke and ash over the countryside as it thundered down the tracks. Choking for some, it was sweet music to others.

Eager to operate Kaiping with the latest methods, Li persuaded British mining magnate C. Algernon Moreing to invest money into the mine. Moreing saw the potential profits and appointed a well-respected young mining engineer to oversee his investment in 1899. The handsome Quaker, Herbert C. Hoover, hailed from the plains of Iowa. He tried to do just what his boss wanted, turning Kaiping into an efficient enterprise that other mine owners could emulate. All the while, he developed an unsavory impression of the Chinese that the West hustled to exploit. "The simply appalling and universal dishonesty of the [Chinese] working classes, the racial slowness, and low average intelligence, gives them an efficiency far below the workmen of England and America," Hoover wrote. Mine managers, he complained, weren't much better. Some refused to descend into the underground chambers to inspect them for safety. Others were so cheap they'd skimp on timbers needed to hold up the mines to adequately protect their workers against cave-ins. "The disregard for human life" sickened him; families of killed miners received thirty dollars for their loss. The only Chinese administrator that Hoover deemed knowledgeable didn't wake up until noon, and then smoked opium. Within a year, the engineer advised Moreing "the game [was] not worth the candle" unless the British took over completely. Moering concurred, so under his command, Hoover won control, forcing the Chinese owners into a subservient role.

America's future thirty-first president, who presided in the White House during the beginning of the Great Depression, had just lit a candle of historic proportions, providing grist for a national uprising. Chinese nationalists seized upon Moering's takeover at Kaiping as a galvanizing event to catapult a political movement. Foreigners backed by superior firepower and science in the land that invented gunpowder had wrested assets, like Kaiping, from their rightful owners for their own benefit. Each additional shovelful of coal from Western-controlled mines profited everyone but the Chinese. Along China's coast, bucketfuls went into ship boilers to move cargos of coal to Japan, an industrializing nation with little native fuel sources of its own. Like Moering, more foreigners would exploit it by the turn of the century, controlling mines outright or in partnership agreements with Chinese firms. Whether by pressure, payments, or combinations thereof, local companies amplified the changeover by granting digging rights to the outsiders. Some of the foreigners, too, had doubled down on their investments in China by putting money into railways there. Next, their executives tried arm-twisting Empress Dowager's weak government to allow their companies to establish factories in Chinese port cities. Japan, in want of iron ore, got its way by provisional deal making. Its banks lent money to Chinese companies on the condition that Japanese industrialists gained access to China's minerals.

Amid it all, the peasant multitudes had exhausted their patience. Food shortages pervaded. Folks were constantly at risk of being evicted from their homes by foreign land-grabs. The Qing Dynasty had no answers. It'd been immobilized, forced into disgrace. This thrust the people into a long stretch of rebellion. The Empress Dowager, who ruled the woebegone nation from 1875 to 1911, was reviled for her inability to stop the Westerners' injecting opium, bloodshed, chaos, and disenfranchisement throughout Chinese society. She hadn't stood up against any of the insults, seemingly hypnotized by her own privilege. Money raised to arm a navy to evict the foreigners delivered no ships. Instead, the people learned she diverted at least some of it to construct an opulent, marble-lined barge for her palace. She and the foreigners had to go.

Chinese students helped push it. A group of them formed a secret society known as the Society of Righteous and Harmonious Fists, devoted to expelling the outsiders. Sun Yat-Sen, a Western-educated doctor, served as an inspiration to the students like an Asian Thomas Jefferson. Sun, the nation's first leader after the Qing Dynasty was overthrown, worried about nearing resource-catastrophe. In 1894, he wrote, "At present China already is suffering greatly from overpopulation… She is confronted with a great many hidden uprisings and frequent famines." At that time, China had 1,479 people per square mile of cultivated land, or just 0.43 acres per person. It was double the number in the US before modern fertilizers, pesticides, and mechanization. Only night soil fertilized the land. When drought struck, with little irrigation in many areas, millions went hungry when all that coal should've been keeping peasants fed.

The student society wanted change, so they launched an ill-fated campaign in 1900 to boot out the foreigners. Westerners called the insurrection the Boxer Rebellion, shorthand for the name of the movement behind the uprising. Hoover lay low during the fighting while the British and other powers pitilessly brought it to a decisive end. China's occupiers demanded retribution for the damage the rebels caused. China had to pay 333 million dollars worth of silver to the Western nations occupying the country of Terra Cotta Warriors.

Unbearable debt or not, the students were determined to right the country before it was fully divvied up. They regrouped into a Republican spearhead aimed at overthrowing the ineffective Empress and her Qing Dynasty. Their campaign succeeded in

1912 and an aging Sun became the first nation's first president, though only briefly. Under pressure from Qing loyalists, he quickly turned power over to Yuan Shikai, who kept only shaky control. He represented the connected Chinese who profited in partnerships with Western companies. As much as things seemed to outwardly change, there was little respite for the masses. Persistent, Sun and others formed another entity—a nationalist front known as the Kuomintang—which was taken over by the remnant of China's Mandarin class. Others signed up with a new Communist Party organized in 1921 with Russia's aid. In a flash, a feverish power struggle between those favoring private ownership and privilege and those seeking communism boiled over into hand-to-hand combat in the streets. The violence brought Sun to despair before his death in 1926. Reflecting on a century of foreign domination, he wrote in 1924, "We are the poorest and weakest nation in the world and occupy the lowest position in international affairs. Other men are the carving knife and serving dish; we are the fish and the meat."

As more blood spilled, the old-time feudalists enlisted within the Kuomintang naturally gravitated toward military leadership, appointing to the top post General Chiang Kai-Shek, who ran away from home after his father died to join the army. Meanwhile, the son of a peasant farmer who earned his fortune trading grain promised those who joined his Communist ranks a future of egalitarianism, land redistribution, and a voice for peasants. It'd be a utopia on Earth, no man greater than the other. Mao Tse-Tung did not succeed immediately, so he bided his time. After the Japanese invaded China in 1937 and indiscriminately killed more than 300,000 in the Rape of Nanjing, which helped instigate World War II, Mao's day had come. He began a revolutionary drive that climaxed in 1949, when he proclaimed to the world that the People's Republic of China had been born. Neither Emperor Qin nor Qianlong would recognize the glory he had in mind.

CHAPTER 3:

THE MIDDLE KINGDOM REGAINED

TALL AND BROAD-SHOULDERED, MAO gazed from a farm field at a nation in ruin when he came to power—physically and socially. Russian occupation of Manchuria, preceded by World War II and, before that, years of Japanese domination in the north and even Shanghai, had devastated the nation's infrastructure and spirit. It came on top of a century of foreign domination that brought strife and civil war. The Japanese destroyed much of Nanjing, attacking it from three sides after bombing the city. They laid waste to industries as far inland as 1,000 miles from China's coast. So as Mao's revolution ascended, the country's scant industrial infrastructure lay crumbled in disrepair and disuse after decades in which the nation's leaders, by necessity, had focused on politics and fighting rather than managing and building the economy.

China's Communists were far from monolithic. Deng Xiaoping, a key ally of Mao, favored meritocracy, modern science and technology, and modest rewards for individual initiative. Radicals—perhaps carrying on a strain represented by the fierce Emperor Qin—favored ironclad party control, smashing symbols of privilege, and kicking out Westerners. Throughout Mao's almost thirty years of rule, the pendulum swung back and forth between the two visions for China, but only after a fierce battle.

As the Red Armies closed in on General Chiang Kai-Shek, he and his Kuomintang forces retreated to the island of Taiwan, which remains a separate nation today. In 1949—filled with dreams of making China into a great, modern Communist power—Mao took over a nation of more than 500 million people who had a less productive economy than in 1929. China was destitute. It had only a small amount of energy capacity, almost all of which came from coal. It was the poor man of the world at a time when Western nations were already advanced coal producers and users, and had become busy drilling for an increasing amount of oil and natural gas. When Mao took power, each average American was supported by an industrial economy that burned 10,000 tons of coal alone each year, plus oil and gas. Each English citizen benefitted from 12,000 tons of coal burned each year. China burned less than one hundred tons a year per person to meet virtually all energy needs. The same was true for iron—a staple material used in making steel for machinery, tools, consumer goods, and construction. The US was busy building roads, airports, housing, and churning out cars, TVs, radios, refrigerators, air conditioners, and the like. Mao looked around and saw a still agrarian nation. Cities were struggling to keep the few lights they actually had on. Elderly Chinese still remember crowded and desolate apartments illuminated by one bare light bulb hanging from the ceiling.

Economic conditions weighed heavily on the Chinese, but Mao's immediate focus was to drive out most foreigners and symbols of foreign influence. Like Qin's armies of old, the Communist cadres took over universities, hospitals, and churches set up by Westerners. They rounded up and brusquely expelled diplomats, businesspeople, journalists, and missionaries. After ending most Western presence, Mao found himself largely isolated, with assistance only from Soviet Russia, not the most scientifically or technically advanced nation. He knew that building the nation into an industrial titan would be a long road given its agrarian roots and large rural peasant population. That's why he first redistributed land to boost agricultural production. He sent his revolutionaries out into the countryside to seize farms from large landholders, seeing them as remnants of China's feudal past. They finished the job by 1952, effectively consolidating power for Mao and his Communists. Next, they collectivized agriculture so profits would flow to the state by keeping peasants on land plots from accumulating agricultural income. It was ironic because Mao's own father had gained stature by making money off grain trading while still a farmer. But the son had little interest in following in his father's footsteps, instead gravitating to politics after the Nationalist Revolution. He saw a bigger picture, so he and the Communists had no hesitation in taking hard-earned farm income instead of letting farmers keep it. They spent it to import Soviet equipment needed for basic restoration of the nation's industries. At the same time, they seized private businesses, turning them into state-owned enterprises. The party celebrated its success with street parades in which former business owners marched to demonstrate their liberation from capitalism. Mao needed several years simply to mend the nation's damaged and inefficient power plants, mines, and other industrial facilities. "The greater part of the first Five-Year Plan was devoted to catching up with the past," wrote Yuan-Li Wu in a 1963 study of economic development and energy use in China published by the Hoover Institution.

There was much need, particularly for mining coal, the mineral that was to fuel the planned industrial engine. In a country almost entirely dependent upon the black rock for energy, Chinese miners still often dug by hand. Coal mined with pick axes and shovels represented twenty-two percent of the total output. Even the other seventy-eight percent was at least partly mined by hand. When Mao gained his grip, the country had only elbow grease, 191 coal cutters, forty-four electric shovels (large steam-shovel like machines used to dig coal), and a limited supply of pneumatic and electric drills and air hammers, all commonly used in coal mining in the West at the time. These few tools, plus the pick axes and shovels that millions of dust-covered miners swung and scooped with, were used to produce all of China's coal. The dearth in coal supply meant that China could not manufacture much. No wonder that before Mao, China imported most of its manufactured goods, including cotton fabric and thread, iron and steel, colors and dyes, paper, chemicals, machinery, rope, petroleum products, and even cigarettes. China exported little beyond bean curd, cooking oil, and raw silk in any substantial quantity, despite some factories set up by foreigners. The vast majority of goods were shipped in and out of the port city of Shanghai.

Industry advanced under Mao, but never reached a scale even approaching what it is today. Industrialization was far from Mao's only concern. The Chairman of the Chinese Communist

Party—as he became widely known in the West—appeared mostly concerned with transforming social attitudes and Chinese culture to embrace communism, a process sometimes called "ideological remodeling." He used massive propaganda programs to erase Western thoughts and inculcate proletarian and peasant revolution in the populace. Loud speakers blared. Cadres marched in parades and held group training sessions. For the Chairman, who was fond of poetry when he wasn't lecturing and issuing statements about correct thinking, the goal seemed to be as much about the revolutionary zeal of class struggle as it was about actually improving the nation's economy. Indeed, as early as 1927, Mao wrote that the "upsurge of the peasant movement is a colossal event." He predicted the peasant movement would "sweep all the imperialists, warlords, corrupt officials, local tyrants, and evil gentry into their graves."

This movement only partially came to be, mostly due to the ancient culture of Qin's tyranny and the fact that the Empress Dowager's corruption never really died. Chou Enlai—a Western-styled figure who became Mao's most important confidant—recognized these spirits within China's culture. That's why he reasoned "class struggle will never end," nor would the environment be paid any heed. Showing China's lack of concern for environmental preservation, he wrote, "In the fields of the struggle for production and scientific experiment, mankind makes constant progress and nature undergoes constant change, they never remain at the same level." Mao envisioned a state of permanent revolution, in which class struggle would free the Chinese from exploitation by foreign powers and the old feudal overlords who'd kept the masses at a subsistence level. Air and water pollution were the last things on his mind at a time when producing enough food and quelling a hundred years of chaos were paramount.

Outlining his goal for China's economy in 1957—when activity had been restored to a prerevolutionary level based on power production records—Mao admitted that China had to "build up a number of large-scale modern enterprises step by step to form the mainstay of our industry, without which we shall not be able to turn our country into a strong modern industrial power within the coming decades." While seeing a role for large industry, Mao urged that "the majority of our enterprises should not be built on such a scale." Rather, the Chairman wanted China to "set up more small and medium enterprises and make full use of the industrial base left over from the old society, so as to effect the greatest economy and do more with less money." In other words, Mao did not envision any more steel mills, chemical plants, and other big industries than needed to gain self-sufficiency for China, plus respect from the foreign predators he and the Communists deemed imperialists.

Industry aside, Mao saw agricultural development as the locomotive pulling China's economic train. Not only would modernized farms provide plenty of food, they would fuel the need, Mao envisioned, for "more and more machinery, fertilizer, water conservancy and electric power projects, and transport facilities for the famers, as well as fuel and building materials for the rural consumers." A rising standard of living would boost light industry to produce goods for China, not for export. To achieve it, rather than relying on money, Mao largely sought new ways to organize and direct human energy and labor. China had just thrown out the Americans and most of the Europeans so it had no accessible market for exports anyway, nor access to capital.

China had only the Communist Soviet Union to turn to for the tractors and other tools it needed. The Chairman also pushed for basic healthcare and sanitation at a time when infectious respiratory diseases like pneumonia and tuberculosis caused twenty-eight percent of deaths in China, compared to the US, where the chronic "lifestyle" conditions of heart disease, cancer, and stroke killed more people than all the other major causes put together at the time. Mao trained the rural peasant population on sanitation practices, repairing and building facilities, including 67 million latrines in the countryside, where eighty percent of the population lived.

Riches still seemed far off, with Mao himself realizing it would take "several decades of intense effort" to make China prosperous. Meanwhile, "diligence and frugality" were his prescriptions for the people. The hard truth was that China still suffered from scarcity of most every necessity, from food to housing. To finally end shortage, Mao launched the Great Leap Forward in 1958. It marked the Communist Party's second five-year development plan, with the plans still today outlining the goals, policies, and programs in areas such as farming, manufacturing, and education.

The Great Leap Forward quickly proved catastrophic in every respect. It included two basic strategies and was dubbed "walking on two legs." There was one program for industry and another for agriculture, which led to the formation of "people's communes." To stoke up industrial production, the Communists organized small industries in communities across China to mine more coal and minerals and dramatically increase production of iron. The goal was to create 800,000 such operations, many involving crudely built backyard blast furnaces that created mostly unusable pig iron. The furnaces squandered coal and iron ore, as they sent smoke and fumes billowing across the nation, even in small rural communities.

Furnaces and kilns used to make brick and block in this period still stand today in many small rural communities with drab dormitory-like housing that seem eerily empty. In new plants built with modern equipment imported from Russia and Eastern Europe, production also failed due to poor management and terrible working conditions. Workers were simply relocated to the facilities with little thought for housing and sanitation needs. They defecated on the factory floor as they endured long hours under the watchful eye of party overseers. The Great Leap Forward left China cluttered with 600,000 "shabby" and mostly small-scale iron and steelmaking factories, 59,000 mostly small coal mines, 4,000 power stations, and 9,000 cement factories. Yet it was small potatoes by Western standards.

The bigger tragedy stemmed from forming 26,000 "people's communes" in the countryside. The Communists forced hundreds of millions of peasants with small garden plots, who also worked on large collectivized farms, to surrender their land and move into quickly improvised dormitories. Children were raised in nurseries to make mothers available as farm laborers; meals were eaten in communal dining halls; wages were eliminated, in exchange for free rudimentary clothing, lodging, meals, and even haircuts. The family structure was split asunder. Mao's Communists then organized the peasants into work crews that toiled long hours, sometimes eighteen hours a day, to clear and till fields, and build more irrigation canals and dams without adequate engineering plans or any basis in agricultural science. The dams quickly failed, flooding and eroding fields. Overirrigation created swamps. Irrigation in many cases also made soils too alkaline for crops.

Soil was quickly ruined. As much as ten percent of China's remaining forests were cut down. Agricultural production fell. Topping that, the commune system eliminated any incentive for workers themselves to care for crops and soil in the traditional way. They stood to gain nothing, since their effort was not tied to any personal profit, reasoned Western analysts. The state took care of them one way or another.

Mao's miscalculations brought almost immediate crop failures and completely destroyed social institutions. Famine quickly struck, killing as many as 45 million people between 1958 and 1962. The exact total will probably never be known. As dormitories and factories began to rot amid the growing chaos almost as quickly as they were constructed, people foraged for roots and ate mud pies. Others rebelled, leading authorities to execute an estimated 2.5 million people in a bid to maintain order. Rumors of cannibalism, perhaps true, circulated. China had again hit rock bottom, after barely climbing out of it as it pressed once again against the limits of nature given its shoddy and limited equipment, haphazard human organization, and lack of scientific knowledge. In the middle of it all, the Soviets broke off most cooperation with China in what became known as the Sino-Soviet split. Soviet Premier Nikita Khrushchev—who denounced the atrocities of Stalin and was succeeding in leading Russia to become a scientific powerhouse with the launch of humanity's first space satellite, Sputnik—ridiculed the Great Leap Forward as fanatical. Mao shot back that Khrushchev had sold out to capitalism.

The failure of the Great Leap Forward, viewed as a "Great Leap Backward" by most of the world and plenty of Chinese, did not stop the population from multiplying in China. It reached

700 million in 1960. This turned the Communists' attention to population control to head off what its rulers knew could bring a larger catastrophe than what the nation had just endured. The party promoted birth control and launched a campaign against early marriage. At the same time, with the chaos of the Great Leap Forward behind it, the nation pursued economic development at a more measured pace—reversing its disastrous communal approach to agriculture—and focusing its revolutionary zeal on education. One of its chief educational goals was to develop proletarian culture to replace traditional art and culture. To improve health care, the party trained Barefoot Doctors, who were stationed in rural areas to provide basic medicine. Each year, Mao also inducted some 750,000 youths turning eighteen into the People's Liberation Army. Coupled with the nation's new atomic weapons—first developed in 1964—plus a buildup of heavy arms, China's turn toward militarism struck fear in the hearts of the West. Amid the technological gains, scientists, engineers, and managers, who were in China's upper echelon before the Communists triumphed, again gained stature. They saw the value of Western science, technology, and capital-intensive development, even though it challenged the revolutionary concept of dictatorship of the proletariat. They became vocal critics of that order.

To counter their growing influence, in 1966 Mao set in motion the Cultural Revolution, which sent politicized Red Guards roving around the country to rout out his educated opponents and destroy symbols of feudalism. Young Red Guards swarmed Qufu, the home of Confucius, toppling and defacing graves, structures, and monuments to the great philosopher and teacher. Local residents, twenty percent of which were his descendants, cowered in the night. The guards targeted people with foreign books, clothing, and foreign-style haircuts, sending them on a Long March into the countryside for reorientation—if they weren't killed along the way—for the transgression of "taking the capitalist road." Mao excoriated high level officials in the party, for instance calling one "China's Khrushchev," forcing them to resign or sit on the sidelines. One of Mao's chief critics was Deng Xiaoping, arrested as a "capitalist roader" while serving as General Secretary of the Communist Party's Central Committee at the beginning of the Cultural Revolution in 1966. His sins? Advocating technical exchanges with the West, to gain access to science and technology to alleviate China's poverty and advocating that the Chinese needed a personal stake in the fruits of their labor. He would eventually succeed Mao, but only after seven years in exile performing manual labor in a tractor repair facility and growing vegetables. The Cultural Revolution's travails highlighted deep divisions in the society and fanned the flames of conflict.

As Mao reached the end of his life, the US enlisted China to coordinate on international security matters as part of its strategy to contain the Soviet Union. Ping-pong diplomacy, in which the US and China agreed to have national ping pong teams compete against one another in a tournament, provided the leading edge to discussions that Henry Kissinger conducted to open China to diplomatic relations in 1972 under President Richard Nixon. Nixon traveled that same year to Beijing to meet Mao. As he arrived in Beijing on Air Force One, the president instructed Kissinger and Secretary of State William Rogers to let him emerge from the plane first to shake Zhou En-lai's hand. A gaggle of TV cameras whirred as Nixon stepped out of the plane to begin an eight-day visit that changed the world. A Chinese motorcade swiftly ushered Nixon and his entourage to the Great Hall of the People. The People's Liberation Army band greeted them, playing "America the Beautiful" and "Home on the Range." The president immediately met with Mao before a Chinese banquet telecast in the US. After a whirlwind tour of the People's Republic, media in tow, Nixon and Mao fashioned an agreement under which the two nations pledged "to broaden the understanding between the two peoples," particularly in the fields of "science, technology, culture, sports, and journalism." They further agreed to pursue bilateral trade and "economic relations based on equality and mutual benefit."

Ever so faintly, the ice had begun to crack. Technical exchanges were easy beginnings to keep the thaw going. Out of that, the US Department of State coordinated arrangements for a Chinese delegation, led by its interior minister, to visit mostly picturesque Southern California to learn about air pollution in the modern city that practically invented it. Around then, the skies of the late-Mao-era were fresher than the blitzing twenty-five years away, but they weren't pristine either, not with so much fumy, big-city coal burning. Jim Birakos, the public information officer for Los Angeles County Air Pollution Control District, was the point man for the entourage. That it was from a mysterious, Communist nation barely mattered. "Mr. Smog," as he was colloquially known in the press, had greeted dignitaries on the clock before. The Soviets had already been there. The Japanese, Iraqis, and others would arrive later.

Then Birakos made the acquaintance of some American strangers. Days before the Chinese were expected to formally shuffle into his building near downtown LA's Skid Row, a group of unfamiliar men approached Birakos. They handed him phony business cards, and asked him to meet them at a local hotel. Inside a room there, Central Intelligence Agency (CIA) officers powwowed with "Mr. Smog." Obviously, the latest in tropospheric science wasn't the agency's interest. They next passed Birakos a list of questions they wanted him to pose to the Chinese to help them better decipher the country's industrial development and who might be a rising party star. The CIA had pictures of each member of the delegation for Birakos to memorize.

When the Chinese showed up, espionage was already on their minds. A security team swept the conference room for bugs and bombs, expecting a set-up. Civil questions streamed next. "They asked about technology, sources of pollution and how to handle them, the cost factor of refinery and power-plant pollution, [even] the sulfur in fuels," Birakos recalled. The meeting stretched about four hours. "They came prepared and had done research." Each time a Chinese official wanted to say something, the interpreter had to run it by the minister for permission first. Following the gathering, CIA personnel debriefed Birakos under the same fake names at the same, nondescript hotel. The session lasted roughly fifteen hours.

While the relationship between the US and China remained rocky in the bigger picture, it seemed that in the 5,000 year arc of Chinese civilization, Mao had brought the nation full circle. At the end of his career, Mao had restored not only a tenuous stability but also respect from foreigners, perhaps for the first time since Marco Polo visited. Mao's hard-learned aphorism that "power grows out of the barrel of a gun" summed up his approach toward foreign nations, pointing at them his massive army and nuclear arsenal. Nixon—in a nation that soon would lose the Vietnam War and face gasoline lines in the grip of an oil embargo by foreign nations organized into a cartel called the Organization of Petroleum Exporting Countries—finally paid the tribute to China that King George's emissary Lord George Macartney never did 200 years earlier. He told aides upon returning from Beijing that it was imperative that the nations end their isolation and be able to talk to one another now that China had nuclear arms. His assessment of China under the aging Mao—expressed in his typical inarticulate and convoluted manner—was "There'd be no power in the world—I mean, you put 800 million Chinese to work under a decent system . . . and they will be the leaders of the world." Mao had established a new dynastic order based on communism, with the Communist Party as the new ruling family.

The transformed nation's new relationship with the US paved the way for Deng's return from exile. As part of a Chinese delegation, he soon went to the UN in New York for a conference on economic development. When he got back, he immediately began planning a modernization program for China, resting upon a strategy of economic development that emphasized international cooperation and investment. As Mao grew sick, his longtime associate Zhou En-lai died early in 1976. Borrowing a page from Confucius, Zhou had always been revered for his humanity and moderation during the revolution, a diplomatic counterweight to fanatics. Meanwhile, Mao's wife, Jiang Qing—who once headed the film division of the propaganda ministry—and her "Gang of Four" purged Deng once more from any role in the party. It amounted to a last ditch effort to maintain a radical approach to the Chinese Communist Revolution. The gang and Jiang—sometimes called "The Great Flag-Carrier of Proletarian Culture"—never could manage to arrest Deng, whom the People's Liberation Army protected. The push for moderation of the revolution had reached a crescendo to become an unstoppable tide. Upon Mao's death later that year, one of the party moderates, Hua Guofeng, became what proved to be only an interim caretaker among the competing factions within the Communist Party, headed by the Gang of Four and Deng. In a surprise move, he arrested the Gang of Four and soon left office as support for Deng consolidated. Deng returned from exile to replace Hua in 1977. In 1978, he introduced the "Four Modernizations." They opened the door for China to become what it's known as today—the world's biggest industrial nation and most polluted place on Earth.

CHAPTER 4:

"FASTER STEPS" AMID THE SMOG

U PON RETIRING AFTER RULING China sixteen years since 1978, Deng Xiaoping traveled the country to see places he had never managed to visit while busy working. Throughout his long career as a central figure and leader in China's Communist Party there is little indication he ever referred to pollution, much less thought about it. It was more like the weather to this looming titan on the world stage, despite his diminutive stature of 4'11". In pictures during the revolutionary war days when he served as a military leader, Mao is seen standing more than a head above Deng. But Deng's slight physique belied his strong constitution. *TIME* named him "Man of the Year" in 1986, describing Deng as "steel hard," a "world class smoker" with a pack of Panda cigarettes always at the ready on the table in front of him. Smoking, he believed, promoted a relaxed atmosphere. So, too, did drinking. Deng loved his liquor, even late into life. At his retirement dinner, he drank five straight shots in a row to celebrate his career, which had put China on the road to becoming the world's most productive nation, with a concentration of power and chemical plants, steel mills, metal smelting facilities, mines, factories, and assembly plants previously unknown in human history.

The first place Deng went upon retirement was the new city of Shenzen, the first special economic development zone he had established after ascending to power. Shenzen was little more than a town west of Hong Kong when he took power. By the time he visited in 1994, it was a mighty city full of skyscrapers, factories, power plants, and home to one of the busiest ports in the world. Deng—then older than ninety—could not wait to look over what his economic reforms had built. He immediately went to the revolving site-seeing platform tall atop the Shenzen International Trade Building to gaze at the city's towering skyline. He sat in a chair as the platform slowly turned, but the buildings were obscured. Only their faint outlines were visible in the grayish-brownish haze.

Along with the great concentration of manufacturing that Deng—dubbed "The Architect"—had built, came air pollution. It would soon threaten a new ecological crisis, just like pushing the limits of China's soil with little scientific knowledge had brought famines that claimed millions in the past. As Deng looked into the gray sky from his perch, he didn't think about how the carbon dioxide emitted from burning massive amounts of coal was warming the atmosphere, even as Japan, the US, and European nations were already debating what to do about climate change. In just three years, they would sign an international treaty known as the Kyoto Protocol, calling for greenhouse gas reductions. Deng was oblivious to the growing national air pollution crisis that was already damaging the health of millions of Chinese. As the murk of industrial emissions grew in the skies over the nation, Deng simply urged his fellow citizens: "Be brave. Walk with faster steps." He was untroubled by environmental pollution and health concerns because China was busy building wealth to restore the glory of its past as the Middle Kingdom, the center of human civilization. It was all about future generations.

At the same time, Deng professed the country would remain a socialist economy employing markets under the firm rule of the Communist Party, though the party would become democratized. All Chinese would benefit and forever escape the dark days. All, under his vision, would share wealth. "I will be happy to be a regular citizen of a wealthy country," said Deng, who favored time with his children and grandchildren. Not only was Deng physically strong, but also psychologically and mentally tough. One US Marine who knew him said he had a mind that "cut the mustard." And despite being exiled from the Communist Party three times before finally coming to rule his nation—marched through the street in a dunce cap and derided as a "capitalist roader" during the Cultural Revolution under Mao—he remained loyal to the party. Even though his eldest son was pushed out a window during the Cultural Revolution, then refused medical treatment by Mao's government as he lay paralyzed with a broken back, Deng did not criticize Mao, remembered in his nation as the "Great Helmsman" for steering China out of the raging seas of catastrophe into a safe harbor. He would only say that without Mao, China would have remained in darkness for decades to come under the thumb of Western nations. "Comrade Mao, like any other man, had his defects and made errors," said Deng. "But how can these errors in his illustrious life be put on a par with his immortal contributions to the people?" Deng observed that it was the socialism Mao championed that had strengthened China. Without maintaining it, Deng said, "China will inevitably retrogress to semi-feudalism and semi-colonialism."

Mao had cleared the way for Deng to open trade with Western nations, but this time from a position of strength and on a level playing field. Deng wasted no time, leveraging China's new power to strengthen the nation and set it on a course toward becoming a world leader. *TIME* described Deng's maneuvers as the "second revolution" in China, "an attempt on a monumental scale to blend seemingly irreconcilable elements: state ownership and private property, central planning and competitive markets, political dictatorship and limited economic and cultural freedom." Ultimately Deng combined communism and capitalism, the *Time* editors wrote, though the tyrannical ghost of the Emperor Qin still haunted the Communists under the champion of modern growth.

Deng learned about the West and its science and technology beginning in 1920 while living in France, where he worked in a Renault car plant trying to earn enough to attend university. He didn't get far with his studies, but he did go a long way after joining the French Communist Party, founded in 1921. As a party activist and volunteer, he ran a mimeograph machine to print the organization's journal for distribution on the street. It earned the young Deng the honorary title of "Doctor of Mimeography." He won notice from the Soviet Union, where Lenin had taken power. The Soviets soon invited Deng to study at the new Sun Yat-sen University in Moscow in 1925. After six months there, he returned to China to join Mao's revolution. From his time in the West, Deng came to see the value of science, technology, and meritocracy. Amid the dark days of the Great Leap Forward, he became convinced that the only way China could escape the clutches of peril was to embrace Western know-how and to reward hard work and innovation. When Deng and Chinese President Liu Shaqi realized that the Great Leap Forward was failing in 1961, they reversed Mao's agricultural policy by allowing peasant farmers to again work private gardening plots. They restored the role of managers and technicians in many industries, removing party bureaucrats from key decision-making positions. Angered when he found out, Mao quipped: "Which emperor decided this?" Eventually the moves, coupled with Deng's general views on how to run the economy, put him increasingly at odds with ideological purists who believed in dictatorship of the proletariat. That's why they were quick to exile Deng from the party when they gained the upper hand during the Cultural Revolution. But even by then, the die was largely cast.

Upon taking power, Deng appeased hard-liners by laying out what he called the Four Modernizations. First, China had to stay on the socialist road. Second, it was to uphold "the dictatorship of the proletariat." Third, it was to maintain the leadership of the Communist Party. Finally, China had to maintain Marxist-Leninist and Maoist thought.

Deng traveled to Japan in 1978 to tour its modernized industries and ride on its speedy trains. Soon China had its first modern steel plant, known as Baoshan. Deng launched development of China's rail system after liking what he saw in Japan riding the bullet train. He visited Matsushita—an electronics company known for the Panasonic brand of televisions, stereos, microwaves, and other equipment—and imagined making China a leader in manufacturing and assembling consumer electronics. Deng sent students abroad to study science and technology and built up China's university system, emphasizing admissions based on merit instead of ideology and making science a primary focus.

Deng's special economic zones wooed companies from modern nations to set up shop, often in joint ventures with Chinese partners. At the same time, he shortened the leashes of potent state-owned industries, opening them up to competition from newer enterprises. Foreign investors and private companies, seeing opportunities amid the new economic elbow room, lunged into China as his reforms unfolded, which included major infrastructure projects—from power plants to airports, ports, highways, and railroads—to support zooming economic activity, much of it financed in part by the World Bank and other international lenders. The Special Economic Zones helped make China an export nation, sending toys, textiles, shoes, and an increasing array of goods to the US and other nations. Hong Kong, Taiwanese, and Japanese businesses were first to invest, seeing the potential to increase profits, but others soon followed.

Deng's reforms did help the Chinese, however. Deng raised the standard of living, doubling average household income. That drove the market for more housing furnished with refrigerators, televisions, and other modern conveniences. However, along with the rising standard of living and increasing opportunity came exploitation of laborers and increasing strains on resources that brought water and land shortages. There was a great outpouring of air and water pollution, as the nation's environment sharply declined. Deng, in effect, had concentrated all of the nation's energy and talent on economic growth, ignoring the environmental consequences. After remaining relatively level under Mao's tenure of twenty-eight years, China's energy usage doubled in sixteen years under Deng from 1978 through 1994. Air quality, of course, worsened. Most of the energy growth came from burning more coal, but the nation also burned more oil, as well as more biomass and waste, putting up the plume of pollution that clouded the sky in Shenzen and other cities. All of this occurred at the same time that the US Environmental Protection Agency (EPA) was cracking down on water pollution during the Reagan era and debating about the impacts of coal power plants on acid rain. By 1990, the US Congress amended the Clean Air Act to require use of cleaner coal and sulfur scrubbers on coal power plants. China continued to ignore air pollution from burning coal.

Dissatisfaction stirred even as the Chinese gained education and prosperity. Students and intellectuals wanted political reform that would lead to the same individual rights enjoyed in the West. They eventually took to the streets to protest Communist Party rule and increasing corruption, gathering 300,000 strong to demonstrate in 1989. They went to the vast, treeless Tiananmen Square, which is hemmed in by the plain gray buildings that house China's government in Beijing. The protests grew more unruly, so Deng soon ordered the army to restore order. Soldiers moved in and the protestors were like fish in a bucket, easy targets who could not escape. The army delivered crushing volleys as troops opened fire on the students and protestors. The number of victims killed remains a matter of contention, but neutral foreign observers estimate the troops killed up to 2,600 demonstrators. Deng acknowledged political reform was needed, but felt that many of the demonstrators were challenging the rule of the Communist Party itself, portending a threat to China's future. It was like Emperor Qin fearing the populace, even in his death. The nation needed to stay the course, Deng reasoned, and not allow an excess of individual rights and personal liberty that could threaten Chinese socialism and the continuance of party rule. His reasoning still lives today, though with a kinder and gentler face as the toughness of the revolutionary period fades.

After all, Deng was the last Chinese leader whose character was formed by the hardships and ardor of the revolution. His designated successor, Jiang Zemin, would go on after Deng's retirement in 1992 to become China's first telegenic president, singing Elvis Presley's song "Love Me Tender" at an Asia-Pacific Economic Cooperation meeting with Philippines President Fidel Ramos in 1995. He hummed a few bars with the army at the National People's Congress that same year. In what uncannily seemed like a confluence of national sensibilities, Jiang rose to power the same year American voters elected Bill Clinton as their president, marking the transition from a nation led by those who had fought in World War II, sometimes called "The Greatest Generation" to a "Baby Boom" figure. Just like Clinton, Jiang had a "soft spot for lavish ceremonies and big feasts" and "a concern for public relations effects rather than substance," remembered Chinese journalist Willy Wo-Lap Lam in his biography of the third Communist ruler of the world's biggest nation. He would be tested in managing public perception of the nation's growing pollution problems, as some of the first environmental protests were to break out during his tenure. He'd also be scrutinized in the US, where concern was rising that China would become a pollution haven for manufacturers, as Congress debated extending permanent most-favored-nation status to China while Clinton was president in the nineties.

CHAPTER 5:

MAKING HAY IN ARKANSAS

WHILE THE CHINESE CHUCKLED watching Jiang Zemin play karaoke showman at state parties on their new televisions, Americans went hog-wild when presidential candidate Bill Clinton blew the sax in dark glasses for a rousing rendition of "Heartbreak Hotel" on "The Arsenio Hall Show" in 1992. From East to West, magnetic, forty-something politicians of the post-Cold War generation—strivers like Clinton and his Transatlantic cohort, British Prime Minister Tony Blair—were changing retail politics. They branded themselves with populist media appearances and town hall meetings that edged them closer to their constituencies than their sometimes-aloof predecessors (Establishment standard-bearers who preferred Nordstrom's and Bloomingdale's).

For his running mate, Clinton tapped Tennessee Senator Al Gore to help unseat incumbent George H.W. Bush. The patrician Republican himself was keenly aware of China's juggernaut potential, having been a former CIA director and UN Ambassador. Gore, same as Clinton, was a Baby Boomer intellectual, plus an ex-journalist, who brought something else to the Democratic ticket besides youthful vigor and Beltway experience. The slow-talking politician with a Clark Kent-like appearance had cultivated an unusual eco-pedigree, as evidenced by his *New York Times* bestselling book, *Earth in the Balance*, published in the heat of the presidential campaign. The Clinton-Gore pairing, whose campaign catchphrase was "It's the economy, stupid," made a formidable team. Pocketbook issues flung them to a victory on generational coattails that reminded some of Kennedy's Camelot. With the Soviet Union dead, the New World Order was less about restraining a nuclear apocalypse than about unleashing international moneymaking. The intertwining relationship between energy and a smoky atmosphere barely rated a blip on the electoral radar. Fossil fuel remained king.

Clinton and Gore's triumph, nonetheless, meant that environmentalists had kindred spirits in the Oval Office, not an old oilman like Bush with industry friends all the way from Houston to the palaces of Saudi Arabia. Before climate change was a term you could Google *ad-nauseum*, Gore was ready to attack it. In his book, he pitched creating a carbon "Marshall Plan" to blunt melting glaciers, rising sea levels, and other effects of global warming on a jam-packed planet. One of the West's paramount goals, he argued, should be to develop clean technologies that "then must be quickly transferred to all nations—especially those in the third world." China should be among the first in line. What Gore championed was grounded in a new industrialism, where manufacturing sins of the past would not defile Mother Nature again. In his mind, there needed to be "a comprehensive and ubiquitous change in the 'economic rules of the road'" by which we measure the impact of our decisions on the environment. "We must establish—by global agreement—a system of economic accountability" for individuals, companies, and nations. To ensure those principles were honored and not conveniently forgotten when it counted, Gore recommended "the imposition of export controls in developed countries (like the US) that assess a technology's ecological effect." In other words, he wanted to make sure that US companies did not sell to China and other developing nations the dirty technologies of the past—cars without emissions controls, banned pesticides, polluting coal power plants—but, rather, the clean technology of the future. Opponents of this model, he cautioned, were already mobilizing, most notably the National Coal Association. In *Earth in the Balance*, he warned that the group was preparing a "disinformation" campaign to sow seeds of doubt about the reality of global warming. Fuel-makers were not about to just wave the white flag.

Gore's environmental bona fides made him a hero in green circles that helped nail down a voting bloc for his two-term boss. A White House had not seen such a focus on atmospheric health since the smoggy late-sixties and early seventies, if then. Nine years later, some of the environmental thrill was gone. The administration failed to construct any backstop of "ecological accountability," especially inside the world's fastest-growing economy. Gore's Marshall plan for the environment never caught on. Instead, decisions in the nineties in Washington under Clinton, the ex-Rhodes Scholar, and in Beijing under Jiang, the karaoke ham, effectively locked China into environmental degradation. Today, the questions about what happened during the nineties burn with the same intensity as the coal that marveled

Marco Polo almost a thousand years ago. Did power players in the Clinton administration hang Gore out to dry, cravenly using him as a foil as they went about cutting trade deals that paid little heed to the vice president's green visions? Or, did Clinton and his team naïvely underestimate China's strength and what their international economic policies would inflict on working people in the US and folks with lungs in Asia? Maddeningly, chances are it was both. The People's Republic exploited the administration's Pollyannaish outlook, motivated by its thirst to deliver short-term profits to US companies and investors—interests represented by two of its top economic policymakers, Robert Rubin, a Wall Street captain, and Lawrence Summers, a Harvard economist who serves as president emeritus of the university today. Both men served as Treasury secretaries while Clinton was president as well as in other federal posts. Throughout the nineties, they ably carried water for Wall Street to deregulate banking and pump up the financial sector of the US economy, which became increasingly obsessed with Main Street companies meeting or exceeding next quarter's "expectations." On Main Street, actually more likely on the outskirts of town along an Interstate highway, Walmart was one company that mastered the quarterly statement, as it grew by leaps and bounds decimating small businesses in downtowns across America in the process. Its key to success was selling low-cost goods made with cheap, dirty energy and by desperate, low-wage workers in China.

Walmart capitalized as Washington theorized about the benefits of trade and China marched to Deng's long-term plan. Clinton, known as the "boy governor" of Arkansas, which is home to Walmart headquarters, would look played in the rear view mirror. The raccoon-eyed, chain-smoking Deng never uttered a public word about smog. Breaking from his ideologically wary predecessors, he attracted a slew of foreign capital and technology to China to grow its economy while firmly proclaiming his nation still belonged to the third world. "Raising people's living standards," he said "is a long-term task which will certainly be carried on for years to come." In other words, economic growth was to take precedence over everything else. As to how to propel that growth, Deng and his successors were savvy enough to know China had no energy supply shortage. Its dilemma was in how to extract fossil fuel, particularly coal, from the hard-packed ground and burn more of it without wasting it, a quandary reminiscent of the Kaiping Mine episode.

By the time the Arkansan occupied the West Wing, Deng's successor, Jiang, gladly took the baton. He stoked up energy production as a linchpin to China's economic ascendancy. He convinced the US and its Western friends to help unlock China's natural resources, though not in the save-the-earth manner that Gore fancied. Rather than cramming freighters and cargo planes headed to the Far East with natural gas drilling bits, sulfur scrubbers, solar panels, and catalytic converters, Washington and its allies were, by the twilight of Clinton's tenure, bolstering China's ability to excavate, process, and burn coal—its go-to power source of the 1900s—under free trade agreements championed by the president and his investment-banker patrons.

Gore in the process became like a famous gunfighter denied a pistol, arguing passionately for a global treaty on climate change that he hankered for China to sign while other administration officials inked sales agreements, only green for the money exchanging hands. Between direct, taxpayer-subsidized assistance from federal agencies and indirect aid through international development agencies it controlled, Washington expedited Western engineering assistance and equipment to help the People's Republic to mine and burn more coal. American and other Western firms benefited, though the transactions boosted world temperatures and propagated the regional smog that so worried Gore. Attached to them was a formal stamp of approval, too. In pressing Congress to support China's Most Favored Nation (MFN) status and a new entity, the World Trade Organization (WTO), the Clinton administration seemed to cover its ears on warnings about environmental safeguards. Without them, some admonished, China would entwine itself into a pollution-haven for manufactured goods on a scale the world had never seen. Here's a little of the timeline:

After the bloody, June 1989 Tiananmen Square massacre and the backlash it stirred about China's human rights record, Washington levied economic sanctions against Beijing along with a threat. Keep up the deplorable abuses and the MFN restored to China in 1980 under the so-called Jackson-Vanik freedom of emigration amendment would be rescinded. (President Harry Truman had originally suspended China's MFN status in 1951 following its occupation of Tibet.) It was up to the president every year to approve continuation of the MFN, with a say from Congress. Dropping that preferential tag would ripple the trade waters by raising US customs duties on ninety-five percent of imported Chinese products. In 1995, close to forty-six billion dollars would've been affected, with Beijing likely retaliating in kind.

Three years after the Tiananmen bloodbath, Clinton and Gore strode into power as self-styled New Democrats unchummy with Big Oil and Coal like Ronald Reagan and Bush. China and economic liberalization remained on shaky ground, though. In mid-1993, Clinton imposed additional human-rights conditions for the next MFN renewal in a gambit the Chinese repudiated. Washington wanted to see China tackle prison-labor abuses, imprisoned dissidents, protection for Tibet, and its interference with foreign media broadcasts. When 1994 rolled around, China's MFN status stayed unchanged, because the linkage between it, human rights, and other bilateral issues were decoupled after Clinton affirmed to Congress that China was making progress, mainly on emigration. In deflecting attention away from *CNN*-broadcast images of protesters in front of tanks and the God-given rights of the individual that other presidents vocalized, Clinton dedicated himself to realizing a long-held Western dream of building a global economy. It was the same year the North American Free Trade Agreement (NAFTA) took effect. As he gained experience and thought about holding his Wall Street constituency that wanted wider profit margins, Clinton gladly assumed the mantle of NAFTA from Bush senior, who negotiated the agreement for trade with few restrictions between the US, Canada, and Mexico in his waning days in the White House in 1992. After getting elected, Clinton and his team worked hard to get it ratified by Congress in 1993. Along the way, he became a true believer in an integrated world economy over which capital would stand supreme. The economic growth it promised—evidenced by the spectacular growth of Walmart in his own home state—made Clinton soften his rhetoric about human rights, focusing on China's progress instead of its shortcomings. Clinton desired what King George III had pictured when he made overtures to China in the late 1700s with the spurned emissary.

As for warnings about China's future environmental record, the predictions were unmistakable. At briefings convened to shape the White House agenda right after the 1992 election, Lynn Williams, international president of the United Steelworkers Union, reminded officials "the environment outside the workplace is only an extension of the environment inside." Like antisweatshop rules, a system was needed to monitor and punish countries that willfully trashed their surroundings as a competitive advantage. "Labor and environmental groups maintain that a failure of a country to establish and enforce its own environmental regulations should constitute an unfair trading practice," Williams said. "Imports to the US made under such conditions should be subject to countervailing duties." Though other union bosses concurred with that view behind the scenes, Williams was the sole voice on a briefing panel for Clinton and his new team, which consisted mostly of chief executive officers from companies like Alcoa, Dupont, Southern California Edison, and Pacific Gas & Electric. They extolled their own programs targeting industrial waste and greenhouse gas emissions, testifying that they saw no inherent conflict between an unspoiled ecology and fruitful growth. The two must go hand and hand, they said.

Many might forgive them for believing these seemingly opposite goals were both attainable for, in 1990, Congress had just updated the pathbreaking Clean Air Act. Twenty years after it passed, Americans were recommitted to ecology. Under the act's latest provisions, fewer toxic chemicals would be permitted, acidic emissions from Midwest coal plants would shrink, automotive tailpipes would belch less harmful exhaust, and industries had to revise their air emission permits more frequently. With this last mandate, the federal EPA and its state counterparts had the authority to force companies to adapt ever-improving antipollution controls. Bush laid the groundwork for achieving these goals by signing the amendments, which Clinton then wholeheartedly embraced. He often behaved like America's environmentalist-in-chief, with Gore his wingman. He decreed that gas-guzzling sport utility vehicles—the new darlings of soccer moms—run as cleanly as conventional passenger cars. He tightened health standards for ozone and fine particulate that spurred a crackdown on numerous industries—furniture makers, printing companies, power plants, refineries, metal and glass makers—to chop fumes causing or contributing to lung diseases, heart troubles, and strokes. Clinton also earmarked federal dollars to develop alternative, low-carbon fuels, revolutionary car propulsion systems generating little exhaust, and advanced renewable energy for homes and businesses.

Despite his boss's ecological bent, Gore found few allies simpatico with his alarm about industrial jetsam rising up in the third world. US Trade Representative Mickey Kantor, a wavy-haired, politically wired Los Angeles lawyer who helped get Clinton elected, instead dwelled on how the trade agreements would enable American companies to comply with environmental standards at home. The world stage was an unusual spot to find the middle-aged attorney best known for behind-the-scenes king making and counsel, conveyed publicly with a winning Southern charm. A fellow Tennessean like Gore, Kantor had moved West, where he spearheaded Democratic candidates seeking the White House and even defended longtime Los Angeles Mayor Tom Bradley against conflict-of-interest charges. Outside politics, he represented local defense contractors, Occidental Petroleum and worked on commuter rail negotiations.

Inside a glass skyscraper in downtown Los Angeles, Kantor remembered China's passion for WTO entry. When a female

Chinese trade negotiator with an aide in the nineties visited his Washington office, Kantor gave her "a five-page, single-spaced memo" about what China needed to do to attain membership. "They came back five weeks later" with promises and answers "that went beyond" what the US sought, he said. "We were very excited. We wanted them in the WTO because now [we] gained some control over" Beijing. At the so-called Uruguay Round talks that created the organization through negotiations that commenced in 1986, Kantor acknowledged that little time was devoted to future air pollution concerns, including the notion that smog could be exported from one continent to another. "Clinton wanted [something]. [But] the Europeans didn't put any pressure on the Chinese to enact controls...The Chinese priority was one thing: growth."

In a 1994 testimony before the Senate Commerce, Science & Transportation Committee, Kantor emphasized to Congress that the trade pact held another perk. It would not impinge on US ability to police whether components in imported merchandise were toxic or released airborne chemicals when used, among other safeguards. As to harmful discharges and waste produced overseas in making these products, the proposed treaties were silent, Kantor admitted. Later in 1994, the year China's MFN was jeopardized with cancellation, Kantor dangled the possibility of a level playing field, telling another congressional committee that trade representatives meeting in Marrakesh had agreed to the "premise that international trade can and should promote sustainable development and that the world trading system should be responsive to the need for environmental protection, if necessary through modification of trade rules." Gore encouraged world leaders at the same Morocco gathering to think in holistic terms. "We are not faced with a choice between trade and environment. We can—and must—have both," Gore said. If there were other administration officials siding with organized labor's view that free trade agreements would open an escape hatch for US companies looking to flee environmental costs, their voices were muted.

But outsiders did not feel restrained. Throughout Clinton's presidency, back-burner debate crackled over American dealings with China. "Trade trumps the environment. Trade trumps human rights. It trumps the security of countries. It trumps the sovereignty of countries," railed Pat Buchanan, conservative media commentator and perennial presidential candidate in the nineties. He opposed NAFTA and opposed most-favored-nation status for China on the grounds its government abused human rights and that shifting production there would undercut American workers. In doing so, Buchanan effectively aligned himself on the question of globalization with blue-collars and the public-interest crowd. As Buchanan served as a loud mouth on talk radio, environmentalists and consumer/labor-rights activists were busy traipsing the halls of Congress in wrinkled chinos looking for ears to bend. However, they couldn't match natty Wall Street capitalists snatching up US manufacturers bloodied in competition with hard-selling Japan a decade earlier. Unshackled from previous financial regulations and freed to invest money around the world, borders were no longer nearly as relevant. A truly globalized marketplace was dawning, and Rubin, Summers, and other administration bigwigs sermonized about comparative advantages for consumers and businesses. American scientific, engineering, and marketing expertise infused into products fabricated by cheap, abundant labor in authoritarian regimes where unions were outlawed and there was no EPA could be a Shangri-la for all. The test was coming, for the WTO was made official in January 1995.

The WTO, in replacing the General Agreement on Tariffs and Trade commenced in 1948 amid the wreckage of post-World War II Europe, would be the new platform where countries negotiated trade deals and hashed out their differences. A wild and wooly new era was going to need it. Lowered trade barriers would conjure semi-borderless global commerce bound by rules, where old ideological feuds—over China's labor camps, allegations of nuclear espionage, and unfair business practices—would be more easily solvable because there are no stakes like economic ones. In his pitch to a wavering Congress, Clinton highlighted America's financial interest in integrating China into the free-trading club. "The bottom line is," Clinton said, "If China is willing to play by the global rules of trade, it would have been an inexplicable mistake for the United States to say 'No.'"

Tyco Toys Chief Financial Officer Harry J. Pearce, in a 1996 appearance before Congress to encourage extension of China's MFN status another year, explained the mathematics of why Asia mattered. Tyco employed 40,000 Americans in design and high-value manufacturing in the US, but had already farmed out toy-assembly work to the People's Republic to reap savings. Without China's preferential standing as a most-favored-nation, Pearce said the tariff rate on Tyco goods would soar seventy percent. He hinted that it might force the company to lay off well-paid engineers and marketing managers in the US. Outsourcing to China was the only way Tyco could remain competitive and, by implication, retain its American workforce intact. Same as Kantor, what Pearce kept to himself was as critical as what he enunciated.

American wages adjusted for inflation had been declining since the seventies. The only way to sustain the middle-class standard of living before it sunk further was to reduce the cost of products and gin up easy-money lending. This unspoken reality precipitated skyrocketing sales in the nineties and first part of the 2000s at big-box discount retailers like Walmart. However, for American workers and communities it was akin to eating the seed corn. For Walmart in Arkansas, Tyco, and other multinationals, it was the ultimate arbitrage deal, not unlike selling opium to China in the eighteen-hundreds by Western traders. They were freed to make hay.

Sam Walton opened his first store, Walton's 5 & 10, in Bentonville, Arkansas in the 1950s. After gaining business experience the folksy Walton, who relished wearing baseball caps, opened his first Walmart in Rogers, Arkansas, at age forty-four. It caught on, enabling the former High School football star and lifetime avid hunter to expand Walmart. By 1976 it became a publicly traded company dedicated to the questionable but appealing business proposition that "a lower cost of living" would improve the standard of living. It would become evident only later that there was an unspoken side to that equation, and a negative one at that.

Selling Chinese merchandise cheaply made at discounted prices was a brilliant strategy for Walton that addicted an American public largely unaware of what was happening. No doubt it would've been controversial in Washington, with Walmart running small downtown merchants out of business by opening huge emporiums on the outskirts of American cities. But Walmart had a little-known advantage, the ultimate insider with pillow-talk access to the president. Clinton's wife, Hillary, had been on the board of directors of the growing retail chain while Bill was governor of Arkansas. She served in a specially created position that was supposed to parlay her interest in greening American business. With a friend like that, it seemed that Walmart never needed a Washington lobbyist. At least that was true until the Monica Lewinsky scandal that broke in January of 1998 jeopardized Clinton's presidency. That same year, with the realization that the Democrats might lose their grip on the White House and the disgraced first family their influence, Walmart hired its first capital lobbyist after company officials met with Senate Republican Majority Leader Trent Lott. He advised them to strike a higher profile in the nation's capital. The big-box retailer concurred, eventually hiring six separate lobbying firms.

Until then, Walmart had ready access to the White House through the First Lady, who even before serving on the board of the corporation from 1986 to 1992 was a partner in the Rose Law Firm in Arkansas, which represented the giant retailer. She joined the law firm in 1976 and became partner within a few years. By the early eighties, when her husband Bill served as governor of Arkansas, Walton had already set up a buying office in Hong Kong, which procured merchandise for the growing retail store chain from Taiwan and other Asian nations, but not China. Sensitive to growing public concern in the US about the effect of imports on employment opportunities, Walton launched a "Buy American" campaign, even as he pursued opportunities to undercut his competitors and widen the company's profit margin by chasing more low-cost labor in Asia, eventually in Shenzen, the special economic zone open to foreign investors that Deng Xiaoping established. After Deng's brutal suppression of student freedom protestors in Tiananmen Square in 1989, Walton decided in the last years of his life to disguise the company's purchases from China by dissolving the Hong Kong buying operation and reopening it as a separate company, though it was hardly at arms-length since it was staffed by all the buyers who worked for the original Walmart office.

Walton died in 1992 and his successor as chief executive officer, David Glass, quickly touted trade with China as the future of business, advising US business students to study Mandarin Chinese. By then, Walmart had shifted its suppliers from Taiwan to Shenzen and other cities on the mainland to take advantage of China's lower wages. It was fueling forty percent annual growth for the Arkansas-based company. Not surprisingly, Wall Street took note, boasting that the company was creating "a major strategic merchandising revolution" that amounted to "breaking from a history of almost exclusive commitment to national brands," (that is, products made in the US, in favor of those made in China) wrote Goldman Sachs. Other companies quickly followed the new model Walmart pioneered.

Seeing the opportunity for his country halfway around the world, Jiang, the singing Communist Party general secretary in big, square glasses, was only too willing to help transform America into a nation of ardent Walmart shoppers. Doing that would nurture China's own latent middle class, furthering Deng's initiative. In exchange for cheaply made goods, Deng and Jiang ensured that China won access to Western factory equipment and scientific expertise. Not long after he was elected president, Clinton met Jiang in Seattle in the fall of 1993 during the Asia-Pacific Economic Partnership meeting. They then met on an annual basis throughout Clinton's eight-year tenure to discuss economic relations and other issues. By the time Clinton was packing up to leave the White House in the fall of 2000, he met with Jiang one last time in official capacity to discuss the details of China joining the WTO.

The resulting explosion of factories and cities expanding like microwave popcorn super-sized China's coal consumption, which increased steadily during Clinton and Gore's first term before plateauing for a few years amid the Asian financial crisis of 1997 and 1998. After transfer of coal technology and perpetuation of the MFN status, China devoured even more spectacular amounts of the mineral. Proof was in the atmospheric pudding. China emitted about 2.2 billion tons of carbon dioxide in 1990, which grew to 3 billion tons in 2000. That was threefold the amount the nation emitted when Mao died in 1974. China's gross domestic product (GDP) had never sparkled brighter, tripling from 357 billion dollars in 1990 to 1.1 trillion dollars in the first year of the new century.

To Clinton, free trade, and not some occupying power, would be its own emancipator spreading liberty and prosperity across a planet gainfully reset by economics. Senator Max Baucus, an Idaho Democrat, reflected the administration's internationalist optimism in 1994 in courting votes to support continuing China's MFN status, and would continue to do so for years to come. Baucus had little zeal to slap on preconditions. Sounding like a *laissez-faire* impresario, he advocated "voluntary action from American business" in the areas of "human rights advocacy; adopting codes of conduct; preventing pollution and promoting workplace safety." Cooperation to him was the yeast needed to ferment progress in China, reprisals the chill that could stifle it. "We should begin," Baucus expounded, "by recognizing that trade itself promotes human rights." Two years later, Baucus acknowledged "there are huge environmental problems in China, which will affect the world environment." However, he urged extending MFN and employing targeted approaches to deal with China's battered ecology. Clinton, in contrast, supported unconditional renewal as a long-run tactic. His secretary of state, Madeline Albright, saw its Blue Sky value. She told the Senate Finance Committee in 1998 that embedding stipulations on US trade with the country would "cripple our efforts to enlist China's support" in reversing environmental damage.

The general public seemed to agree. Clinton was popular, American technology companies (and their stocks) were sizzling, and the nation was at peace. Only a few were willing to stridently challenge the prevailing view that trade would be a boon for environmental protection globally, namely, unions, some environmental groups, and a few members of Congress. AFL-CIO Secretary-Treasurer Richard Trumka, who cut his labor-movement teeth as a West Virginia coal miner, foresaw a day we might regret the trade policies. Trumka maintained that China denied labor and basic human rights, just as it always had, and conditioned foreign investment "on harmful export and technology transfer requirements" in its favor. He also predicted in 1996 that the US trade deficit with China, then about twenty-six billion dollars a year, would balloon once American companies flocked there to take advantage of its lack of workplace protections and air- and water-quality standards.

The next year, while Congress reviewed China's MFN status, Rep. Richard Gephardt (D-MO) came out swinging. Gephardt, the fair-haired Midwesterner and future presidential candidate with a deejay-smooth voice, already saw Washington was unlikely to eliminate Chinese trade preferences to force Beijing to become greener. Why should it when it had the US over a barrel in its dependence on cheap imports, and later China's trillion-dollar ownership of US treasury bonds? In Gephardt's estimation, unless the US got tough by writing enforceable provisions in trade law as criteria for Beijing's right to export goods here, "the benefits of US action on the environment may be quickly nullified by China's and other developing nation's inaction."

Gephardt might as well have been talking to the wall, ignored as he was at the other end of Pennsylvania Avenue. There, Clinton's cabinet was busy angling to finance sale of more coal technology to China while Gore lectured Beijing in 1997 with a chart on global warming, illustrating the need to lop greenhouse gas emissions. He advocated solar and wind power and suggested that he and Clinton were interested in enlisting China into the Kyoto Protocol's carbon cap-and-trade system. "If a US company needs to reduce emissions of carbon dioxide," Gore explained, "we'd like to let them do that by investing money and transferring technology to China." Gore, true to his word, played a key role in negotiating the Kyoto agreement, but the Senate never ratified it.

Whether Gore comprehended it or not, America's helping hands with developing nations like China were smeared in coal dust. Both the US Export-Import Bank and US Overseas Private Investment Corporation in the nineties invested a combined 4.2 billion dollars for nineteen different coal-fired projects abroad, the Environmental Defense Fund discovered. One of the deals was the Export-Import Bank's 1996 loan of 409 million dollars to further the sale of six 350-megawatt (MW) coal-fired boilers for the Yangcheng Power Plant in China's Shanxi Province by New Jersey-based Foster-Wheeler Energy Corp. Every year, this plant funnels 15 million tons of carbon dioxide skyward. And that's just one of 101 plants like it in the coal-laden province west of Beijing. The World Bank, led then by Americans Lewis T. Preston, a J.P. Morgan executive, and James Wolfensohn, a corporate attorney, additionally helped finance twenty-nine coal-power projects. The only reason agencies like these ceased spending was that by 2000, US companies were no longer competitive with foreign competitors selling coal equipment on the global market. Other nations could do it less expensively.

Though a beleaguered, lame duck president wobbled by scandal and Al Qaeda's first attacks, Clinton at a March, 2000 news conference broadcast utter confidence, even intellectual surety, that the trade deal with China was a no-brainer to consummate. "This is an agreement about the conditions under which China enters the WTO," Clinton said. "The United States doesn't lower any tariffs. We don't change any trade laws. We do nothing. They have to lower tariffs. They open up telecommunications for investment. They allow us to sell cars made in America in China at much lower tariffs. They allow us to put our own distributorships over there. They allow us to put our own parts over there. We don't have to transfer technology or do joint manufacturing in China anymore. This is a hundred-to-nothing deal for America when it comes to the economic consequences." Pressed by a journalist recounting Gore's own comments that if he were president he wouldn't strike a WTO-deal unless it included hard stipulations on environmental and workplace standards, Clinton said it wasn't possible in multiparty talks, and then self-congratulated his administration for including them in the NAFTA hard-print. "So I know a lot of the people who wanted [environmental safeguards for China in the WTO] aren't satisfied that we've done as much," he said. "But it was a really groundbreaking effort."

So, try as he did, Gore never could hatch a twenty-first century industrial economy based on global environmental protection or his ambitious environmental Marshall Plan. Ironically, he depicted the result by riding a lift to the top of a giant chart during the 2006 documentary *An Inconvenient Truth* to dramatize the upward spike of carbon dioxide into the atmosphere. The booming economy during the nineties caused exponential increases in greenhouse gases. Gephardt's forecasts were vindicated about global warming, about menacing Far Eastern smog, and the balance of trade. It turned out to be quite unbalanced, tilted in China's favor.

Nobody knows how a Gore administration would've reapproached the Kyoto pact and China, since George H. W. Bush's namesake son beat him by a chad-hanging whisker in the contested 2000 presidential race. Clinton's formerly lengthy coattails had shortened several sizes with the Monica Lewinsky impeachment affair. But the system of unfettered, environment-be-damned trade was set in concrete. George W. Bush moved briskly in requesting that Congress grant the People's Republic permanent MFN, which it did within months of his taking office, but only after Clinton had done the heavy lifting. Activists echoed the dark warnings voiced by labor leader Williams. Friends of the Earth President Brent Blackwelder even conjectured that agreements like the one that launched the WTO, which China joined in 2001 right after the fateful day of 9-11, would "foster the growth of pollution havens around the world," enabling transnational corporations to go rogue. Looking back now, Kantor admits China's air is an apocalyptic-like health disaster and that the US should have pressed more during the nineties to include clean air provisions in trade agreements, as the administration insisted with NAFTA. "From 1993-2000, the WTO worked," Kantor said. "What we didn't do was have strong environmental provisions. We didn't make that happen...Today, when you land in Beijing and taxi to the airport, it takes your breath away." Meanwhile, chalk one up for the ability of Gephardt, Williams, Blackwelder, and others to read the tea leaves. One way or another, we all became Walmart shoppers.

CHAPTER 6:

PARTICLE DAWN

MAYBE IN HINDSIGHT WE should've been peeking over the emerald horizon where those factories began to decamp. Rather than titillating ourselves with clunky cell phones and a White House intern's stained blue dress, perhaps we should've battened down the hatches against industrial capitulation that Clinton and the free trade crowd hastened in their bull rush to crack China open. For whatever reason, though, few outside the Washington/academic wonkosphere seemed to have noticed that China of the nineties resembled nothing of the arthritic, old Far East reciting Mao's Little Red Book to anyone who cared. Ditching austerity, it was whooshing at the speed of one of its bullet trains in its evolution from manufacturing pipsqueak to leader of the pack.

You know that sensitive, overweight kid so introverted that bullies he easily could've gotten into a headlock drove him indoors to wallow? Well, that was China, international punching-bag of the last two centuries, before it marshaled its girth to carve for itself what it'd missed out on so far: a fat piece of the world economy. Nothing illustrated its early victories like gross national product that more than tripled over the decade, from 357 billion dollars in 1990 to 1.2 trillion dollars in 2000. Outsiders' big money—ones with lots of zeroes—deserve some of the credit. Nearly a century after the Boxer Rebellion had shunted British and US firms from Asia, direct foreign investment to China by 1997 had almost reached half a trillion dollars.

The Clinton administration, hell-bent for a policy reset there, bankrolled a portion of those outlays with taxpayer's dollars in hopes of accessing markets inside the world's most populous nation while exerting more sway over its government. Monies not earmarked from the American treasury cascaded through the World Bank and other global financial institutions that Washington steered. The billions didn't wend through the typical rabbit holes of foreign aid, where dictators' cronies and in-laws suddenly got rich. They subsidized nuts-and-bolts public works—roads, ports, highways, and such—essential in animating China's export business. In effect, the West was lubricating the chute for Asian manufacturing, one that in a few years would undercut countless made-in-America brands, be it snowboards or semiconductors.

Of course, few were that vulgar about the pattern set to emerge. Most experts chiming in saw it as unfolding globalization, where streamlining the path from Chinese production lines to American checkout lines would showcase the exquisiteness of a tariff-free paradigm uniting former Cold Warriors. Deng championed the association. But he was a realist. When in the early eighties he famously quipped, "To get rich is glorious," he might've prefaced his remark by explaining what it required. In his nation's instance, there was no way to fabricate merchandise at the impatient clip world markets demanded if the raw materials and finished products couldn't be as efficiently transported as, say, a UPS distribution center. From harbors to super-roads, China was swapping sun hats for construction helmets. America's credit card helped with the tab.

China wasted not a second, either, pouncing on its opportunity to become wonderfully profitable. At the opening of the decade of tech stocks and grunge rock, it registered a slight trade deficit of ten billion dollars with America. In a turnaround that startled many economists, it enjoyed a net eighty-four billion dollar surplus with its former nemesis by the dawn of the new millennium. US imports of Chinese wares registered more than 300 billion dollars—about the size of the defense budget under Reagan—by the juncture Clinton completed his economic handiwork in 2000.

Interestingly, Chinese imports were less than half that when his wife, Hillary, sat on Walmart's board of directors before he ran for president in 1992. Nobody said the Clinton-Walmart connection was fishy, just as no one could dispute that Walmart was turning the land of Mao into a manufacturing archipelago of plants, distribution centers, and contractors whose sprawl was almost extra-planetary.

◘

BLEAKLY, CONFIRMATION OF ASIA'S renaissance was also visible beyond hectic ports dominated by giant, praying mantis-looking cranes. Over many crowded spots, skies were surrendering their cerulean gleam to smokestacks panting fumes from galaxies of new factories, along with the first wave of privately owned automobiles. The artificial haze was not only an optical obstruction. It was forensically detectable in the lower troposphere, or the space between the ground and 1,500 feet up where smog generally confines itself, in a preview of coming envelopment. Some major cities where residents were getting their first taste of the nation's embryonic consumer economy were being swathed in rising nitrogen oxide seeping from power plants and vehicles. In municipalities exceeding 2 million people, the gas violated limits in four-fifths of them. To thrive, in a sense, was to cough.

Number-crunching health experts might've sputtered themselves in 1995 after the Massachusetts Institute of Technology issued a divining analysis that should've given would-be globalists a collective flop sweat. Lost production from Chinese left ill by particulate-matter and ozone pollution above background levels had popped fivefold (to 112 billion dollars) from 1975 to 1995, as Asia's infrastructure binge and proto-reforms advanced. Seemingly, it only took the sidelining of certain people exposed to certain airborne contaminants that hadn't existed a decade or two ago to begin tearing at society. MIT had sniffed something big. Another report from the era, this one from the World Bank in 1997, stressed that if China merely complied with its own relatively slack rules, 178,000 unnecessary air pollution deaths could be averted yearly.

Of all the threats, the public health tsunami whipping around coal was the most chilling. Before most had heard of the Internet, researchers in Tianjin south of Beijing were discovering that Chinese living near power plants and companies fashioning steel, dyes, chemicals, and locomotives fueled by the nugget lived in a pulmonary gun-scope. They were four-and-a-half times more likely to contract bronchitis, asthma, allergies, and other illnesses than those in less industrial enclaves. Scarier results were plumbed in Nanning in southern China near Vietnam during a 1991-2002 study deciphering lung cancer rates. Residents close to factories there in some cases faced double the odds of getting the disease than their urban neighbors. Children's health was its own pathogen rain. Experts tracking 6,000 youths aged thirteen to fourteen residing near plants in rural, southeastern China were twice as likely of developing allergies or asthma than peers not near those generators. Rates of the chronic, often deadly disease— the top cause of childhood hospitalization—jumped over the last two decades. Epidemiologically speaking, coal burning was China's elephant in the room.

While no one pumped the economic brakes to contemplate what these multiple studies were foretelling, China's national leaders during the nineties weren't completely sitting on their hands, either. They did the obvious and the unexpected. They strengthened air quality regulations countrywide. They then prodded some heavy industry out of the capital. In another novelty, they even enlisted the national media they customarily gagged to expose tens of thousands of the country's highest polluting factories. The unusual coverage was nicknamed the Green Hurricane. It'd only gust for a few years before the 30,000 or so government censors manning the Great Firewall of China busied themselves tamping down environmental turmoil.

Beijing city authorities got their own fingernails grimy charting pollution about then. Every day, technicians sampled averages of three smog-related compounds: sulfur dioxide, nitrogen dioxide, and miniscule specks of carbon-family discharges less than ten micrometers in diameter, technically known as "particulate matter" (or PM-10 for short). What the Chinese regarded as a good day under their emerging Blue Sky program, American regulators would've contested as an unhealthy one by applying sterner EPA limits. Naturally, that assumed they could perform side-by-side comparisons. Yet that was impossible since Chinese officials squelched the data they were collecting by sequestering it in-house. Releasing the numbers, they later admitted, might've elicited public scorn, questions about their stewardship, and inflamed what they dreaded most—social unrest that could topple them from power one day by disagreeable means.

Beijing city hall also thought small, vent-small, focused on the thousands of smoky residential heating systems, where coal was tossed into home and apartment building furnaces to combust at high temperatures. Exhaust from this antiquated warming method for years puffed from rooftop chimneys barely above street level. Plumes would drape neighborhoods on freezing, windless nights, casting a grey pall in the early morning through which bundled-up children walked to school and people scurried to work.

Overseas, meanwhile, West Coast researchers were circling a different sort of weather disturbance. The swirl that captured their attention on satellites was often milky-white, predisposed to springtime appearances, and capable of traversing the Pacific Ocean on a parabolic, eastward trajectory over Alaska in four to ten days. China's fierce dust storms were twirling up into the atmosphere and across the ocean snaking ribbons of grit, each drift weighing tens of millions of pounds, much of it dappled with industrial particles. Because the concentrations of copper, lead, zinc, and arsenic were low, they were yet to enflame environmental concern, only mild consternation among scientists intuiting a flattening planet before the term became talking-head chic.

There were no stunners here—not about coal, not about Trans-Pacific drift—under the Faustian bargain contoured by Deng and perpetuated by Jiang and his likeminded successors. China would rejigger the calculus of great nations by shape-shifting into an export-manufacturing colossus dedicated to Western store shelves. This model was its chance to vault out of its excruciating past, to erase those centuries hostage to foreign occupation and shuffling backwardness. Bottom-barrel wages, slack red tape, pliant locales, and sheer size conferred to it transcendent advantages that Mexico, Taiwan, and other non-Western factory bastions could never sustain. As the world's friendliest landing pad for outsourced production, air quality would have to take it on the chin, at least for now. Under this creed, rules that had been tightened in 1996 were loosened in 2000 to accommodate boundless, new capacity for China's two-pronged drive to industrialize and modernize.

In November 2001, the ruling elite of the People's Republic got the signatures they so craved as the rubble was being bulldozed away in Manhattan and Washington, DC following the Al Qaeda attacks. Grinding, sometimes-rancorous negotiations about China's future had its oddly quiet denouement in the Persian Gulf emirate of Qatar. Troops and guards adorned in purple camouflage and white robes tightened into a security perimeter against supposed terrorist threats for the membership induction. The admission ceremony granting China the trading rights of any capitalist nation was over in an affable blink. WTO Director General Michael Moore hugged Chinese Trade Minister Shi Guangsheng, said a few words, and it was official. Who could've predicted what would be more earth shattering: the ascension of Islamic radicalism or 1.3 billion Chinese capitalists?

The year 2001 couldn't have gone more swimmingly as China's year of legitimization. In July, the International Olympic Committee (IOC) announced that the capital of 20 million people had trounced cosmopolitan Toronto, Paris, and Istanbul in the vote to host the 2008 Summer Games. Only a wizened clairvoyant could've predicted the labor required to invert the city's smog-tableau into green exemplar once the economic afterburners were lit, or how the soupy air would soon be blamed for killing Chinese in droves from exposure to microscopic bits unloosed by the country's double-digit GDP. Even a fortune-teller might not have believed the atmosphere could be so sadistic.

Was this really what Clinton's White House meant trumpeting new "economic rules of the road" of shared technology that fostered an environmentally healthful future for all? An era where brackish skies no longer clouded? Over a few years, that quixotic idea lost its moral currency, its voices supplanted by a deal-making philosophy that the faster Asia's industrialization occurred, the better it would be for both sides. So instead of avoided, inefficient, fume-prone technologies entrenched themselves in the factories and gear works of a China the West helped reimagine. Those early warning health studies by MIT and the World Bank—studies that might've been Gore's ammunition to lobby for treaty provisions to contain the filthy smokestacks that he dreaded would proliferate—just didn't seem to mortify anyone else in power as much as the vice president.

◘

COMBINE CAPITALISTIC TOE DIPPING of the eighties with broad economic trends and trade pacts adopted in the nineties, and the society legendary for its herbal medicines and reliance on nature by the early-2000s was under chemical bombardment hard to exaggerate. Some of the experts' admonitions during the WTO debate about emissions dumping from North America to the Far East on the luggage rack of the free trade bandwagon were looking downright soothsaying. From cities where housing complexes rose weekly to towns with the crudest of services, tens of millions of tons of sophisticated compounds circled over peoples' heads, infiltrated their food, contaminated their water, glommed to their homes, and stunted their crops. The sources were as many as their ill effects—coal fed into humongous plant furnaces casting brilliant red sparks and cavalcades of big rig trucks thundering every which direction. Cement scooped up from enormous, sandy pits and liquids extracted from drums that spruced up electronics' screens and forged plastics slotted their own waste legacies. For the most part, they'd all materialized within a generation.

On the air pollution front, the Chinese saw four chemicals drench their skies. Nitrogen oxides are brownish-orange gases that escape from automobiles, refineries, power plants, heavy industry, and other origins. When it reacts in bright sunlight with hydrocarbons—vapors from gasoline, diesel fuel, solvents, paints, and such—nitrogen oxides convert into ground-level ozone that disperses as microscopic bits able to invade the lungs. People, understandably, conflate two types of ozone, partly from cultural misperceptions that have blurred their meaning. The upper-atmospheric variety protects Earth from the sun's deadly ultraviolet rays. Its invisible, lower-level cousin is what's hell on the lungs. Ozone inflames the respiratory tract, making it taxing to breathe. It can aggravate bronchitis, emphysema, and asthma as well, raising the chance of respiratory infection while making you antsy for shelter.

Not to be forgotten in China's chemical lineup are sulfur dioxide and directly emitted fine particles. Sulfur dioxide, the primary ingredient in acid rain that the Eastern US, Canada, and Europe wrangled over in the seventies, is a respiratory irritant especially noxious for asthmatics, children, and the elderly. Through the atmosphere, it transforms into sulfate particles that can evade respiratory defenses. Machines burn coal or oil laced with sulfur plume it, which is why the nastiest concentrations of sulfur dioxide usually linger around power plants, boilers, and similar operations. Fine particulate matter less than 2.5 micrometers in size, or about thirty times smaller than the width of a human hair, may be the most insidious compound of them all. Its infinitesimal mass is like a diplomatic passport that allows it to bypass different membranes, where it can penetrate the lungs and enter the bloodstream to wreak biological havoc. Versatile in its capacity for damage, PM-2.5 impairs lung function and worsens asthma. Scientists have associated it with cancer, heart attacks, irregular heartbeats, and premature death in people with existing cardiovascular ailments and other woes. Motor vehicle exhaust, power plant emissions, steel mills, and construction sites spew most of it. Also, because it's so light, PM-2.5 can be lifted astonishing distances by local winds and the jet streams alike. Most nations consider it the best, single barometer for air pollution out there.

A gallery of heavy metals and industrial compounds absolved from smog formation constitute a whole hazard category unto their own in contemporary China. Among them are dioxin—one of the most poisonous compounds known to man—mercury, lead, paraxylene, polycyclic aromatic hydrocarbons, fluoride, ammonia, black and organic carbon, chromium-6, cadmium, arsenic, and other materials with skull-and-bones health implications. Not only are some carcinogenic, they can also compromise immune, nervous, and reproductive systems, weaken the heart and blood production and inhibit childhood development. Smelters, power plants, steel plants, and recycling graveyards for castoff electronics are fingered most for discharging them into Asia's clotted skies.

Now for all the meteorology you need to know; Chinese smog is frequently its most tortuous when high-pressure weather systems whirling in from Siberia clamp over its territory, generally in winter and early spring. Contained in these weather systems from the north is a layer of cool air that sinks toward the earth, pressing the contaminants down like a lid on a cauldron, sometimes for days. If the conditions stagnate overhead, winds die off and don't blow the filth away with much urgency.

◘

ELEVEN YEARS AFTER THE WTO accepted them, China's membership papers could've doubled as coronation parchment. Using 2012 as a baseline, the once-forgotten Middle Kingdom—now the Kraken of carbon dioxide, acid rain, and nitrogen oxide discharges—was still on its tear. Asthmatic and all, Asia's tiger boasted a 5.8 trillion dollar economy that emplaced it as the globe's second largest, behind only the US and ahead of sometimes-archenemy Japan. Being number one in big categories landed it there, and the People's Republic was the preeminent overall manufacturer, with exports swelling geometrically since 1979. Nobody fabricated more steel, chemicals, solar panels, and wind farms than its workers. In size-matter metrics by country, China maintained the longest sea-bridge and high-speed train, the second busiest airport, and the penultimate number of billionaires. Its freshly built infrastructure made Westerners salivate. More automobiles are purchased there than any place else as part of a bubbling 1.7 trillion dollar consumer market that can't snap up enough kitchen appliances, cell phones, and Swiss watches. A market, incidentally, just beginning to be whetted by fattened incomes, if not a hankering to live more American.

Demographers predict that come 2030, nearly two-thirds of its population will be city-dwellers. Multinationals Pfizer, GlaxoSmithKline, and Colgate-Palmolive, along with the major US automakers, have sunk billions there. Besting them all is Walmart, which operates some 350 stores employing 100,000 people. Shanghai alone has constructed the equivalent of 334 Empire State buildings since 1998. "You can't be an elevator company and not be in China," explained the CEO of United Technologies, which produces Otis Elevators. In central Chengdu, Louis Vuitton, Gucci, and other upscale European brand-makers field stores on the avenue giving way to a statue of their former dear leader, Mao. Direct foreign investment that stood at 430 million dollars annually in 1982 had whooshed to 92.4 billion dollars by the year of the Beijing Games. By 2013, to no ones surprise, China's annual four trillion dollars in trade knocked the US off its perch as king of the import-export hill.

In spite of these blazing advancements, the country that also owns trillions in US treasury bonds remains terrifically impoverished. China ranked midpoint of the World Bank's

181-country index of wealth per citizen. At 13,700 dollars, the average Chinese earned about a third of the typical American. While hundreds of millions of Chinese are no longer destitute, two hundred million remain so. The ruling body reflects this duality as a classic police state able to jail or execute just about anyone it pleases while maintaining a cult of self-enrichment, where hordes of Community Party members stuff their pockets with ill-gotten gains and perks denied commoners.

Air pollution had never migrated over such a paradoxical concoction—sunny, gullible Los Angeles included. Neither did it dilly-dally. By the time the world hyperventilated about the Y2K bug frying computers, China's airshed, rivers, and lakes downstream of factories were shading into preepidemic gray. Premier Zhu Rongji, a straight-shooting pragmatist, brashly predicted how air pollution tramples health, unconcerned about what his colleagues thought about his forthrightness. On the eve of the twenty-first century, he offered this fatalistic comment on smog that epidemiologists later corroborated: "If I worked in Beijing, I would shorten my life at least five years."

CHAPTER 7:

FULL BODY BACKLASH

A T SEVENTY-SEVEN, THE OLD man had a simple wish for his pitiful story. "I just hope I can die sooner," he told *Agence France-Presse*, tears dampening his face. "I gave my life to the Communist Party, yet I have nothing now." Even on his deathbed, he spoke anonymously, frightened of retribution. What the party loyalist could claim as his in 2006 was lung cancer that he ascribed to polluted air and water from living in Liukuaizhuang village in the city of Tianjin, roughly seventy-five miles southeast of Beijing. The chemical companies that had rooted there and the neighboring town of Xiditou in the nineties had apparently yoked residents with an annual cancer-diagnosis rate of 2,032 per 100,000 people, which was almost ten times higher than China's national frequency for the disease. (American men during 2006-2010, by comparison, logged an annual rate of about 436 per 100,000 people.) Yet more disturbing than Liukuaizhuang's place on the Bell Curve was the grim, new tautology that people who shriveled up and perished there from cancers of the liver, bone, lung, breast, and blood epitomized in China 2.0. They were the casualties of hundreds of unofficial cancer villages. Unbridled industrialization celebrated with stiff propaganda and ceremonial pens had flipped the script. Where it had delivered swift prosperity in the post-WTO era, it now served up company towns brittle with heartbreak.

Tests confirmed that Liukuaizhuang's dull, green waters were infected with high levels of poisonous hydroxybenzene, a water-soluble, acidic derivative used in manufacturing that's toxic when ingested. Fluoride and bacteria were detected, as well. How much hydroxybenzene (also known as phenol and often crystalline-white in color) had taken flight on the local winds was anybody's guess. Its prevalence wasn't. Plants molding resins and plastics devoured the substance, and then it devoured the village. Trying to corral its outflow into the river, the local government ordered the area's large-scale polluters to cease work, but smaller ones continued operating with a wink and a nod from their pals in office. Those with the cash to split town did. Had the dying, old man been an American, his family might've sued for compensation and justice to spare future victims of gut-wrenching demises like his. But in China, where citizens have no Bill of Rights, there was little winning precedent for such responses, much less a city hall defending them.

South of there in Xiadian, hospitals were awash in patients with cancer of the stomach, liver, and other digestive organs. Fifty of them had died since 2004. Like most other cancer villages, adulterated water was the primary culprit. The Baoqiu River, where untreated wastewater downstream of a paper mill, steel factories, and a bone-processing plant gave the waters a red or creamy tint, was the probable source. "We only realized there was a problem in the past three or four years," a female shopkeeper said in 2009. "People began dying…only a few months after getting cancer and couldn't be cured." Local authorities, she noted, recommended that citizens sell their land to developers and relocate. Those unable to do so had to rely on adjacent Dacheng County for their water. Basically untouchable, Xiadian's industries refused to curb their toxic discharges.

Beijing tried staunching some of the damage in 2008 with the Ministry of Environmental Protection's (MEP) agreement to spend 134 million dollars—about one-third of the 400 million dollar Bird's Nest stadium—to erect wastewater and sewage treatment plants nationwide. Compared to the immensity of the challenge, officials realized those millions were a drop in the bucket. Maybe not even that. As the MEP itself conceded, *one half* of the nation's 800 million rural population lacked safe drinking water, much of it ruined by agricultural and factory run-off, as well as human and animal waste. As a subset, more than 250 billion people struggled to get enough water. Lined up, China's thirsty masses equaled the combined populations of Europe's five largest nations: Germany, France, England, Italy, and Spain. Few in Europe, however, had to fret about cancer from their faucet.

The scope of the problem certainly crested over regulators too shorthanded to reverse the decay in Xiadian. Or chase down polluters elsewhere that funneled toxins through secret discharge pipes. Or dispatched goons after complaining villagers. Or bought silence with bribes. While ministries responsible for water resources, construction and agriculture had associated roles monitoring contamination none had "Environmental Protection" in its name. But only about 300 staffers in the mid-2000s worked at the MEP's Beijing's headquarters, with another 3,000 or so at its five regional offices and sister agencies. In contrast, the EPA, which policed an area about the same size as China with a population a quarter as large, employed 17,000 people nationwide. The EPA, in other words, was six times the force of its Chinese counterpart that faced multiple crises stacking up one atop the other. Given's the MEP's skeleton numbers, it wasn't foolish to wonder if the Politburo had on its payroll more state-backed cyberwarriors, a gaggle of them already allegedly hacking American energy-industry networks from a People's Liberation Army building in Shanghai, than it did guarding the land? Finances, after all, telegraph priorities.

A sunshine-pumping propagandist could still argue that comparisons between the EPA and the MEP were specious since employees at China's local environmental protection bureaus shouldered the burden of watchdog inspections. On organizational trees, the bureaus answered to their superiors in Beijing. In practice, they received their marching orders from GDP-swooning city halls. These municipalities, according to noted Sinologist Elizabeth Economy, provided them with their lifeblood: "budgets, career advancement, number of personnel, and resources such as cars, office buildings, and employee housing." Little mystery, then, where their allegiances lay, or why polluters so casually disregarded them. Even after it bulked up its workforce to inspect 70,000 facilities in 2008, the ministry admitted that ten percent of the operations it shuttered for regulatory shortcomings restarted without permission. When you toted up other evidence of rogue plants, you might say the ministry's hammer had Nerf material in it.

Blending methanol made from coal into Asian gasoline is another example of derelict enforcement, albeit one that scarcely wins attention. China has enough small coal-to-methanol plants to replace half its traditional gasoline with the alcohol-based fuel, despite rules that limit mixing it with gasoline because of its damaging effect on car engines. Methanol's carbon footprint also shows its blemishes. When you include the energy needed to synthesize the fuel additive from coal, it emits up to eighty-four percent more greenhouse gases than traditional gasoline, said Chi-Jen Yang, a research scientist at Duke University's Center on Global Change. But nobody at either the central or local government level evidently cares enough to monitor the laws. The result? Up to five million tons of the bootleg fuel is stirred into gasoline each year. The ill-gotten gains of black market blending, Yang contended, are just too attractive to pass up, even greater than if the comingling were legalized, since the windfalls are akin to narcotic-trade markups.

Travel through China as we did and you'll appreciate it's the human environment that distinguishes seedy collusion from a capitalist variant of the Confucian order. Typical of the often-incestuous relationship between municipalities and wealthy industrialists is Taihe County in Anhui province west of Shanghai. When Haiquan Liu, chief executive officer of the Anhui Jinggong Group Company, phones his local city hall, the mayor and his entourage materialize quickly at the firm, seemingly with all the time in the world. And why shouldn't they? "Mr. Liu," as he is known, is busy rebuilding the heart of the city in the heart of the county. A one billion dollar mixed-use project framed with concrete from his nearby cement plant is underway thanks to him. Consequently, gleaming, new condominiums with handsome landscaping and public amenities like his are fast replacing old USSR-inspired housing of China's yesteryear. The Haiquan's of the

People's Republic are the mortar of a new society skewing toward Western tastes. They coexist with less honorable industrialists able to manipulate authorities through "red envelope bribery" and other means in *produce-profit-now* circles. People within striking range of factory effluents expedited by improprieties usually just adapt. In doing so, they join history's other disenfranchised people whose birthplaces became more company than town with every smokestack belch.

Shangba, a tiny village surrounded by shamrock-colored paddy fields in the far south near Myanmar, required no homily about dire circumstance. Something wholly unnatural was exterminating living things there. The shallow river that wended through the town of about 3,000 was rife with heavy metals painting it sometimes burnt-orange. Water that generations once drank to survive or channeled for farm irrigation killed all the fish. Chickens and ducks floated dead, too. Not even diluting the river by a factor of 10,000 times could keep any aquatic organism in it alive more than twenty-four hours. "If you put your leg into the water, you'll get rashes and a terrible itch," young rice farmer He Shuncai complained in 2009. Citizens saw no whodunit in the septic river. They blamed mining operations for sheening the water with cadmium and zinc, which then permeated the food supply. Excavation tailings dumped near the paddy fields further spread the metallic remnants. The hand of disease touched repeatedly thereafter. Awful cancers of the colon, kidney, liver, and stomach became almost humdrum. One report suggested 250 villagers had succumbed to them since the late eighties.

Isolated in their misery and forced to decide between starvation and poison, some townspeople ate the toxic rice and even sold it to others. For the emaciated, their choices were no morality play. It was how they stayed alive. "We have appealed to the mine and to senior officials to stop this," lamented He Shouming, Shangba's local Communist Party official. "But so far nothing has happened. I have one family of three young children who lost their mother and father…we are stuck here." In certain hot-zones, entire towns were nearly wiped out as if a super-virus romped through them

From the rural climes of Xinglong in the southwestern Yunnan Province, residents around several chemical companies and a paper mill sprouted tumors, too. Industry had puked the air with chemicals and colored the water with vivid red and yellow slicks. Interrogated about the whip-spray of toxins, one of the factories impugned the previous firm occupying its site. County regulators trying to monitor wily polluters, meanwhile, often felt a step behind. "It's like police trying to catch a thief," complained Song Bin, a staffer with Luliang's Environmental Protection Dept. Among other subterfuge, companies flicked their treatment systems off when electrical supplies were low or sneakily under the cover of night.

A nearby cancer village tried the less submissive route to connect polluters with the polluted. Environmental groups in the former boondock farming town of Xiaoxin, where people's bodies developed ominous lumps and the cattle died strangely, filed a then-rare public-interest lawsuit against the Yunnan Luliang Peace Technology Company. The objective: to force the business to establish a 1.6 million dollar compensation fund for the suffering it caused employing chromium-6 for leather tanning. The chemical, a widely applied rust inhibitor/industrial solvent used to fashion steel, paint, plastics, and other materials, was made infamous in the hit movie *Erin Brockovich*. Ingestion of the yellowy compound is known to cause digestive cancers and leukemia, among other maladies. Activists investigating tips that the company dumped 5,000 tons of the stuff, some of which migrated into the Nanpan River, stumbled across 140,000 additional tons buried in Xiaoxin and nearby Xinglong. For a material whose lethality is obsessively measured in parts-per-billion, that's a lot of death spread around. Villagers had unwittingly been tapping some of the infected soil for homes and road paving.

As with so many of these episodes, it's not altogether apparent what happened with the litigation in Yunnan, where the worst of the pollution was fenced off and a few scapegoats detained. One environmental attorney wasn't sanguine it'd make a dent in his nation's evolving justice system. "Our circle of lawyers has a saying: in China, the big cases are about politics, the mid-sized cases are about influence and only the small cases deal with law." A film entitled *Hopeful* by a Chinese non-governmental organization (NGO) and lawyers from the American Bar Association retold the incident. "Why was the factory built here and not Beijing and Shanghai," a resident asked rhetorically, perhaps after attending too many wakes. "Because in Beijing and Shanghai, there are people watching."

The villager might not have realized how attuned his cynicism was. Shanghai wasn't always today's cosmopolitan Shanghai of fabulous stores, museums, and apartment towers, where high finance meets lifestyle decadence. In the nineties, there were still open fields grazed by oxen and attended by "coolies" (unskilled laborers) in what is now China's largest city, population 23 million. Conjuring a first-order metropolis required jutting skyscrapers, welcoming cars, and industrial ribbon cutting, so it was goodbye to the wandering livestock and hello to feverish construction. On cue, viscous smog blanketed the city 700 miles from Beijing. For roughly one hundred polluting industries located there, it was a fast ticket to inland provinces. "Once situated," a cynic clucked, "they resume polluting, out of sight and mind."

But did that make orphaned Xinglong a place irreparably doomed or unfairly stigmatized with cancer? Not necessarily in the dearth of scientific and medical attention stranding cancer villages, which Communist leaders only acknowledged in 2013, and elliptically at that. In the US, stamping an area a confirmed cancer cluster is exceedingly difficult; the Centers for Disease Control and Prevention defines them as a "greater-than-expected" number of cases that occur "within a group of people in a geographic area over a defined period of time." Never mind the suffering catalogued in places like Hinkley, California; Tom's River, New Jersey; Camp Lejeune, North Carolina; Woburn, Massachusetts; or Fallon, Nevada. Meeting the accepted threshold is rare. Indeed, a National Institutes of Health analysis of 428 investigations since 1990 determined that just three locations had links of varying certainty between hypothesized exposure and the hundreds of cancers of concern. That said, experts flummoxed by unproven connections in the West gulped at what was stewing in the Far East.

Foreigners probably first heard of China's cancer villages in 2009 after they learned of its killer smog. An investigative journalist and microblogging ace named Deng Fei penned an explosive story accompanied by a highly circulated Google map pinpointing one hundred of them. The non-technical term, which describes a post-reform phenomenon with fundamentally the same definition as US cancer clusters, took off with a blaze of publicity. Deng, a square-faced young man often pictured glowering at the inhumanity his articles uncovered, had first made his name with exposés on child trafficking and organ harvesting. Now he seemed to have defined a new chapter of Asia's eco-despair.

In truth, there'd been sporadic academic and Chinese media attention on the topic since the late-nineties. Government restrictions on journalists and limits on the power exercised by NGOs just kept it under wraps. The state's capacity to shut people up on these topics was impressive. A Yunnan Province doctor who diagnosed 111 kids with lead poisoning later had to publicly eat his words, saying he'd mischaracterized their health. A party secretary who disclosed cancer rates in Henan was cashiered for "leaking state secrets." Today, researchers suspect there are 459 cancer villages at a minimum, though no meticulous count has been issued. In addition to authorities censoring what people can reveal about the chemical hotspots by persecuting or threatening them with jail time or the loss of their jobs, a cultural taboo cuffs a fuller assessment. Because Chinese are traditionally associated with their hometown villages, intrepid sorts who identified themselves as hailing from an area overrun with disease can jeopardize investment, tourism dollars, even their own reputation in the process. But someone had to speak up for the dead and dying. "China," wrote Lee Liu of the University of Central Missouri in a groundbreaking study in *Environment* magazine, "appears to have produced more cancer clusters in a few decades than the rest of the world ever had."

Ringing China's eastern coast, Liu discerned, was a "cancer belt" that accounted for eighty-six percent of the disease-ridden villages. Forming the crescent-shaped grouping were six coastal provinces and their six inland neighbors in a patchwork banding from Hebei in the north to Guangdong in the south. Though twenty-nine of the country's thirty-one provinces had at least one cancer village, Hebei and Henan provinces sported the highest concentrations. Much of the contamination behind them speckled major rivers and tributaries that bucolic Chinese had relied on deep into their lineage. The geographic exodus of the modern toxins had economic logic to it. When China embraced foreign manufacturers and investors in the opening hoopla of Deng's reforms, it was along the eastern part of the country where the plants first towered. As time went by and scrutiny increased, new factories plowed inland to capitalize on what they reckoned would be tepid resistance from the yokel-locals.

Scholars also mapped a pattern that their colleagues who'd studied ports, industrial parks, and dumps worldwide could appreciate: environmental injustice demarcating the haves and have-nots. Chinese cancer villages usually festered in destitute areas afield more affluent ones blessed with improving regulatory and medical care. In Guangdong's mountainous regions, decades of strip mining for iron and copper leached cadmium, lead, and other heavy metals into the water and soil. In Henan, where those same chemicals, plus sulfur dioxide, feast on the vulnerable, more than three-quarters of the young are sick year-round. Jiangsu province, with one of China's shiniest sub-economies, harbors its own chronically ill. Alongside one highway there is a sign reading "Investors are our Gods" not far from seventeen advertisements for cancer treatments.

Greenhouse gas measurements from consumer-product factories inside China are also magnifying—or revealing—the wealth gap in what's touted as a class-free society striving toward Marxist plateaus with capitalist élan. "Highly developed" areas in

Beijing-Tianjin and provinces to the south, for instance, import eighty percent of the low-value, carbon-intensive goods from provinces outside their borders, one multiuniversity analysis concluded. These New Money consumption zones benefit the most from Asia's export goldmine, with more shopping and less heat-trapping gases in their everyday affairs. People manning factory posts in central, northwest, and southwest China, conversely, must wipe sweat from their brow, disconcerted about their raw deal. In a sense, they've become a mini-pollution haven trapped inside of a bigger one.

Some Angelenos can sympathize. For decades, the working-class families living around the jangling ports of Los Angeles and Long Beach responsible for tens of billions of dollars in economic activity yearly—much of it from handling imported goods boxed in the Far East—haven't breathed the same as people in Beverly Hills or Arcadia. Dockside neighborhoods there are aggrieved on a micro-level of what the Chinese are buffeted with nationwide: disproportional childhood-asthma, heart, and lung diseases, and uneasy cohabitation with the town's chief moneymaker. Trucks and machinery running on particulate-matter-spewing diesel fuel are the main instigators of compromised health. But globalization is a transit game. Sorties of big rigs and trains haul merchandise from ports to warehouses managed by big US retail companies across the West. The operation has even warranted its own Chamber of Commerce-type handle: "Driveway to the Nation." Residents near them burn through pallets of inhalers, with blocks around them afforded their own nickname: "Asthma Alley."

◘

INCREDIBLY, GUANGDONG AND HENAN might have ducked the worst effects from Asia's manufacturing lollapalooza. Global consumers' unquenchable yearning for snazzy electronics, specifically devices engineered with built-in obsolescence so they must be replaced faster than other items, has conjured up a sub class of woebegone Chinese towns about as opposite of shoppers' euphoria as you can find. Even characterizing these places where the toxic skeletons of the digital world clutter pits and mounds haloed in pewter smoke as Dickensian smacks of sugarcoating. Electronic waste, also known as e-waste, may just be the Far East's most environmentally sinister import, if not its most ironic.

For all the billions of dollars of assembled products China 2.0 ships across its borders, it also allows back in what millions of people no longer desire. As of the late-2000s, the People's Republic was on the receiving end of as much as seventy percent of the 20-50 million tons of worldwide e-waste generated annually, the majority of it from overseas. (Nigeria and Ghana are the other leading depositories.) Officially condemned, decried by activists and banned by treaty, ending the practice, nonetheless, has been like trying to grab smoke in your palm. Hence, televisions, personal computers, laptops, cell phones, refrigerators, washing machines, and other gadgets unable to be repaired or donated to charity in their purchaser's homeland go for dismantlement in ramshackle villages. Once unloaded, people for as little as one hundred dollars a month harvest the castoffs for subcomponents and materials they sell to recycling outfits. Enough e-waste went yearly to China to pack dozens of super-freighters.

With the toxic contact involved, the labor makes dead animal collection appealing as an alternative profession. E-waste workers must melt and strip wires to yank out a product's copper core.

Done there, they heat computer motherboards to reclaim its gold. They burn and crack picture tubes and plastic coatings to mine silver, palladium, and other valuable metals. Old-fashioned acid baths, shredders, broilers, pliers, and open fires are tools of the trade. Wage differentials persist in making the revolting business lucrative. Allowing a developing nation to perform the grunt work is one-tenth the cost of what it would be in the regulated West. Treaty loopholes, payoffs, and shady recycling outfits willing to bend the rules lubricate the system geared to cannibalizing anything with a microprocessor.

Glumly, the disassembly process is often a biological cannibal itself. Workers handling the electronics not only expose themselves to unsafe materials breaking down the gizmos, but in lighting fires to further strip them or reduce the size of the heaps, they and others near them are susceptible to a veritable periodic table of toxins that float into the air or worm into the soil and water. Besides heavy metals like cadmium, lead, chromium-6, and mercury, other freed e-waste poisons include fluorine, dioxin, bromine, and polyvinyl chloride. Best not to be around them too long; many of the compounds precipitate long-term damage to organs, nervous systems, and blood-production, raising cancer risks. Especially virulent are fumes from polycyclic aromatic hydrocarbons (PAHs), a class of one hundred different chemicals that researchers believe sparks lung cancer. Lead poisoning is another e-waste occupational hazard. In fact, air samples drawn from one Chinese village handling e-waste averaged *sixty-five* times higher than samples collected in the US and Canada. Overaccumulation of the metal in blood can trigger learning and nervous system difficulties, arrested growth, and lower IQs in kids. Children growing up around smelters, battery plants, and mines can be sitting ducks for having too much of the junk in their circulation.

Dioxin, which scientists classify as one of the modern world's "dirty dozen" toxins for its persistency and prevalence, is another malicious body gatecrasher. Most people consume it through the food chain; it's tainted cooking additives in Europe, pork in Ireland, and milk in Germany. But a slew of hard-hat jobs—recycling, smelting, chlorine bleaching of paper pulp, waste incineration, herbicide-pesticide production—can bubble it airborne into unsuspecting populations. Dioxin's unusual lethality stems from its molecular capacity to lurk in fatty tissue. Lying dormant for seven to eleven years, it can wait to strike before disrupting people's hormones, fraying their immune system, goading cancer, or short-circuiting child development. A 2007 study warning of the danger to childbearing women and infants determined that one Chinese e-waste recycling site registered dioxin levels at least twenty-five times above international standards. The DuPont Corporation slogan coopted by the sixties counter-culture of "better living through chemistry" was never hummed in certain Far Eastern villages.

Considering the peril, those ripping open the plastic and metal casings in e-waste centers attack their trade spectacularly unprotected. Usually. Few have ever heard of hazmat suits, let alone tested one out. The majority only dons gloves, forsaking (or never receiving) masks or other defensive clothing. Some entrepreneurial Chinese strip circuit boards right in their own kitchens and yards instead of in open commercial pits. Migrants or unemployed farmers willing to do anything to eke out a decent living constitute most of the workforce.

Guiyu, a town of 150,000 in the southeast Guangdong province, might hold the unwanted distinction of being the Big

Apple of e-waste recycling. Tests of children's blood there have turned up PAHs five to ten times higher than in American children. Still, it's a paycheck. "In Guiyu, people often live literally alongside piles of discarded electronics, or sleep just a story or two above their e-waste cluttered shops," a Yahoo! News report found. Playing next to them in that carcinogenic miasma were their unkempt kids. Imagine the reaction of customers in faraway countries if that scene was displayed on packaging at their local big-box retailer piping in hip-hop during the Christmas rush, where the latest gadgetry are always hot sellers.

Guiyu would've had no shortage of lip-biting shots if environmental guilt ever spanned that far. When *Sixty Minutes* aired a piece about the squalid activity there in 2008, it discovered components from Apple and Sun Microsystems at a reclamation site that the mayor and thuggish businessmen tried futilely to prevent from being filmed. The town, *Sixty Minutes* reported, recorded the highest levels of dioxin on the planet. Also unnerving was a US General Accounting Office study that fingered forty-three American companies for their willingness to illegally ship e-waste computer monitors rich in lead to China.

High-tech garbage didn't wind up there inadvertently. It'd been whistled in for years. In September 2002, before the e-waste term had been coined, the customs office in Zhejiang province opened a 360-ton shipment from America. Inside the containers were busted TVs, computer monitors, photocopiers, keyboards, and other dead electronics. Most of them were probably flash-made in the People's Republic before the veil of secrecy around cancer villages was even lanced.

CHAPTER 8:

HU'S GREEN WASHOUT

For OUTSIDERS PEERING IN, Chinese President Hu Jintao had all the personal charisma of an encrypted computer. His disinclination for public speaking and flat expressions encrusted the man whose thick, black hair a Gobi Desert sandstorm seemingly couldn't dishevel with a frosty coat of technocratic detachment. Whereas Deng occasionally cut loose, wearing a ten-gallon hat during a Texas trip, and Jiang sang and pounded shots with the best of them, Hu was the bespectacled sphinx whose nation's relentless economy appeared to be conquering the world. Inscrutable. State media contorting to humanize the dark horse, elected China's top man in 2003, portrayed Hu, then in his early-sixties, as a paragon of modesty. He was easygoing, consensus seeking, exceptionally bright—a man of the people, too. A Xinhua profile was impressed by how he'd "braved" a rainy, New York night to personally thank fans bowing at him outside his hotel. Tibetan separatists who remembered his suppressive tactics as party chief of the region in 1988 insisted ruthlessness coursed through him. The son of a poor tea shop owner from Anhui province was such a closed book that college yearbook-type information was regurgitated. Supposedly, the hydroelectric engineering major could bust some moves at the ping-pong table and on the ballroom dance floor.

This we know. China's robotic leader was capable of nimble movement. Risky as it was for his presidency, the eco-damage smoking out of his nation's trillion-dollar GDP had become too uncontainable not to act on. A year into his tenure, the World Bank estimated that smog-related destruction alone gouged four to five percent from China's total productivity. An unpublished analysis by the Chinese Academy of Environmental Planning that came next contextualized the math. Lung cancer, heart disease, and other maladies enflamed by air pollution were prematurely killing 300,000 people annually. Fast on its heels was a study by prestigious Peking University tabulating that 24,000 died from it just in Beijing, where particulate-matter levels often equaled that of LA, New York, Chicago, Atlanta, and Washington, DC, combined. Not a *single* Chinese city in 2006, in fact, met World Health Organization (WHO) recommendations.

Hu, indubitably, was briefed on these morbid particulars that China's peasant class was still forbidden from hearing. Average life expectancy that'd corked up a sensational thirty-three years between 1949 and 1980 was beginning to fizzle, lagging behind more pedestrian economies in Colombia, Malaysia and elsewhere. Along the swiftly industrializing Pearl River Delta that gashes deep into southeastern Guangdong province, workers and families exposed to emissions hiccupped by prosperity were dropping by the thousands. Hu, lampooned as "Wooden

Face" behind the scenes, might've gone pale at the historical symmetry. Just before his death, France's Napoleon Bonaparte in 1816 had described politically fractured China as a "sickly, sleeping giant"—a term Western nations later recycled when they ransacked the nation's coal and neutralized its citizenry with cannonballs and opium stashes. More than a century later, with the People's Republic speeding into its WTO-fueled Gilded Age, it must've been nauseating for Hu to dwell on how the expression "Sick Man of Asia" was now literal.

At first, the analytical warning shots had all the pop of an air rifle. Iraq, Afghanistan, Hurricane Katrina, sizzling home prices, Facebook—in the US, the distractions were everywhere. For the environmental community itself, smog was largely passé— yesterday's news, wholly unsexy—whereas rising Arctic seas stranding polar bears on ice floes warranted all hands (and a few celebrities) on deck. Enough urgency, however, built internally that Hu felt compelled to bound onto the health study merry-go-round while his colleagues took a more head-in-the-sand approach. Under his direction, the environmental ministry attempted to take stock of the destruction wrought by pedal-to-the-medal growth. Their so-called Green GDP calculation would be an "environmental yardstick" that subtracted from the overall GDP the cost of China's human and ecological fuckups. It'd also serve as a kind of scorecard to judge how well every official across the land was performing in guarding Mother Nature under his or her care.

Hu received more than he bargained for, because the first Green GDP produced in 2006 theoretically reduced China's stated GDP growth rate by nearly one-third, from ten percent to seven percent. Toxins previously unaccounted for in government ledgers were registering monstrous effects. Some provinces were so mangled that tabulating what it would take to restore them dragged them into zero-growth territory. For Hu, the roundup was a dart popping the Establishment presumption that there'd be time later to reconcile industrial wealth with their poisonous legacy. Ignoring it after he'd sworn to harness "scientific development" to narrow the gap between the nation's rich and poor would've been a dereliction. He'd already pursued official corruption necessitated by the task-masking side of the job; in some years, more than 140,000 party members were sanctioned for venality. Bottling up escalating Internet traffic in the march toward the 2008 Beijing Summer Games was another obvious step. The Green GDP was Hu's back-door method of shouting, "Time Out!"

For the party and those making coin they'd never conceived, Hu's numbers were a buzzkill, an idea to bury. For unaligned experts with the skinny on the ecology, the three percent figure that Hu had gambled to compile was a joke worth harrumphing. Whatever the rationale, the Green GDP, they believed, grossly underestimated reality as a deceptive, politically-rigged percentage unable to mask the carnage obvious to anyone hostage to a Beijing smog attack, downwind of a coal plant, or astride a dead-zone river. It didn't take a Sierra Club membership to appreciate that some of the numbers in Hu's equation were problematic. For one, damage statistics covering soil and groundwater that would've added billions to the tally were excluded. Secondly, some local officials who'd ridden high for years on their hometown industry stonewalled information requests from the ministry. Papers just sat on their desks.

Many of the local technocrats grumbled they'd been set up for failure. Why, they railed privately, should they cooperate when their Beijing superiors for years assessed them mainly by jurisdictional economic performance? "Good statistics," one proverb chimed, "lead to promotion." Provincial and township agencies underreporting grey air or black water, or exaggerating their successes to make their numbers look spiffier, were only playing the game they'd been taught since Deng's era. A successful game it was, too. Chinese mayors who invested in cleanup machinery like wastewater treatment had less chance of advancement than colleagues who oversaw roads and similar improvements, one US analysis concluded. Tell them again why they should be proselytized into becoming green crusaders?

Resistance surrounding it, Hu's environmental ministry dashed out a separate report suggesting that ten percent was the more accurate ecological drag on China's GDP. Heresy to some, gutsy truth-telling to others, this meant that China's gaudy economic output was in the same, zero-growth fen as the worst of its provinces. Washington was obviously watching the issue ripple through China's body politic. American diplomats in Guangzhou, one of southern Asia's industrial spokes, termed the conditions there so "alarming" in the mid-2000s that it'd be "politically difficult" for any reformer hoping to sharpen monitoring, cables released by *WikiLeaks* showed. "It is a sad irony that this region of China—seen as a beacon for poor migrants who want to find fame and fortune—has actually become more harmful to those migrants and others," one missive read. "Officials will have to determine how high a price in terms of the environment and health they are willing to pay..." another said.

All the same, what the truest number was few on the outside would ever learn from insiders, be they fawning technocrats or frothing do-gooders. The warring calculators across the bureaucracy proved more obstreperous than the upper crust in China's Politburo and State Council could tolerate in sausage-making politics, Communist Party style. By 2007, the Green GDP ceased to be published, a remnant of dreamers and academics.

Hu's bid for antiseptic light on a poisoned ecology had failed. Its essence, even so, would soon gush.

If there was ever a single document that shook the green community's Birkenstocks on the topic, it was the World Bank's 2007 takeout. Gracing the cover of "The Cost of Pollution in China" were bicycle riders strapping on facemasks to endure mud-shaded skies and a rancid, trash-strewn channel. The country's State Environmental Protection Administration (later renamed the Ministry of Environmental Protection) over several years had cooperated with the organization in writing the 128-page document. As the statistics made evident, the human price of smog smashed every previous conceptualization. The raw figures rung of Biblical pestilence. They estimated that 350,000-400,000 people annually died prematurely from outdoor air pollution, 300,000 more from indoor air pollution and another 60,000 from water-borne contamination. Each year, man made pollution was sending 710,000-760,000 Chinese to their makers unnecessarily early.

According to the World Bank, more than half of China's urban population inhaled particulate matter (so-called PM-10) in concentrations over one hundred micrograms per cubic meter ($\mu g/m3$). That level was quadruple what WHO deemed safe for a twenty-four hour period. Crowded southern provinces such as Shandong, Guangdong and Jiangsu absorbed the harshest of it. As occurred in other production beehives, China's air pollution chemistry had evolved with nuanced changes in its industrial

DNA. Tailpipe exhaust from the explosion of millions of new automobiles and trucks spit out cloudbanks of hydrocarbons and nitrogen oxides, which then mingled and reacted with particulates, sulfur dioxide, and heavy metals leaking from coal-fired power plants and factories. In only about twenty years as an export-manufacturing dreadnought, the Asian power was cornering the market on aerial flotsam. Enough of its toxic ash swirled to fill an Olympic-sized swimming pool every two-and-a-half minutes, according to Greenpeace. The group believed China was sitting on at least 1 million tons of carcinogenic industrial waste. The country's sulfur-based smog—the type behind deadly toxic episodes in Europe—was off the charts, too.

The People's Republic's monumental water crisis was another hazard the World Bank report seized on with empirical oomph. Parroting other studies, it claimed 300 million to 500 million rural Chinese lacked access to local, clean water or municipal supply, and that half of the nation's main rivers as of 2005 were too unsafe to provide drinking water. More than one in ten people with digestive cancers had contracted it from these rivers. Chemical fertilizers, whose application doubled between 1990 and 2004, as well as pesticides fanned most of the diseases. The price tag for the human grief rattling hospital rooms and residences was trickier to nail down, for it depended on how one appraised life. When the World Bank calculated the cost of air and water pollution using conservative techniques, it pegged it at a relatively trifling 1.2 percent of China's GDP. After it substituted that method for numbers reflecting society's inclination to pay whatever it takes to avoid environmental mortalities, the figure more than tripled.

With the Green GDP fiasco still lingering, Beijing treated the World Bank's death figures like classified missile launch codes. Once the report's draft version was finished in 2006, Chinese officials requested—as in insisted—the organization excise statistics detailing premature mortalities. Beijing, taking its usual fallback argument, claimed the numbers were sensitive enough to provoke social unrest. A retired ministry official who helped coordinate the research furnished a varying, if comical, justification. "We did not want," said Guo Xiaomin, "to make this report too thick." Begrudgingly, the World Bank removed what the Chinese sought, including a map of where the most deaths were recorded. Overall, about one-third of the document was expunged. By summer 2007, the redacted material didn't matter. The numbers went public, then viral, turning the World Bank's analysis into the go-to referral about an ecological Pompeii able to manufacture a coffee maker, dog bed, or solar panel in a production heartbeat.

Also weighing in was WHO, which itself pulled no punches averring that China experienced more preventable smog deaths than any other spot on Earth. Outdoor and indoor air pollution, WHO's statisticians estimated, removed about 650,000 Chinese from the planet each year, along with another 95,600 from diseased water. Neighboring India was runner-up on the smog death-scale, with 527,700 succumbing annually to those causes. By comparison, the US, which had undergone its own plenty-fatal Industrial Revolution at the beginning of the twentieth century, suffered about 41,200 yearly casualties to impure skies. Worldwide, WHO contended that air pollution—an urban blight around since the time Marco Polo explored China in 1200—annually packed 2.1 million people into graves that should never have been dug.

The effects of backward living indoors added immensely to whatever death toll was bandied. Household air pollution, though

142

frequently a topical stepchild to more lurid environmental drama, strafes people without electricity who burn wood, coal, or even dried animal feces to cook or heat in residences lacking decent ventilation. While awareness about the danger it poses is widespread, solutions are thorny. In Shaoguan City in the southern Guangdong province, many natives depend on lumber and crop trimmings in chimney-less houses to keep them warm and fed in a quaint manner of feudal times past. In doing so, they lightly poison themselves with carbon monoxide and particulates that have nowhere to escape. Blocked, they coil inside, entering people's lungs by themselves or alloyed with tobacco smoke or teeny dabs of modern building materials like asbestos. Once outside, townspeople there receive little succor. They're double whammied by air spangled with heavy metals from nearby industry in a loop of chemical inhalation.

Presented this scene, only government spinmeisters had the temerity to rebut the shakeup in China's pyramid of diseases. By the 2000s, cancer had become the nation's predominant cause of death, responsible for a quarter of fatalities nationwide. Common killers in the tumbledown third world of shantytowns and outdoor toilets—infectious disease, malnutrition, and infant mortality—were being replaced by disorders of spreading Far Eastern affluence. China's lung cancer rates had climbed fivefold since the seventies, though the nation's consumption of thirty-eight percent of the world's cigarettes also factored into the equation. In swelling metropolises like Beijing and Shanghai, the disease accounted for roughly thirty percent of all cancer deaths. Rural inhabitants lived in their own shadow of terminal diagnoses. Chinese farmers, experts said, were three times more likely to perish from liver cancer than the average global citizen.

Topping those unwelcome odds, China's stomach cancer rate was double that of the rest of the planet.

Diseases from tiny cell mutations borne by industrial toxins paralleled horror tales from Asia's coal-belt. Tales you'd suspect were outlandish science fiction, à la *The Island of Dr. Moreau*, until the maternal screams reverberated across the hospital floor. Infants were dying or pronounced deformed at rates not even the most rabid growthsmogogist—our vernacular for a leader who prioritizes GDP ahead of healthy air—could ignore. In one inland province, newborns entered the world fundamentally unassembled because of neural tube defects in which their brain, skull, or spine during gestation was either improperly connected or missing altogether. That bombshell find emanated from a decade-long investigation by researchers from Princeton, Texas and Peking universities. Most of the malformed babies they studied perished before their first birthday. In Shanxi province alone, it afflicted 140 per 10,000 births, twenty times the US rate. Manufacturing solvents and incineration byproducts, especially PAHs sired when fossil fuel is unable to fully combust in chambers of sun-like fire, added to the deformities. Health-wise, areas like this were the last place expectant mothers should reside. Babies developing DNA and metabolisms, in general, lack the defenses against pernicious chemicals that adults' with a mature immunse system can at least joust.

Even if they survived, children whose mothers lived near PAH-discharging power plants during pregnancy were frequently consigned to a tragic existence. Neurologically dinged, they failed to grow like their peers, had a fraction of their motor skills, or were stumped for answers that most kids understood, other experts stressed. Parents around a Chongqing coal-fired power plant didn't need any tweedy PhD or attentive physician to recognize that something was wrong with their offspring. They only needed to compare their children's tiny heads with their playmates' normal-sized ones. What was a future mom to do? Hold her breath for nine months? Seek hardship emigration? In vitro exposure to particulate matter was an even broader risk to infants. Affected babies tended to either be born dangerously underweight—a phenomenon observed not just in Asia but Brazil, Spain, and America—or preterm, the globe's paramount cause of neonatal deaths. (A preterm baby is one that arrives before thirty-seven weeks of gestation). Still, the correlation was most pronounced in China, where concentrated mists of fine particles ranked the highest (in other words, around heavy industry or rampant coal burning). Scientists believe the sooty, toxic grit hastens an immune-system response in mothers baleful for the growing person inside them. Antibodies roused to neutralize foreign chemicals can also suppress folic acid needed in the placenta, which supplies the baby with oxygen and nutrients essential to their survival. In the last twenty years, the People's Republic looks to have cornered the market on swaddled offspring not right inside, with birth defects surging seventy percent, or 900,000 annually, the Ministry of Health acknowledges. A recognized Nanjing University professor hypothesized that one out of ten birth defects in China were instigated by contamination. "Their cities are in big trouble and so are their babies," a University of Texas expert told *Environmental Health News*. The statistics don't lie.

Meteoric energy consumption, up seventy percent between 2000 and 2005, was darkening conditions beyond childhood disfigurements—way beyond. Emissions of sulfur dioxide in that same time frame had mushroomed forty-two percent more than government targets, positioning China as the globe's leading source of acid rain compounds, a kind of liquid sandpaper that can wear away the façades off limestone buildings. The caustic spray regularly drizzled one-third of the mainland, with southeastern China shellacked the most. Winds scudding it east have fried crops a thousand miles away in Japan, as well as South Korea, Taiwan, and the Philippines. In fact, before anyone's britches were knotted over the regional drift of Asian smog, half of the airborne acid settling in Japan in 1996 was produced in China, inducting its neighbor into what environmental historian J.R. McNeill crowned the "unhappy downwind club." The fizzy rain no one ever called romantic, which causes billions of dollars of damage a year, so troubled Tokyo that the government once offered to lend its mammoth neighbor 125 million dollars to install desulfurization equipment.

Japan knew to be on guard from Chinese smokestacks. When acid rain drenches rivers and lakes, falling pH levels can kill or hamper the breeding of aquatic life. Absorbed into the ground, sulfates can delay the natural decomposition of dead animals, overloading the land with so many chemicals that soil overhardens, reducing fertility. Some of it later flakes into rivers, causing secondary pollution in another rabbit punch to the ecosystem. Farmers detest it. Aluminum ions that build up in the soil impede plant root systems. Harvests of rice and winter wheat in China's east, researchers posit, might be as much as thirty percent more bountiful without acid rain defiling it. On top of that, sulfur dioxide has effectively chain sawed some Chinese forests by penetrating the outermost tissue and membranes of leaves, which are then unable to metabolize nutrients or reproduce properly.

Timber! Acid rain since 1980 has destroyed almost half of the mason pine on Nanshan Mountain in Chongqing and ruined all but four percent of similar trees in Sichuan province's Caboa Forest. For those pines, the air carried death.

Junfeng "Jim" Zhang cut his teeth as one of the world's foremost air quality experts on public health by tracking Chinese acid rain in a conservative, witch-hunting era. Zhang, from Guangzhou province, had fantasized since middle school of being a scientist at a most unscientific time. As with so many, the Cultural Revolution blew through the family's house, with his mother afterward forced by the state to teach at a village elementary school. When Deng finally came to power, education was relegitimized, and some wounds mended. The feats of Curie, Einstein, and Newton inspired young Zhang to reach higher, and in doing so became the first from his province to attend Peking University, which is akin to China's Harvard. "It was a big thing," Zhang said in an interview from a spanking new global health building owned by his current employer, the University of Southern California. "The mayor and officials came to congratulate me."

Beijing of the early-eighties was hardly the "Airpocalypse" gagging today. Zhang remembers more nighttime stars and vegetable fields than hissing cars. "Everybody was still making the same as everybody else, whether movie star or factory worker." Graduate studies eventually seated him on a Soviet-made, People's Liberation Army airplane with his professor measuring sulfur dioxide in clouds. "It was very bad," he said of the levels. He'd spent three months in the south tracking the compound in coal power plants. At night, he bunked in a small room he shared with other students, half of whom smoked. Years later, in 1999, authorities blocked Guangzhou's ace from entering an e-waste village to study it. In hindsight, that was okay. Zhang would be making Olympic-sized headlines in the future.

To be fair, some environmental tread-damage predated Asia's post-WTO growth spurt. Desertification and other soil damage from centuries of excessive cultivation, overgrazing, and the parched, rugged climate has persisted, affecting *one quarter* of the country's territory. Here, China's ecological overshoot, mainly to prevent millions from dying of starvation, was history that never receded. While farming restrictions, the globe's biggest tree-planting campaign, and relocation of nomadic herders off grasslands have kept these flatlands from widening, an area six times the size of Great Britain still remains covered there in either sandy dunes or gravel from the Gobi Desert like a beige horizon without borders. The windblown lands that some deem China's biggest green crisis may take another 300 years to reverse, if fortunate, as global warming spins its consequences.

The takeaway from the blistering sands? Even a dominion blazing Mach speed economically can't always outrun its tracks.

CHAPTER 9:

WHEN PEASANTS ATTACK

Wang Hui beckoned his friends to listen carefully. *Shhh.* With the police hot on his scent, these words were probably the last of his old life. Here was the plan. Should the cops not release him from jail in due course, his chums had to harden themselves for action, semi-suicidal action, in fact. Together, they were to bang the town gongs to assemble other villagers with chutzpah to bust him out of the station. That's right: a people's rescue, how—through a rickety window, by explosion—wasn't specified. Pulled off, the jailbreak would be a sonic boom, a raised middle finger at the Establishment, liable to end painfully for his ragtag emancipators. Wang himself knew how viciously authorities treated rabble-rousers, because he was one of them as party secretary in Huaxi Village, an unglamorous outpost on China's eastern coast not far from Taiwan. An indefinite stay in a dank cell, reprogramming, worse: that was his future for truth telling. Deep down, Wang might not have cared about the hole they intended for him. Populist fires stoked by toxic overload were bigger than him.

The insurrection about to engulf Zhejiang province erupted as so many inspired by it would: as a come-hither to industry from civic bosses under the gun to cultivate potent economies. It was the chemical companies the local chiefs wanted to sweet talk here. Those wise enough to listen would find favorable land-use terms, breaks on energy bills, an accommodating city hall—you name it. Not surprisingly, the industrial headhunting from Huaxi (later known as Huashui, and sometimes lumped in with the Huankantou area) perked up ears. Before long, too, plants making plastic products, herbicides, and other chemicals signed thirty-year leases to operate in a sprawling manufacturing park. Assembly lines within a few years of that were formulating something else: a combined twenty-five million dollars in annual revenue that brightened the local economy and, by trickle-down theory, everyone touched by it. For some off-the-grid locales in the late-nineties, the Pied Piper of heavy industry warbled an irresistible ditty.

Just not for all.

As time lapsed, the mood around one of the factory zones close to where 12,000 people resided was nowhere near the cheeriness radiated in government corridors. Huashui's bucolic twinkle, beautified by mountains on two sides and open fields on the other, was being smudged in homes and across cropland. Maize and rice stopped growing. Hillside pines abnormally held their buds. Occasionally, factory waste gases were so astringent, so overpowering, that some children couldn't even pry open their eyes. Nearby, schools sealed their windows and doors. Already, there'd been half a dozen babies born dead and whispers of birth defects. Festering grudges over land grabs at the industrial park shifted into quiet panic that a chemical killer had taken up camp.

By the early 2000s, Wang, an otherwise faceless party apparatchik, could barely stomach it anymore. Then a fertilizer outfit called Dongnong Chemical Industrial Company sidled in next to the other manufacturers. Wang must've developed an ominous feeling, or received a tip, for he started digging less like a blinkered administrator and more like an ardent detective. Dongnong Chemical, he learned, should never have been waved into the Huaxi area. It'd been booted from another town after its handling of fungicide spoiled the surroundings. Executives who'd tried moving the firm elsewhere ran smack into a local wall of opposition there. In limbo, Dongnong Chemical attempted retreating to its earlier home. Once reporters outed them, that didn't work, either. Much of the industrial musical chairs Wang recounted in an open-letter-style article that became an underground bestseller after he printed and helped circulate about 1,000 copies. Even before his missive came out, he'd refused to sign the lease for the industrial park's latest tenant. Motivated by his stand, it wasn't long before 600 area residents inked their names in a signature campaign expressing their grievances about the factories.

Wang's premonition about his own demise was about to be realized, though. Police or orders from above hunted for their comrade (also known as Wang Wei), the seditionist, after someone ratted him out. His pals needed to remember what he said about hammering those gongs. So worried were some townspeople about him that, when they recognized an official in a local restaurant-bar, they dragged him outside to coax out answers. Irked with his responses, a mob of them "clashed with the militia." Next, they chased factory workers from their dorms and, for good measure, wrecked thousands of dollars in plant equipment. Soon after that, in October 2001, Wang and eleven others were arrested for their impudent behavior. No one dared ramming a getaway car into the station to break him out. This wasn't Hollywood; too many sharp edges for storybook endings.

But jail walls for Wang, whose unknown personal details are juxtaposed by his very public acts, settled little. Two years later, unfiltered wastewater stinking with herbicide was dumped into the rivers. The crops it irrigated were so extensively tainted that all the rice harvested in one village was judged uneatable and had to be thrown out. Proud farmers could only kick the untillable soil at the turn of events. For years they'd been accustomed to selling their products at market like any free-enterpriser. Now they were forced to purchase big-city vegetables for their own families' dinner tables. Overall, there was little joy unifying Huashui, only pent-up frustration about what the embrace of manufacturing had inflicted on the unfortunate.

Clamoring for relief, villagers lodged complaints up the official ladder in China's haphazard legal system, where not all complaints are investigated equally or at all. They petitioned two cities, the regional environmental protection wing, even the central government in Beijing. Desperate, one citizen traveled to the capital hoping to sway a reporter to expose the predicament. A female journalist who did visit around then only exposed paranoia; she was detained for possessing materials without the "requisite application" to authorities. Outsiders, just the same, noticed printed slogans declaring that residents wanted their earth back, and that "when poison gas gets released," people cry but "corrupt officials get rich."

Despite it all, nobody rushed in to save the day, perhaps because they didn't know it required saving.

Provincial leaders shaken by the popular discontent had no intention of loosening their grip in a compromise. They acknowledged to townsfolk that six of the offending plants *were* violating regulations to save money, even as they allowed them all to keep their machinery spinning. Among them was a factory that killed some of the trees and crops with hydrogen fluoride gas. Anything else was incidental. In Huashui, people had to realize that economic priorities were obliged. At least they were, anyway, until 2005.

When residents bidding to speak their mind with Dongyang's mayor at a March reception were spurned, the anger under people's roofs boiled over into activist theater. It was like a Chinese version of sixties America (minus the tie-dye and Bob Dylan anthems). Authorities hadn't publicly revealed the nature of the industrial leases they ratified. They'd barely refuted crackling rumors that the factories' high-profit margins were lubed by city hall bribes. And what about the toxins? Villagers exasperated by the suffering and deceptions finally put their own necks on the chopping block, just as Wang had with his subversive article. They blockaded the road into the industrial section with a dozen makeshift tents they lashed from bamboo. Senior citizens insistent that the chemical and fertilizer plants relocate from Huaxi acted as watchful guards. Who'd mess with them? Vested interests—that's who.

Eight days after the barriers went up, roughly one hundred police and cadres stormed into the demonstration zone to torch the bamboo barricades. Disrespect like this had to be snuffed out before it gave malcontents in other cities ideas. The villagers took it in stride. They weren't dandelions apt to crumble in the first stiff wind. They simply reproduced their little fortress from new bamboo timbers. Sympathetic merchants donated free bread and noodles to them while they did.

Foaming at the mouth, the local government in early April reasserted itself with reconciliation and intimidation. It announced that all thirteen factories would suspend production to address ecological issues. Protesters roiling the social order—a "small bunch of ill-willed criminals," in officials' eyes—were instructed not to tempt fate again or they'd be "severely punished." Police had already arrested the man who'd placed himself in the bull's-eye by scouting for media interest in Beijing. The barricades had to come down, especially with an approaching storm, officials insisted. The protestors remained, unwilling to budge. Twice, elderly "nightwatchers" lit fireworks to summon help to their side when the police tried provoking them.

Authorities within hours mounted the raid they probably expected would snuff out the nuisance permanently. Beijing would applaud how decisive they'd acted. This time, 3,500 police, hired security, and administrative personnel deployed in a caravan of buses, sedans, ambulances, and coroner's trucks. Unlike before, the show-of-force kicked a hornet's nest yet unseen in free trade China. A crush of residents estimated 20,000 to 30,000 strong flocked to defend Huashui's protestors. Clammy police attacked the bamboo tents with scissors and watermelon knives as rocks flew at them and nostrils flared. A few wrinkled seniors lay down in act of civil resistance to keep the government vehicles and their outflanked forces from retreating. In the sweaty chaos, a pair of agitators was allegedly killed when public-security bureau vehicles ran over them. "I personally saw two wounded elders being tossed into the funeral hearse," one eyewitness said.

The battle intensified. Surrounded police swung truncheons and sprayed tear gas. A few activists stumbled into polluted ditches. "The [protest] cleanup must be done even if people have to die," some uniformed individuals shouted. Scores of locals were killed, thousands hurt. Among the seriously injured was the deputy mayor.

Sizing up the anger channeled their way, a passel of cops and government workers fled. Behind them were dozens of vandalized government vehicles and the destroyed BMW owned by a "certain town cadre." Protestors soon got their mitts on potentially incriminating documents and 200 red envelopes with bribes to police from an unnamed source. "The Communists are even worse than the Japanese," raged one villager. "I don't feel regret about what we have done," added another.

The hostilities did have its kindnesses, including a knot of villagers who tended medical aid to wounded police. Revelations came from it. Many personnel enlisted for the second raid, it seems, were initially told they were headed for a mountain hike or firefighting, not an environmental scuffle. Some of them wavered when briefed about the real intent. "Inside their hearts," an observer quipped, "they were with the villagers." Whose idea was it to attack the demonstrators? Someone acquainted with an injured police-station director pointed toward his hospital bed. "He's not a people's hero. He's a people's idiot."

Government censors warned China's mainland press, which they'd unleashed before with the "Green Hurricane" environmental coverage, to ignore the conflagration in Huaxi. Breathe not a word. News of the "peasant rebellion" disseminated anyway on foreign outlets. Hong Kong media characterized it as a "large-scale riot." Propagandists countered that an insidious minority with "ulterior motives" were the bomb-throwers who'd ignited the fighting. Few minds were swayed or grudges extinguished by the back-and-forth scapegoating. The MEP, China's equivalent of the EPA, and their regional counterparts had no choice but to swoop in to investigate and defuse. The event in a culture notorious for information-control had fostered remarkable national attention once it'd dribbled out. Two publications that laid bare the details, Hong Kong's *Phoenix Weekly* and a Woodrow Wilson Center Journal piece, later made sure of that.

Ultimately, the biggest polluters, including Dongnong Pesticide, were boarded up or moved away. Skeptical citizens nurtured their doubts things had changed, nonetheless. They refused to disassemble their bamboo obstructions until they personally saw industrial equipment being carted off. In December 2005, "justice" was meted out for sixteen of those involved. Eight officials, among them Dongyang's mayor, were punished. For some that translated into a slap on the wrist. The eight arrested villagers received no such leniency, with sentences ranging from a year to months to nothing. Not for Wang, Huaxi's plucky Nelson Mandela; he earned three years jail time for "gathering a crowd to disrupt social order." Good luck finding his photograph or anything much else about him.

Still, because he'd done what he had, raw street emotion over ecological illness, as well as corruption, property seizures, and other social inequities in a China of adrenalized GDP, had a name people could chant: *Huaxi!* A *Guardian* newspaper correspondent there five days after the uprising ceased depicted an awakened David in countryside no longer so serene. Crumpled police cars, dented buses, scuffed riot helmets, discarded machetes, and truncheons were testament. "[These] are the trophies of battle in which peasants scored a rare and bloody victory against the Communist authorities, who face one of the most serious popular challenges to their rule in recent years...," *The Guardian* wrote. "Residents should be bracing for a backlash. Instead, the mood is euphoric." Exactly how many were hurt and whether anybody died under the wheels of official cars was contested. Less refutable was people's admiration. Tourists and others drove in to survey how a rebellion looked. "Aren't these villagers brave?" said one taxi driver from a local city. "Everybody wants to come and see this place."

The protest smoke spiraling there could've been brushed aside as an anomalistic uproar bound to happen, a regrettable misunderstanding, except that it fit into an undeniable pattern growing by the day in the mid-2000s. Chinese commoners were exerting themselves with astonishing moxie and resourcefulness in ways that the Politburo likely never anticipated.

Within the eddy of noteworthy revolts was a November 2004 tussle between employees of the Ningbo Huanguang Stainless Steel Company in the Beilun District southeast of Dongyang and residents who blamed it for heavy dust emissions and noise. "We used to eat the bayberries after picking them from the trees without washing," one middle-aged woman reminisced wistfully. People ceased that simple enjoyment, she said, after the factory opened and most of the village's fruit rotted. The air now smelled odd. A peppery dust sprinkled windowsills. Upset villagers accused workers of beating them. Unlike Huaxi, a sit-in to seal off a key road failed. When the district government ordered the steelmaker to overhaul its waste treatment, the company refused. Not until 2011 did the facility close.

With each of these incidents the populist ghost of Tiananmen Square was kept alive in a green war beginning to fissure governmental explanations. Dipping into Far Eastern history, there was ancient precedent for citizen snapping points. Recall how the laborers who constructed the Great Wall for the Emperor Qin later raided the sadist's tomb, smashing his beloved Terra Cotta Warriors and torching the structure? Just as rulers then ascended, corrupted themselves, or were deposed when crop failures led to starvation or hopelessness, China's modern-day ecological hammering was bleeding into a political conundrum for the leadership. Bungle it, disregard citizens howling about neighborhood poison, and not even real-life sentinels might save them when the crowds assembled.

A collection of residents in Changxing went on the offensive in June 2005, three months after Huaxi. They muscled into the Tianneng Battery Company amid disclosures that 200 local children had tested positive for lead poisoning. A week later, while Americans celebrated Independence Day with hot dogs and beer, the fur flew near the Xinchang Jingxin Pharmaceutical Company after villagers requested compensation for odor discharges and rice-crop damage they pinned on the factory. Production was suspended, but the truce was brief. Believing the operation was stealthily restarting, residents from town and an estimated 10,000 sympathizers from nearby villages wrangled with police. Arrests and stronger plant regulation ensued, as if scripted in the tapestry of revolts, while mostly oblivious customers half a world away stuffed their shopping carts with products emblazoned with the innocuous phrase "Made in China."

People's indignation against manufacturers cropping up in their hometowns exhibited itself in another geyser of populist venom when a notorious chemical entwined two far-flung cities resisting the *same* company. An innocuous-sounding conference in Beijing in March 2007 was where the fuse was lit. There, a university chemistry professor and others on a technical panel broached the upcoming construction of a large paraxylene (PX) plant near Xiamen, an affluent city with a history of war and scandal close to the Taiwanese Strait. The committee hemmed its attention on the petrochemical used to fashion polyester, plastic, paint, and cleaning solvent, disclosing information some had yet to hear before. While not exactly the biological kryptonite that dioxin is, PX is not to be trifled with; it's a harsh irritant that if ingested or inhaled can damage the liver and kidneys and poison the blood. It also can enflame the nose, eyes, and throat. Aware of its toxic bite, the committee suggested the factory be constructed someplace else. Xiamen politicians caught flat-footed by the recommendation were none too excited by the prospect. Quickly, they gathered to "unify thinking," one peeved group said. The maverick professor, they said, should be disregarded and then eclipsed. Out poured a charm offensive with articles and press conferences exalting how the PX-plant would strengthen the local economy. The government's counteroffensive only polarized camps.

Now that they knew more about the pending manufacturer, Xiamen residents—housewives, students, academics, white-collar workers, and others—mobilized to bat it down with the scant means at their disposal. Demonstrations at public hearings were staged, Internet campaigns spearheaded, letters to higher-ups penned. When none of that succeeded, they turned their cell phones into guerilla walkie-talkies. Even as cyber-cops tried preventing them from organizing online, people texted the coded phrase to "take a walk." And walk they did. On June 1st, thousands flooded city streets in a peaceful protest, some of it uploaded in video clips. The MEP interceded reflexively as it had in Dongyang, this time requiring an environmental planning assessment for the whole city. At a televised public hearing, eighty percent of those surveyed opposed the plant. Leukemia, birth defects—the economic benefits of PX, they said, was not worth its cost in flesh. The city finally agreed.

But the PX soap opera wasn't over, for one town's relief balled into another's headache. Shortly after Xiamen was taken off the hook for the future plant a rumor tore through the grapevine. Fujian provincial officials, it went, planned to move the operation to a rural, island town to the west, in the Gulei Peninsula in Zhangzhou. Shockwaves vibrated. Even the suggestion they'd be the dumping ground for a chemical works that another city had agitated against jolted thousands of Zhangzhou's citizens in February 2008 onto the streets. Townsfolk and police skirmished before a single ounce of PX had been uncorked.

Other long shot victories were achieved with individual tenacity, not collective punches. Take Zhang Gongli, a mild-mannered, poorly educated, middle-aged farmer with a receding hairline. Zhang had no aspiration to be a crusader in Quigang, a small village of about 2,000 in the Anhui province east of Shanghai. He never intended to defy China 2.0. It was the factories that shook to life there in 2004, pumping out dyes, pesticides, and other substances that reshaped him into an environmental folk hero. The pain was 360 degrees: searing air and water, healthy children gone sickly, fish and wildlife flopping sidelong dead in a blackened river. The regulations on the books barely mattered, either. Only leverage did. Plant honchos immune to accusations of bribery, inspection cover-ups, and savagery against villagers were the industrial mafia. Somebody, Gongli decided, needed to don a cape.

Recognizing they were outmatched, he and some of Quigang's citizens locked arms with Green Anhui, a fledgling NGO. Along the way, a posse of residents and student activists caught the eye of award-winning filmmakers. "I feel scared—I really don't want to be a hero," Gongli confided to them. "But the next generation will suffer. We risk our lives for their happiness." Over three years, cameras followed him as he skirted brick-throwing, gun-firing thugs, pep-talked friends and neighbors in his squalid hometown, and beseeched federal officials for intercession. The resulting short-subject documentary, *The Warriors of Quigang*, was nominated for an Academy Award.

Busted on a big screen format, Quigang's worst polluter, the Jiucailuou Company, packed up and decamped a few miles away from its prior industrial neighborhood. What it and other plants left behind was soil and water still ungodly poisoned but at least not rotting further. As a microcosm of a desperate citizenry, the film about Gongli is alternatively bleak and ennobling. But so, too, is the arc of Lou Liquan, a fish farmer who banded with the NGO Chongqing Green Volunteer's Alliance to detoxify one of China's heartland provinces after he lost his inventory to factory waste. Villagers persecuted and imprisoned there for "disturbing social life" when they sought relief were so grateful at the arrival of an activist that they kneeled down before him at the town's entrance. Between the NGO and media attention, only three of the chemical companies whose production was idled were permitted to resume. Gongli and Liquan, two citizen environmentalists learning on the fly, had made industry blink.

Neither of them was jailed for muckraking. Wu Lihong was less fortunate after his decade-long campaign to cleanse Lake Tai in the lower Yangtze River Delta. Hundreds of plants manufacturing food additives, adhesives, solvents, and other materials had turned the waterway, sentimentalized for its limestone banks and family gardens, into their own private dumping pond. The stocky, ex-factory salesman had grown suspicious about it on after-dinner walks smelling nauseating odors. In a jiffy, Wu deputized himself to learn why. From his motorcycle, he gathered evidence from gooey, fishless waters. He mailed photographs of factories discharging undiluted wastewater to officials and pinpointed hidden outflow pipes. When in 2001, Wen Jiabao, then China's vice premier, traveled to Lake Tai to inspect the fouling Wu had publicized, Wen saw little of it at a dye factory. In a well-staged charade ahead of Wu's visit. Plant workers refilled the nearby canal with fresh water and carp and positioned fisherman around. Dead lake? Where?

After years of harassment and ruses to entrap him with job offers and gifts, authorities in 2006 finally charged Wu with blackmail and extortion. Just before, the National People's Congress had honored him for his courage. Behind bars, Wu alleged that his jailers deprived him of food and forced him to stay awake five straight days until he signed a confession. Mystical Lake Tai was the "land of fish and rice" no more. In 2007, toxic cyanobacteria (pond scum) colored China's third largest freshwater-body neon green. Millions who relied on its waters for cooking and drinking were instructed not to touch it.

◻

WHETHER THEY PEAKED IN bloodless "regime changes," indiscriminate carnage, or courtyard executions for tyrants, history has taught us that revolutions have erupted over less than the neighborhood-level pushback rocking China in its first years as the planet's manufacturing Godzilla. Along its path to economic celebrity, sped no doubt by its zeal to be the world-leader in chemical production, Beijing had fundamentally misread how much death, injustice, and official neglect its citizens would stomach before reaching for their pitchforks (and cell phones). China's ruling party for years had justified peoples' misery as the transitory consequence of rapid-fire development from poor, agrarian state to industrial juggernaut, something no different from the growing pains endured by other countries. What, a growthsmogogist might ask, was the loss of a fractional segment of society each year to pollution compared to the tens of million who perished in China's famines, natural disasters, and warfare? The philosophy had the ring of an insurance company actuarial: environmental grief that could fill blocks of Bird Nest-like stadiums with victims was tolerable collateral damage worth briny rivers of tears. Whether the rationale of short-term sacrifice on the altar of economic prosperity was spot-on accurate or attempted brainwashing will fall on historians to distinguish. But one truth was undeniable. In the People's Republic, everybody and nobody is charge of Mother Nature.

Out of pure self-interest, provinces and city halls often guarded polluting industries as if moats were dug around them. Even when chastened by superiors or the companies were fined what their Western counterparts would spend on a corporate retreat (7,000 to 8,000 dollars), many officials gave factories *carte blanche* once any ruckus subsided. Why would locals sell their neighbors out, in some cases for an envelope crammed with Yuan from their favorite plant? Because towns trying to hang on as metropolises grew and traditional farmland shrunk were at a crossroads of unpleasant options. They had to forge deals that richer areas spurned, which was why the first wave of "environmental mass incidents" careened through remote villages off the tourist map.

Every day in the mid-2000s, while Chinese cargo containers piled up Lego-like in US ports, townspeople from some Asian village or another staged protests as a result of shotgun marriages between heavy industry able to prop up the tax base and residents forced to cohabit with them. Of the estimated 100,000 to 180,000-plus citizen protests a year during this era, rallies involving smog, water, sanitation, fertilizers, and the like accounted for a sizable hunk of them, perhaps a quarter. Folks watching loved ones shuttle between morphine injections and radiation treatments frequently had little choice except to take their chances defying hometown polluters. Under China's political system, they had no constitutionally guaranteed rights of expression, organization, representation, or appeal. Blocking the public's ability to participate in the decision-making constructed top-down without sufficient "pressure valves"—i.e. lawsuits, initiatives, elections— baked confrontation right into the system.

Beijing had seen it all coming, too, quarterbacking within a few decades a national makeover that other countries required generations to complete. It was the tactics the party chose that were less original. Cutting industrial corners, okaying energy-squandering plants, hiring too few inspectors, turning a blind eye on violations: these were frequently China's flywheels to success. If state rhetoric counted, later-era growth was supposed to have been more sensitive. China's cabinet, the State Council, in 2006 required, or at least reiterated that officials must consult the citizenry on projects affecting their air, land, and water. The MEP itself in not so many words voiced that there needed to be transparency. Yet in most antimanufacturing scuffles, information flowed lamely after the fact.

The slack reins lent the impression of administrative fecklessness. From all evidence, the MEP was incapable of enforcing its one hundred or so laws, punishing dirty industry in ways that deterred criminal behavior, or even knowing how to stay ahead of crises. How their political superiors in the Great Hall of the People acted with riots flapping was a separate dynamic. Communist leaders, experts saw, generally acquiesced to middle-class demands for quality-of-life issues provided any revolt was localized, not blatantly political, and did not jeopardize their GDP-centripetal doctrine. Protestors in urbanized Ningbo, Xalian, and Dalian, thus, were treated less barbarically than ones in underdeveloped villages. President Hu, the man whose Green GDP unnerved the Establishment, toed to this party line. When Mongolian herders resisted displacement from their traditional grazing lands to make way in part for extensive coal mining, Wooden Face refused to intercede. Then again, if there was one subject the party feared brushfire-dissent over, it was its bedrock determination to reshape those desolate lands into China's energy insurance on tomorrow.

All in all, the uneven responses encapsulated the weak, decentralized control that Beijing imposed on its provinces. That it was more environmental paper tiger than watchful overlord. For some local bosses, regulations were advisory, not mandatory. "We don't think these decisions apply to us," one Guangdong official said of pollution controls. But why should they when a country nominally committed to greening was still dominated by patronage, with more clout to obstruct Blue Sky improvements than ministers had to enact them? In straining to impose their will in areas swimming with toxic leftovers, the country's supposedly in-charge men seemed only to reinforce an old maxim: "The heavens are high and the emperor is far away."

◼

IN 1955, A DOZEN years after a gigantic smogbank bushwhacked downtown Los Angeles with such eye-smarting intensity that some freaked that it was a Japanese chemical-warfare attack, the world's first, dedicated air pollution agency was sweating buckets. Scientists then were still unsure whether the gray-brown tendrils spreading from the mid-city to the suburbs were a temporary annoyance or the slaughter of thousands of innocents about to pounce. In a worst-case scenario, where heavy contaminants oversaturated the airshed, officials were shaky on how best to notify residents to scamper indoors and off the freeways. Should they sound civil defense air horns wired to warn of nuclear attack? Dispatch low-flying planes fitted with loudspeakers? Blink the streetlights? After lengthy debate, a radio-teletype system with big factories and contracts with the media were approved in a tiered, alert regimen able to halt trash burning and big industry, among other precautions. As was frequently the case, blowback reared. The oil company that would become Atlantic Richfield, as well as other prime manufacturers, was rankled that their operations could be tugged offline. Where the bickering stopped was the nodding consensus that the region's smog generals needed to shield the population of a booming, car-crazy metropolis.

Los Angeles County's Air Pollution Control District, having overcome a fractious adolescence marked by blame mongering, turf battles, political grandstanding, and junk science, was a force cobbled from scratch. Even if the murky skies bothered Hollywood directors and civic boosters the same as the average nine-to-fiver, sometimes grooving the impression of an unsolvable crisis, the district had made great headway since the appearance of the primitive "smogometer" air-testing contraption in the forties. Slowly, incrementally, the mystery fumebanks were being analyzed, their sources regulated and policed. The air district hired engineers and weather forecasters for a new vein of atmospheric management. It contracted with epidemiologists and researchers. It debuted a public relations bureau that communicated routinely with citizens and journalists. It funded health studies with USC, UCLA, and others. While Mao presided in a Beijing that hardly manufactured anything, Southern Californians were standing up against a nemesis of their own making.

Cranks and conspiracy theorists aside, Angelenos had faith in the air district as an entity answerable to them. Groundbreaking experiments by its star consultant, California Institute of Technology biochemist Arie Haagen-Smit, illustrated that local smog was a photochemical reaction formed when automobile exhaust fumes reacted in sunlight with other gases. It wasn't a sulfur derivative, as some industrial interests and quasi-scientists hollered. S. Smith Griswold, a square-jawed, ex-Stanford football player who became the APCD's second chief, told the public what it didn't care to hear: that the air might deteriorate further before it got better, and that GM and America's other major automakers were sandbagging the West Coast with delaying blarney about engineering their vehicles to run cleaner. Griswold even volunteered to spend two hours inside a Plexiglas smog chamber to better empathize with the physiological and emotional tolls shouldered by the masses on those rasping days. He survived it coughing and dizzy, pleading never to return, but in doing so became a man of the people.

Smith's agency likewise involved citizens on the front lines. It proposed a ban on their beloved backyard incinerators, dispensed health alerts, goaded them to keep an eye on smoke sources, and briefed them on laws in the pike. When the blurry skies refused to dissipate quickly enough, Griswold's crew invited ideas from anyone around the world, qualified or not. Within weeks, the APCD was avalanched with thousands of schemes, some worth chasing, most bound for the shredder. In letters and blueprints, folks suggested drilling venting-holes through the San Gabriel Mountains, pumping dry ice into the troposphere, piping smog to exhaust stacks up near the clouds, or concocting a time machine. Also lurking were more civic organizations, industry trade groups, and think tanks than you could count on in a sometimes-earsplitting exercise of democracy. Everybody, nonetheless, was in it together.

Gradual progress, coupled with the people's desire for faster relief, drew regulators into the game. California was suddenly a bellwether. In the sixties, its newly minted Department of Motor Vehicles required millions of automobiles to be fitted with primitive exhaust trappers. The state, after years of the cold-shoulder treatment from Washington, was then able to convince lawmakers to nationalize emission standards to bring the powerful carmakers to heel. Impressed by the state's arguments, if not the 500,000 public letters encouraging action that were dumped on the Capitol steps, Congress passed a breakthrough waiver allowing California to establish tailpipe regulations tougher than national limits. Not long afterward, Congress approved the US Clean Air Act, granting citizens and environmental groups the right to sue polluters and government agencies if they failed to protect them. Breathing healthily was now a civil right.

The EPA, charged with targeting chemicals from smog to lead and monitoring states' actions, was founded in the same flower-power epoch of 1970. Earth Day was, too. The California Air Resources Board, already on the job for three years, bared its teeth with the waiver ratified and the Big Three automakers—General Motors, Ford, and Chrysler—wounded. It disseminated rigorous tailpipe standards that domestic and foreign carmakers agreed to adopt, some more gracefully than others. Americans had demanded relief from whiskey-brown skies. Government listened.

The moral? China is hardly the first dawning power to industrialize its way into a smog guillotine. Indeed, it's not even the first Far Eastern one.

Japanese air pollution, which had first hazed over mines and smelters in the late 1800s, had become something horrid by the sixties. In buffing itself into an industrial/electronics comer from the ashes of World War II, the country had pumped too much grime into the air. Reeling, citizens demanded that local governments require industry to adopt pollution-control equipment. Just as LA mothers with Marge Simpson hairdos (and kids in tow) browbeat regulators to do more, Japanese women did the same. Asthmatics in one area even sued a petrochemical complex.

Despite all that, it still took a grievous smog attack over Tokyo in 1970 to shake Japan's central government into a more decisive posture. New laws were enacted, among them emission standards modeled after America's. Resourceful engineers next tackled energy efficiency. The improvements were inhalable within a generation. Compared to a decade earlier, Japan by the nineties only consumed one-third energy per unit of production from before and could claim automobiles running ninety percent greener. Hometown control delivered. "Japanese municipal and prefecture officials became very responsive to citizen concerns, disciplined more by local elections than Tokyo," wrote McNeill, the historian. "This tempered the tendency to sacrifice local environments (and health) for the greater glory and progress of the nation." Lungs from Tokyo to Osaka to Hanshin exulted.

The "Killer Smog" that paralyzed London in December 1952 further carries nuggets about flowering from murky events. England's Victorian era had ushered in hundreds of thousands of coal-burning residential chimneys and steam engines to what was then the world's largest city. Jolly, old England was mechanizing. Its resultant combustion, though, was not trivial. Coal burning regularly domed the skies in pea-soup-thick sulfur clouds. Conditions had become ripe for the type of disaster that petrified California officials: a chemically sponged atmosphere kept in place by listless winds. One such day, that darkness lunged. A British writer described a sun in retreat, hanging "sulkily in the dirty sky with no more radiance than an unlit Chinese lantern." Healthy Londoners sputtered to breathe; those with ailments barely could. Four thousand perished within the first five days, another 8,000 in the months that followed. London hadn't lost so many people in the century since the 1918 influenza contagion.

Like the Japanese would, Londoners militated for change and investigators demanded answers. Lawmakers provided both when they approved Britain's 1956 Clean Air Act. It outlawed most dark smoke from chimneys while promoting smokeless coal and other alternative household fuels. Coal, responsible for three-quarters of England's energy in 1958, became a mineral non grata. Seeking its replacement, public and private explorations settled on natural gas after North Sea reserves in the sixties were drilled. A fuel-mix revolution was underway. By the Beijing Games in 2008, blue-flamed natural gas furnished England with forty percent of its needs. Oil accounted for a little over a third, with coal, the old scourge, at just sixteen percent.

The lesson? A hijacked sun can be rescued, public spirit willing.

CHAPTER 10:

BLUE SKY, DARK DEATH

IN CHINA'S WIZARD-OF-OZ-LIKE, ONE-PARTY rule, nothing was official—including the lie that big-city air pollution was fog—until the elders standing behind their hammer-and-sickle curtain sanctified it as fact. To many of the growthsmogogists in the bunch, e-wastelands, popular uprisings like Huaxi's, and cancer villages were white noise to be drowned out by more uplifting storylines of the glorious 2000s. Village waters gone surreal red, foamy as bubble bath, or so marbled with dead fish and trash you could practically walk across them, were better left for ministerial attention. Why even publicly confront the nation's ecological blistering when, for the first time ever, dozens of cities were disclosing pollution levels that for years they'd kept locked in file drawers. Mothership Beijing was even better PR, a whirling dervish of greening with the Olympics only a handful of years away. These were reasons to celebrate how far China had advanced, not repent.

The Blue Sky program that the central government introduced in 1997 about fifteen years into Deng's reforms was one of China's core air quality initiatives. Under it, three mainstay pollutants—nitrogen dioxide, sulfur dioxide, and PM-10—were measured, monitored daily, and assigned a numerical value. Whichever one averaged the highest over the previous twenty-four hour period dictated the daily Blue Sky rating on a scale of one to 500 on an Air Pollution Index (API). China's system was laxer than America's, which revolved around a more conservative, worse-case-scenario approach. China's methodology, where cities with APIs below one hundred were in compliance with standards for commercial and residential sectors, also exceeded benchmark guidelines recommended by WHO. But any day with an API below that magical one hundred still made it Blue Sky.

From the fish-eyed view, government's willingness in 2000 to publish an API for forty-two urban areas connoted a slight democratization. Leaders' prior refusals to disseminate basic smog data had been a sore spot precipitating snippets of dark humor, if not a dose of public nihilism about the government's mistrust of them. "You can believe something," the Chinese maxim went, "when authorities deny it." Apparently they'd now seen the light in the steely air, and wanted credit. "Releasing the numbers is a revolutionary concept for the people and the government," an official explained. "We were worried people would complain that air pollution is too serious. Instead, the consciousness of the people has been raised. And they feel the government trusts them with the facts." By 2007, eighty-six cities were posting API readings.

Question was, were they "facts" or bureaucratic smog and mirrors? Cities, among other technical decisions, had excluded from their initial API ground-level ozone considered traditional, urban smog before scientists lasered in on particulate matter readings. Steven Q. Andrews, a previously unknown American environmental consultant with glossy associations (Princeton University, the Natural Resources Defense Council) unearthed all of this and more in the late 2000s as a kind of one-man statistical wrecking ball. To this day, there's been nothing like his numbers-debunking journal piece *Seeing Through the Smog*. Fishy math, Andrews saw, had rigged results. In one biting deconstruction covering 1998, he found that roughly eight out of ten Chinese cities with populations over two million exceeded national limits for tailpipe- and smokestack-disgorged nitrogen oxide. Yet as if by hocus pocus, *none* of those 559 cities that had tested for the pollutant violated the standard seven years later, even though everyone knew Asia's smog crisis had deepened. Sham or statistical miracle?

Another skew hooking Andrews' attention was the bait-and-switches of the monitoring station locales. From 1998 through 2005, Beijing technicians culled data from seven central-city stations with hefty traffic and other urban activity in order to tabulate API readings. The next year, however, two of the devices near traffic vanished, and were replaced with three stations *positioned distant* from automobile congestion. For Andrews, who'd first visited Beijing in the cornfield-Blue Sky era of 1984, the shell game greatly explained how the capital achieved ninety-three additional Blue Sky days in 2006 and 2007. The next year Beijing added three additional testing units, all of them set up beyond its main urban district. Guangzhou and other cities may have borrowed this same deceptive tactic.

Andrews' analytical knife had so much to slice. The MEP's little-publicized decision in the year 2000, for instance, to measure

175

nitrogen dioxide instead of nitrogen oxide in API calculations cleverly masked how unhealthy the air was, since the latter had exceeded limits more than any other contaminant pre-2000. "Blue skies are here again in Beijing, just in time for the Olympics— or are they?" Andrews wrote in a lacerating, January 2008 *The Wall Street Journal* editorial. "Last week the Chinese government rolled out new statistics claiming that air quality has dramatically improved between 1998 and last year. But a closer look...casts doubt on the...sunny claims."

Chinese officials prickled by Andrews' findings answered with condescension, not personal harassment that they've marshaled against native-born activists and reporters. They said they had patience for the "small group of people" who still misunderstood the city's clearing airshed. Not everybody, however, was in on the trickery. Word later dribbled out that some of the legerdemain went undetected by the Politburo until after the fact, making the nation's leadership appear either morally coopted or unforgivably ignorant. Reached in Beijing, Andrews explained that his enthrallment with the subject began with statistics that "looked incredibly suspicious. Everyone thinks the Chinese numbers are manipulated and distorted, but at the same time these numbers are incredibly important," he said. "One of the things that astounds me is that a lot of government officials know what's going on... There's actually less transparency now than in 1998."

Ordinary Chinese befuddled by the chasm between Beijing's APIs and its cruddy air had every reason to wonder if the statistical chicanery that Andrews and others teased out was standard operating procedure nationwide. Fence sitters need only ponder what was reported between 2001 and 2007 in thirty major cities like Chengdu, Tianjin, Dalian, and Chongqing for clarity. Each one of them in that interval reported an astonishing percentage of API readings just below or at one hundred, the threshold allowing them to classify their air quality as "good." Sure was serendipitous; only when the API reached 301 were healthy Chinese advised to reduce their outdoor activities.

Blue Sky days, consequently, were all in the definition. Ten years before the Beijing Games, the capital experienced one hundred of them. Ever since, they'd increased, pinnacling to 244 near the end of 2007. Funny that it did, since the city that very year weathered *265* days where at least one station registered PM-10 of 150 µg/L or higher, according to Andrews. By comparison, not a single Los Angeles monitoring station that year recorded particles at that level.

Technocrats understood the gains were a hard sell amid these conflicting numbers but they tried anyway. "People used to ask me whether the ratings are scientific, or if we are playing tricks," Du Shaozhong, deputy director of Beijing's Environmental Protection Bureau, once told a journalist. "But this is the most advanced scientific equipment in the world."

True as that may be, the machines don't operate by themselves.

◼

AGGREGATED, CHINA MIGHT'VE RENAMED itself The People's Modern Republic of Coal, Toxins, and Chemicals. By the MEP's own reckoning, the country yearly was cannoning skyward roughly 22.7 million tons of acid-rain–causing sulfur dioxide, a near-exact tonnage of smog-creating nitrogen oxide—both the most of any nation—and 12.8 million tons worth of industrial dust. Grouped together during the 2000s, it was deluging the atmosphere with well over one hundred million tons annually, without even including secondary industrial poisons floating about. A bottomless gullet for raw materials amplified it. Chinese assembly lines might've boxed up more finished television sets than any competitor, but by 2005 China was also the reigning production-kingpin of cement, steel, aqua-cultured food, and fertilizers, and runner up for most chemicals, textiles, and pesticides. On the intake side, it consumed forty to fifty percent of the planet's supply of aluminum, zinc, copper, steel, nickel, and, of course, coal. The docks never slept.

As you're seeing, the materials craving was sloppily handled. Because many of China's heavy manufacturers depended on antiquated or wasteful technology with shabby pollution filters, the country's overall energy efficiency was half the world's rate. Companies burning coal to produce ammonia for fertilizers and clothing required forty to eighty times the water than similar operations powered by natural gas. Now ponder a whole country littered with energy-hogging, vapor-billowing industries. Imagine, as well, what happens when factories manipulate the basic metals they import minus the right controls? Exotic fumes lift off. China, according to one little-read EPA-supported study, is far and away the predominant single-country source of emissions of mercury, non-ferrous metal, gold, pig iron, and steel. Besides those, China, between 2000 and 2007, released half of the estimated 8.2 billion tons of fossil fuel gases discharged globally.

Unsettling as those discharges are, it's China's stubborn addiction to coal—which influences smog, heavy metal dispersal, and climate change—that screams the most for intervention. The country's dominant industrial fuel grimes its troposphere like cigar smoke in a closet. Coal burning by the country's electricity generators, industry, and other sources emit two-thirds of its nitrogen oxides, eighty-five percent of its sulfur dioxide, and seventy percent of its soot, according to the Chinese Centre of Disease Control & Prevention. Exposure is known to trip heart ailments, respiratory problems, and cancer. Something else baleful hides in it, too. In its flaky ashes can be found carcinogenic mercury, arsenic, cadmium and lead, even some radioactive material, none of which anyone willingly invites into their homes. Some of that effluent goulash rides the Jet Stream and Gobi Desert storms to China's neighbors to the east and around the planet.

Closer to the ground, fumes and particles from China Inc. were tunneling into all sorts of delicate spaces. Engineers at Intel Corp. examining the chassis of computers that'd been in East Asia or India probably felt violated. A dark film of contaminants had smeared the machines' inner-surfaces. Sulfur had rusted the copper circuitry, wrecking the computers' motherboards so they couldn't conduct electricity properly. Restless about the implications, the chipmaker experimented with corrosion-resistant gold as a possible replacement. When it was determined to be too expensive for mass production, Intel veered onto another path. At its Oregon facility, it spent 300,000 dollars for a smog chamber to test the pressurized effects of chemicals on computer parts. A year into it, no bulletproof answer materialized.

◼

CANCER VILLAGES AND ASHTRAY-SKIED towns, where facemasks should've been sold in vending machines, were only extreme portraits of China's rutted environmental skin during the twenty-first century. In truth, the character of provinces distinguished over the millennia by their cooking and dialects, their handicrafts, ethnic mix and legends were being overlaid with industrial personalities. Emissions profiling was in swing.

Lunch-pail enclaves, such as Hebei and Shandong, brimmed with traditional, large-scale polluters, though central areas like Tangshan and Chongqing were coming on fast as manufacturing New Turks. Coastal Shandong, known for its tasty prawns, kelp, and tobacco, was swampy in fumes from power-generators, chemical plants, and construction-material work as a three-legged polluter. Eclectic Jiangsu, home of the Tianning Temple that's been destroyed and rebuilt five times since its inception in 655 AD, vented those same contaminants, as well as vapors from chemical, steel, and cement factories, not to mention emissions from lighter industries such as paper and textiles.

To the west in Shanxi, where birth defects were common, coking mills fizzed the air with oxides of sulfur and nitrogen plus dangerous hydrogen sulfide, phenol, and benzene. The skies in once-forlorn Inner Mongolia to the north, a center of religious art and clans that still worship mythical animals, were a grab bag of undesirable gases themselves, souped with the same compounds as Shandong and Jiangsu in addition to flotsam from petrochemicals, non-ferrous metal smelting, coal mining, and steel-making. Sichuan, an ancient area near Tibet home to hot springs, giant pandas, and sizzling, peppery fare, slow-cooked pollution from materials processing of cement, glass, and ceramics.

Whatever their differences in bulk emissions, Shanxi, Hebei, and Shandong were cousins in one respect. Green lighting so many coking-coal plants elicited air furry with benzo(a)pyrene, a hydrocarbon of particular nastiness. People who inhale or ingest it can wind up with cancer, a compromised immune system, or hampered fertility. Another source of industrial-belt carcinogens were heavy metals flung into the atmosphere, especially by smelters. The metal particles from them that settle into the land and water can be ten to one hundred times more virulent than fertilizers containing them.

Landmarks from dynastic China of scraggly beards and sly innovation weren't so much diseased by these chemical whorls as slowly munched by them, history being no match for witchy combustion. Coal dust in northern Shanxi province hoarded like snowflakes on enormous statues carved from "golden sandstone" by nomadic invaders in the fifth- and sixth-centuries. Oxidizing acid rain in Sichuan province scrabbled at an 800-year-old sculpture of Guanyin, a hallowed Buddhist depicted with a thousand arms. Not even the Terra Cotta warriors arrayed for eternal protection could rest; one professor is championing a glass wall around them to shield them from aerial threats that paranoid emperors of old rarely fretted over. Preservation has only restored so much.

In post-WTO China, something creepy was only a hot furnace away.

CHAPTER 11:

POTEMKIN VILLAGE OR GOLD MEDAL MIRACLE?

Like "swallowing glass." American runner Amy Yoder Begley's description of competing in Beijing's hellish air, in this instance during a 2002 event, awoke others' bronchial memories. Judging by the comments of her peers training for the 2008 Summer Games, they might've preferred sweating for hardware around the cobras of the Sahara Desert than the city where your oxygen sometimes came spiced with black char. US triathlete Jarrod Shoemaker was so winded from breathing in a previous race that he could barely speak. "If I tried to laugh," he recalled, "I'd be doubled up with pain."

In bidding for the Olympics in a destination ridiculed for its airshed, the Chinese understood they'd set themselves up for humiliation beyond pale if their pesky friend tormented people during the seventeen days in August. The nation's awaited moment for international adulation was the Hu administration's crucible, too. Should it misstep, leadership would be red meat for late-night comedians and Web lampoonery. What company would want to move there then? Even the IOC, which had its own reputation hanging by choosing Beijing, diplomatically phrased the city's task "an environmental challenge."

The Chinese, all the same, were nothing if not steely-eyed in their conviction they could simultaneously erect first-rate Olympic venues while achieving landmark clean-air by the time the traditional "Let the Games begin!" pronouncement echoed through the Bird's Nest on opening night. There'd be no grandstands full of coughing and eye watering, officials assured, not after their billions of dollars worth of preparations. Just wait. In the run-up to that anticipated August evening, the city devoted itself to wringing Blue Sky days from its sooty atmosphere. Bursting public coffers from the nation's export bonanza was its banker. So bullish were officials that the capital's skyscraper-building, coal-burning, engine-running rhythm could be tempered that they'd set the bar up there with the pole vaulters. They'd operate a "Green Olympics," endowing Beijing with a legacy that'd remain long after the tourists departed.

Once the competition kicked off, the metropolis, whose exotic, tile-roofed palaces were fading like yellowing souvenirs, would go even further ratcheting down its high-combustion modernity. During its bid, Beijing had vowed to meet twenty goals in a punch-list offering everything from new rail spurs, wastewater treatment plants, and natural gas pipelines to clean fuel usage and vegetation safeguards. None of that, however, would mollify public opinion unless chewy smog was sent packing.

The Olympic Action Plan that Beijing released a year after the IOC awarded it the Games was obsessed with that vey mission. Segmented into fourteen stages, the outline brimmed with approximately 17.4 billion dollars worth of environmental components, many of them troposphere-aimed. The money would slash industrial vapors and vehicle exhaust through factory relocations and shutdowns, and pay for administering Draconian commuting restrictions. It'd enforce bans on open fires and promote energy efficiency, be it at giant power plants or apartment-house boilers. By the time sprinters hit the track, technocrats swore that Beijing's levels of sulfur dioxide, nitrogen dioxide, and carbon monoxide would meet WHO standards, with PM-10 measurements similar to "major cities in developed countries." The city's catchall effort would leave little untouched for the sake of an uncharcoaled sun.

Patriotic numerology depended on it. The People's Republic intended to bang its gong (not the one in Huaxi) commencing the XXIX Olympiad on the eighth day of the eighth month of the eighth year of the new millennium. This kickoff date was no arithmetic providence. The harmonic calendar, where eight was both sacred and lucky, had to be feted. And it would, thanks to all that cash.

Public transportation for a gridlocked city was among the first beneficiaries. Beijing's subway grid was expanded and 400 miles of fresh expressway grooved. Sixty thousand dirty taxis and buses were replaced with low-emission models, and 4,000 natural gas-powered coaches—supposedly the world's largest contingent of them—sallied forth. Done there, it was off to industry. Whether permanently, before, or during the Games, the capital's heavy-hitting polluters could no longer vent waste as normal. Two hundred factories were ordered to adapt to cleaner production methods. Four power plants were instructed to burn high-grade, low-sulfur fuel. Also into slowdown mode would go the Beijing Coke and Chemical Plant and assembly lines at the Capital Iron and Steel Company (which by itself released 18,000 tons of particulate matter yearly); the Beijing Dongfang Petrochemicals Company and Dongfang Chemicals Factory would do the same. In lockstep were cement, lime, and brick makers. Even the city's top polluter, the state-owned Shougang Group, employer to 120,000 workers, curtsied to regulators. It acquiesced to curb its steelmaking operations ten miles from Tiananmen Square by three-quarters, and then transfer its entire setup a hundred-plus miles eastward by 2010.

Not finished yet, officials insisted that 3,000 construction sites responsible for whipping into the atmosphere two-thirds of the area's dust go quiet during the Games. As sprinkles on this eco cake, a 1,750-acre forest fleeced with thirty million trees and roses would be planted north of the Olympic village to suffuse it with oxygen and color. The landscaping job was only twice the size of New York's Central Park.

Beijing, the tinkering chemist, also blocked a million automobiles from the roads to distill the smog effects a year before the Games. Months later, during a summit for African heads of state, the city kept 800,000 vehicles in their garages and parking spaces in another dry run. Nitrogen oxide dropped by forty percent. When the Olympic zero hour arrived, the city knew what it had to do: it'd effectively snatch the keys from freeways full of cars. Some two million drivers, or about one-half of all privately owned vehicles, would be prohibited from entering certain parts of Beijing under an odd/even license plate system. All high-emitting cars and trucks would be forbidden from *any* section of the city. The chemist had spoken.

Public grumbling by NGOs and others feeling marginalized by the preparations, meanwhile, were dimly heard. In one adjacent region, farmers simmered over getting the shaft. To ensure Beijing was well hydrated during August, the government had diverted what it labeled "emergency water" from Hebei province to a municipal canal being dug in the capital. After some Hebei crops withered, farmers had to couch their frustration in martyring nationalism. "For the country, the [Olympics are] a good thing," one man from Beijing's less developed, provincial little brother told Reuters. "But...sometimes you wonder if they need all the water more than us here."

You had to give China's showpiece town credit nonetheless for believing it could make smog jump through its hoops with such a high degree of difficulty. Mega-phoning speedy edicts while continuing to rubber stamp *build-build* urbanization bespoke national bravado as much as it did metropolitan agenda. Smokestacks were retrofitted with sulfur scrubbers. Natural gas appliances supplanted fumy, old boilers near Beijing highways locked in standstills. Each day, the city greeted roughly 1,200 new cars and trucks to the existing 3.1 million vehicle load already more than half of Los Angeles County's 5.8 million. They motored around 1.7 billion square feet of new construction since 2002. With apartments and high rises blooming everywhere, Beijing's unofficial crest could've been the construction crane. The capital, *The New York Times* opined, "is like an athlete trying to get into shape by walking on a treadmill yet eating double cheeseburgers at the same time." And dust from that "treadmill" was as relentless as the pollution crumbs. Doubters only needed to inspect billboards advertising the Green Olympics in a city where the average life expectancy of a traffic cop working in that sticky exhaust was forty-three. Up close, one observed the signs were splotched with atmospheric grit and drab particles. Why not just announce a nursery school in the slithering Amazon?

◼

TIME NEARED FOR THE Olympics of pulmonary dread. Athletes watching the clock tick down toward the starter gun kept one eye glued on the API. Beijing's oath to muffle tailpipes and factories, to throw its urban gearshift into neutral, slammed into a sea of doubt among the *crème de la crème* of the globe's fittest people. Teams from European powers, including England and Germany, trained in Japan or South Korea, scheduling themselves to arrive in China at the last minute to reduce their fumebank intake. Once there, many said they'd wear facemasks when not competing. American triathlete Matt Reed, who strained for breath after an asthma attack at a September 2007 track meet clobbered him, would not hesitate. "We race all around the world, but I've never noticed pollution so badly as in Beijing," he said. "Sometimes we'd go for a bike ride before the race, then you'd get back and blow your nose and it's all black." For Kara Goucher, one of Yoder's fellow runners from fresh-sky Minnesota, the smog was "much worse than I imagined. It's a bit eerie how the sun never comes out all day."

Before long, China's Olympic brass was wincing as much as them. In March, marathon champion Haile Gebresallie of Ethiopia announced that he'd skip his signature event and only run in the 10,000-meter race—a precasualty of Beijing's reputation. When CNN and the BBC broadcast his controversial decision not to participate in the marathon, Chinese censors quashed the segments. "The magnitude of the pollution in Beijing is not something we know how to deal with," acknowledged David Martin, a respiratory expert counseling US marathoners. "It's like feeding an athlete poison." US boxing team physician Frank Filiberto had reckoned the capital's air had been unfairly demonized—until he visited. Only six of eleven boxers could complete a twenty-minute training run. Jog in the hotel instead, they were told. Some claim smog even penetrates there.

Anticipating a swell of anecdotes like this, Beijing's Olympic Organizing Committee tried reassuring everyone not to prejudge. Targeted smog constituents, it reported, had already plunged nearly fourteen percent since the city was awarded the Games in 2001. The MEP's deputy director, Zhang Lijun, vouched that once all the measures were activated, there would be "no problem" for the city to meet its green commitments. The whole country would be pitching in, not just factory bosses idling or tightening the screws on machinery. During the competition, big industry far afield of the city in the Shandong, Hebei, and Shanxi provinces, as well as Inner Mongolia, would suspend production of electricity, buildings, cement, steel, etc. The Bureau of Weather Modification, hot for a role, was conducting test-runs for multiple contingencies, too. Atmospheric challenges were its bag in a culture that prided itself on manipulating the clouds. Since 2002, the Bureau crowed it'd induced or prevented rain hundreds of thousands of times (though it couldn't always keep VIPs from being drenched at national events). But never was the stress ratcheted up like this.

Chatter about cloud seeding and industrial lockdowns, though, only jacked up the anxieties. In an unprecedented admission in spring 2008, the IOC publicly expressed its reservations that the Chinese could achieve their lofty objectives in time. Copious

189

smog, the IOC said, was disquieting on two counts: it could hurt the wellbeing of athletes who'd sacrificed years for their moment, and present obstacles for those chasing world records or personal bests in endurance sports such as the marathon, long-distance biking, and the triathlon. The committee alerted the host there'd be no pussyfooting around. Acute conditions could lead to postponements or cancellations. Face-saving was irrelevant. As it were, the IOC's medical commission and others would jointly meet daily to evaluate whether certain events could proceed. They'd already heard from international air-quality experts who concluded that Beijing's weather wasn't as lousy as its reputation. The commission in April, all the same, asked about contingency plans. City officials reportedly answered that they had "hard measures" in their back pocket. Coercing more factory workers as well as Beijing's civil servants into mandatory, last minute vacations was a phone call away.

The US Olympic Committee (USOC) applied the latest science in case Beijing's skies proved uncooperative. Medical personnel jetted back and forth to the Far East to determine if athletes would require inhalers or other breathing medications. Activated-charcoal facemasks were offered to every team member. For extra precaution, a senior US physiologist planned on toting a pneumotachometer, a breathing gauge attached to a laptop, to measure lung function. Asthma, hyper-lung sensitivity, bloodshot eyes, oxygen-starved muscles, an irritated heart: each part of an athlete's anatomy could be jarred. Asthmatics had to be careful with the medications they took, since common inhalers with "beta-2 agonists" were banned as performance-enhancing stimulants by the World Anti-Doping Agency. Everyone on team USA was also cautioned about overusing the painkiller ibuprofen to counteract smog effects in the East Asian cradle of them.

Déjà vu had hurtled fully back into China's face. Besides its manhandling of dissidents, Beijing's pollution was one of the reasons that the IOC in 1993 tapped Sydney, Australia in a nip-and-tuck vote to host the 2000 Summer Games. This despite intense lobbying by China to snag them—and some veiled threats that it might boycott the 1996 Games in Atlanta in retaliation. Now, with redemption in sight, could the capital be so enshrouded that its image never recovered? "Once upon a time, staging the Olympics in Beijing would have been much easier: Build some big stadiums, fill them with loyal party members, keep the foreign guests well fed, and declare victory," *Wired's* Spencer Reiss clucked. "But successful cleanups in other developed cities have raised expectations. China wants to take its place as a world leader, not just the new heavyweight champ of carbon emissions. Scenes of marathoners in gas masks, beamed around the world, would be a PR disaster that no amount of glossy Bird's Nest blimp shots could offset."

Beijing Mayor Guo Jinlong, newly installed in 2007 as an ally of President Hu Jintao, apparently was on the hot seat over it. Guo, a smiling, veteran party boss who reportedly spent his off-hours message-board surfing, would be shown the door if the city failed to achieve the Blue Sky relief it outlined, one source said.

Maybe more than anybody else, Peter Ueberroth could appreciate Guo's predicament. Los Angeles had tapped the no-nonsense, travel-industry businessman to oversee the 1984 Summer Games when the region was at the tail end of its stinging dalliance with photochemical smog and still in the jaws of perpetual congestion. "Johnny Carson was hammering us on TV... Several learned professors from universities painted a doomsday scenario," he recalled in an interview. But Ueberroth and company invested in practical thinking. Calculating they needed to eliminate just eight percent of freeway traffic to avoid bottlenecks, they aimed for an eighteen percent reduction as their cushion. They cajoled delivery trucks to roll in during non-peak hours and big corporations to commit to carpooling. Downtown hotels where visitors stayed scheduled buses to venues. Smog and traffic as a result mostly kept their claws off the '84 Olympics. "People to this day were stunned," said Ueberroth. Not only had he debunked urban cynicism, the first privately operated Games in history turned a 238 million dollar profit. Ueberroth's feat helped earn him *TIME*'s Man of the Year and a job as Major League Baseball Commissioner. When the USOC went fifty million dollars into the red amid allegations of mismanagement and ineptitude in 2004, Ueberroth was cherry-picked to save the day as its chairman. Which meant time for him in China. "They faced other issues than we faced," he quipped, ever diplomatic.

Western activists, be they in human rights or workplace-protections, harped on China's state-sponsored behavior in the months before the Beijing Olympics. Market economy or not, they said, mistreatment of individuals that'd derailed US-Sino relations winding back to Nixon was as prevalent as ever. There was record-breaking imprisonment of journalists, persecution of critics, abuse of migrant construction-workers, pre-Games demolition of housing settlements, Internet bullying. Folded into their topical greatest-hits was China's pilloried ecology, albeit more as supplemental material. Activists cited smog fatalities and birth defects, colossal greenhouse-gas emissions, and plans for 500 new coal-fired power plants. Most Americans didn't care.

For our purposes, Gore might've lipped the most show-stopping, pre-Games comment—if a social-justice champion hadn't uttered it instead. "Both multinationals and consumers in the West need to recognize," said Robin Munro, research director at China's Labour Bulletin, "that if acceptable labor standards are to come to China, the cost of China's exported goods will have to rise." Precisely the same could've been repeated about air quality standards, but the complaints generated little buzz in an America slumped in two unpopular wars. Tack on the West's fingerprints on climate change and exported Asian pollution and moral authority was in the eye of the beholder.

Hillary Clinton, then a senator from New York, wasn't shy about conveying her opinion. She recommended that President George W. Bush on principal skip any personal involvement in the Olympics' Opening Ceremony to protest China's violent repression of Tibet and its unwillingness to stem atrocities in Darfur. Nothing was said about untainted air as a fundamental right.

◘

A WEEK BEFORE THE opening ceremonies, a nagging haze clung overhead. A cooling rainstorm that spritzed days earlier, breaking a hot, steamy spell, must've felt like celestial relief. Mindful that smog owed them no pity, city technocrats tried being proactive. They'd initiate the contingency plan the IOC wanted kept handy. If contaminants hung around, they'd shutter 200 additional factories, embargo more cars from driving, and shut down some construction sites still operating in Beijing and Hebei. Curiously, Beijing's API remained in the "good" category as the pressure built to push the emergency button.

But good was not enough with the Games around the corner. Near midnight on July 28, a succession of dull booms exploded over the city for about half an hour. It wasn't organic thunder. It was the Bureau of Weather Modification shooting its load, or, in this case, specialized artillery shells filled with silver iodide, dry ice, salts, and/or other materials. Warheads had detonated inside the clouds with the aim to coax diffuse water molecules inside of them to band together into large enough raindrops for a last-ditch, air-sanitizing deluge. Several downpours were reported, along with a few cracks of lighting and even some azure sky the next day. The weather bureau, normally engaged during national droughts or loitering urban smog, pronounced itself equipped for any forecast. Like an insurance rain poncho, it would modify those same chemicals to decrease raindrops' size and resulting precipitation if they jeopardized the Games' opening-night show.

The Chinese were not blowing smoke, at least not on this. Over the years they had stockpiled more weather-manipulating munitions than some banana republics owned in combat weaponry: 7,000 antiaircraft guns, 4,000 rocket launchers, thirty aircraft, plus a reserve army of 37,000 members to manage them. China's customs might be subtle, but its public engineering was a silver platter of gigantism. Weather tweaking, sometimes satirized as a "meteorological enema," began in the People's Republic in 1958 when the friendly Kremlin transferred cloud-seeding expertise to its Asian comrade. Half a century later, the Chinese were spending 150 million dollars on a single rainmaking effort, a sliver of the fifty-five billion tons of moisture they claimed to unleash a year. Independent scientists have remained unconvinced if the rockets catalyze the clouds to do anything they wouldn't already. The theatrics, nonetheless, had value. As a Beijing weatherman told *Vanity Fair* in 2008, "People believe what they will, and government must be seen to take action."

Temporarily diluted by rockets, the smog resurged as the Olympic hordes flew in. With a day to go before the opening, one headline typified the mood: "Beijing Leads in Race for Most Polluted Olympics." PM-10 during the 1996 Games in Atlanta, Georgia averaged 31 µg/m3; in LA in 1984 it was around 70 µg/m3. While complete data wasn't available during its Olympics, Seoul, South Korea reached 170 µg/m3 sometimes. Lined up next to them, Beijing was an emissions outlier, *averaging* 111 µg/m3 since July 20. "Pray to the Mongolian weather gods" for purgative northern breezes, atmospheric chemist Kenneth Rahn had once joked the capital might need. Unhappily, typical summer winds carried grit from the south.

Accompanying those particles were a couple of illuminating, diplomatic-type incidents. In early August, four American cyclists arrived at Beijing's airport wearing antipollution, antigerm facemasks. Photographers clicked their shutter buttons as they strode past, and the images galloped across the Internet. Before China could get testy, the USOC declared its revulsion that the group had offended the host country so soon after it unfurled its red carpet. Under Olympic rules, athletes were barred from wearing any clothing with protest messages, and likewise could not engage in demonstrations involving government, religion, or race. Two African-American sprinters who'd notoriously raised their fists in a black-power salute on the medal stand during the 1968 Summer Games in Mexico City had been expelled for their gesture. The masks, thus, could be interpreted as a political statement the same as a "Free Tibet" button could, subjecting the transgressors to possible disciplinary action. They could even be sent home.

A few days after the facemask photos splashed across the Web, the USOC issued a statement expressing regret on behalf of Mike Friedman, Sarah Hammer, Bobby Lea, and Jennie Reed. Forgive them, it said. Yet it was the committee at fault, for it'd dispensed the masks to about one-third of Team USA as a pre-Games training recommendation, and then expediently forgot it had. It wasn't until after the Olympics that the USOC apologized to the cyclists for the "confusion" in a *mea culpa* that felt too tardy to one of the alleged offenders. "We were called a disgrace to the United States team and were belittled and embarrassed by the very people that are supposed to be advocates for us," Hammer ranted. "They treated us like we were just stupid athletes and like we didn't matter." Other competitors tried blanking the subject from their minds. Distance runner Shalane Flanagan said the only way she'd quit was if she were "coughing up a lung."

President Bush, in Beijing for the Games, wasn't all that warmly received, either. Thirty-three years earlier, he'd accompanied his then-ambassador father on a trip to the capital after graduating from Harvard Business School; there, they'd played a jetlagged game of tennis against an unimpressive skyline. In a speech in Thailand before arriving, the younger Bush now reproached the Communists with familiar rhetoric for American presidents. "The United States believes," he said, "the people of China deserve the fundamental liberty that is the natural right of all human beings." A Foreign Ministry spokesman parried with government-speak. The People's Republic, he claimed, already promoted "basic rights and freedoms," meaning: Butt out of internal affairs!

Except for the air quality, the Opening Ceremony drew raves. The choreography, in fact, was so immense in scope, so enchantingly presented, all of it climaxed with twenty-nine sequential fireworks bursts, that one nearly forgot the evening's point. The real headliners, athletes in colorful getups from 204 nations led by Greece, would soon be parading around the track.

The spine-tingling showmanship would lose some of its Kumbuya aura as its contrivances were revealed. Days after Chinese President Hu proclaimed the "historic moment" had arrived emerged revelations of a terrorist threat to blow up a jetliner over the stadium during the inaugural festivities. During them, authorities kept prominent dissidents in jail or under house arrest. Among them was artist Ai Weiwei, one of the stadium's designers. He was trapped in a windowless cell, required to ask the guards' permission just to touch his face, on a three-month sentence for knocking state behavior. More downers were en route, too. The angelic-faced little girl handpicked to sing "Ode to the Motherland" in actuality was lip-syncing to somebody else's voice. Another trick of stagecraft involved the pyrotechnics spectacular, the majority of which was outed as a made-for-TV computer simulation. Of course, had viewers and stadium attendees fluttered high over the Bird's Nest arena for a more bracing, ecological glimpse of everyday life here, their appreciation for the night's magical footwork might have curdled into something more puckering.

Beijing's Environmental Protection Bureau, for its part, had other excuses to be snippy besides the masks' kerfuffle. Foreign journalists were continually snapping photographs of dinghy-gray or manure-hued skies and publishing smog articles, many of them caustically written. State censors, maddeningly, weren't allowed to spike any of it. Unsurprisingly, neither side believed the other. The BBC and the Associated Press, which had lugged along their own monitoring devices out of mistrust for official numbers, reported that Olympic-time air pollution violated China's own standards. Beijing authorities denounced the findings, snarling at the Western press for atmosphere sampling outside athletic venues. People "should judge whether there is pollution by scientific statistics, not by what our eyes can see," the Bureau reminded its detractors.

Trouble was, there was so much of it to view. "Take a deep breath, click your heels three times, and repeat after me: 'There's no place for smog...'" a *Christian Science Monitor* reporter satirized in a post-mortem after Chinese suits upbraided the media for its reluctance to appraise the city's air quality by their readings. Still, for every gibe about Beijing's ham-fisted propaganda and vignettes depicting six-pack-chiseled athletes gagging on the 3-D airshed, nobody could dispute the city had genuinely tried to dress itself in green threads. From the rainwater-capture system at the Bird's Nest and energy-efficient lights at Tiananmen Square to garbage trucks powered by lithium-ion batteries, this was no charade.

For a third of cyclists, unable to finish their 158 mile race in the muggy, chemical air near the Great Wall, trying just didn't cut it. But IOC President Jacques Rogge, in a pretzeling explanation that elicited some media snickers, was unsure what athletes had inhaled at the event. "The fog you see is based on the basis of humidity and heat," Rogge said. "It does not mean to say that this fog is the same as pollution. It can be pollution, but the fog doesn't mean necessarily that it is pollution." Evidently, China's balls-out, antipollution campaign had impressed the IOC's commander-in-chief so greatly he'd become its atmospheric defender.

Somehow, either by miracle or man made effort, good fortune or geo-engineering, Beijing's skies obliged halfway through the

Games. The sun took the wheel and smog clambored into the back seat. It was bronchial victory at last, a jubilant Games that would've made Mao proud. Even Yoder Begley, the decorated, blue-eyed runner from Indiana, said conditions weren't as harsh as they were in 2002, when her lungs and nose were afire. Guo Jinlong, Beijing's message-board-cruising major, got to keep his job.

◼

CLOSING CEREMONY WRAPPED UP, the post-Olympic environmental reviews that cascaded in were, to put it nicely, devastatingly mixed. Billions had been doled out, sacrifices made—and this is what it bought? Peking and Oregon State University researchers, along with the Associated Press, the BBC, and Beijing's own Environmental Protection Bureau, each reported that pollution levels from August 8–24, to varying degrees, exceeded WHO recommendations the Chinese had so vehemently sworn to attain. Never mind those continual sunny days. Fine particulates broke international standards every second, the joint-university study determined. A MEP official attributed whatever haze there was in the capital to nitrates, sulfates, and black carbon from vehicle exhaust. Still, that was neither apology nor explanation.

A UN analysis framed a rosier portrait. From July until the end of the Olympics, both nitrogen dioxide and black carbon had fallen noticeably, with PM-10 unchanged. Beijing rainfall, almost double its thirty-year average for the August timeframe, deserved an assist, the UN added, for helping to strip soluble gases from the troposphere. Whether that unusual amount of rainfall was elicited by cloud seeding or meteorological kismet was unascertained, though common sense tilted to the former. The National Bureau of Economic Research, a US nonprofit organization, added its two cents. It concluded that Beijing's skies were almost one-third healthier during the Games than a year earlier in "the largest natural experiment in air cleaning" in memory. The normally dubious NGO Institute of Public & Environmental Affairs (IPE) gave even higher grades, estimating "the average level of pollutant concentrations had plunged forty percent" during the first twenty days of August 2008 relative to the same period in 2007. The battle of statistics had no outright winner.

With so many conflicting findings, somebody with a political agenda could always tweak the results to bolster their argument. A novel lab experiment conducted during the Games, even so, furnished insight on a more molecular level. A team of American and Chinese scientists led by Junfeng (Jim) Zhang, the former Guangzhou science whiz who'd earned his bones studying acid rain, certainly recognized its once-in-a-lifetime opportunity. Now a professor at New Jersey's Rutgers University, Junfeng was thinking Beijing. Months of preparation by him and his colleagues delivered a troupe of professors and students to Peking University's hospital. There, 125 resident doctors of both sexes were recruited as lab rats, every one of them non-smokers in good health. Zhang's bunch treaded carefully every step organizing them. The government still wasn't releasing full pollution data then, and discouraged researchers from publicizing smog-mortality rates. Wise to all that, Zhang demurred when NBC courted him to be an Olympic air quality commentator for a gig that many would've prized. Assigned to such an incendiary topic, Zhang characterized his team as worried but focused. Keeping one's head down couldn't hurt.

Potemkin Village or Gold Medal Miracle?

The would-be doctors averaging twenty-four years of age were examined before, during, and after the Olympics. Researchers recorded baseline levels of systemic inflammation, signs of blood clotting, heart rate, and blood pressure. When the fiats against driving and other activities went into full force, it was obvious inside the young physicians. Biomarkers in them associated with blood coagulation, a signpost for potential coronary-plaque buildup, exhibited "significant reductions." Circulation in Zhang's human smog-meters had markedly improved. Once the Games ended and Beijing's chemical skies roared back, the negative biomarkers returned with them, upping the risk of future heart attacks and strokes. The trailblazing results webbing ephemeral air quality changes with instant cardiovascular health were later published in the *Journal of the American Medical Association*. Zhang laughed that with the money the government spent on the airshed, his experiment cost over a billion dollars a day to perform. "There were two messages," he explained. "Your body is constantly making adjustments to day-to-day conditions that may hurt you, and your [anatomy] is less sensitive to air pollution if you're exposed to a lot, though you're still at risk for long-term disease." As a whole, Zang added, the millennial test subjects acted unbothered by his stark discovery. Tell that to their coronary arteries in a few decades.

Beijingers everywhere had to treasure the fresh skies while they sparkled, because they wouldn't for long. A year after the Olympics, roughly sixty percent of that air quality improvement had evaporated, the National Bureau of Economic Research claimed. All that manpower and money for a forty percent greening touted as a heady first step seemed more than ludicrous. It was an indictment of the folly believing you could engineer your way out of growth as no modern state ever has. Veteran China-traveler Aaron Heifetz, press officer for the US women's soccer team, sampled it in the spectrum. Beijing smog, he recalled, was "a non-issue" during the 2008 competition, including the title match the Americans won, in spite of the hullabaloo about its potency. Three years later during an event in Chongqing, the atmosphere had its talons out. "The complaining [by the athletes] was more, 'this is depressing,' not that they couldn't breathe, because it was so dark and dreary," Heifetz said. China "is like a big, uncontrollable, city-sized factory. It's a fascinating place."

The capital's frittering, post-Game improvements were catnip for those looking to extrapolate bigger failings. In particular, it savaged a line of political thinking that authoritarian governments able to maneuver at will without messy public discourse, citizen input, and other democratic mechanisms were better positioned than free societies to tackle gargantuan societal problems. Where republics were oxygenated by disparate voices, a Politburo that answered to no one could move mountains. What were champions of that theory spouting now that smog had doubled down across the whole country after the Games? Smog's brutal honesty to haze exactly where it should when summoned by man, machines, and weather had shut them up. Better symbiosis between public efforts and private investments, some Western academics chest-thumped, would have engrained improvements that didn't peter out. Totalitarian government had flopped.

From our soapbox, it's the tired, old thinking that has failed. The Communists, more capitalists than ideologues by the 2008 Games, had paved world-class byways over mud roads, some with hoof-prints still in them. They'd built dams of Paul Bunyan-esque proportion and hatched into being a middle class that few

Sinologists imagined was plausible as recently as the poufy-hair, Sony Walkman eighties. To us, drawing a line between China's feats there and its heretofore-slippery commitment to ecological restoration is selective jabberwocky. The economy of the People's Republic today isn't like the lumbering Soviet's was, even though its government frequently acts like a Kremlin-style puzzle palace. Nor is its manufacturing ethos comparable to Hitler's prewar Germany. Europe, the US—it's not comparable to them, either.

New species that it is, China 2.0, some believe, will eventually succumb to the "Environmental Kuznets Curve" that plot-points the intersection where a modernizing society demands better air and water from its caretakers. *Yeah, right.* Neither we, nor the experts trying to untangle this quilt of ambiguities, can predict how and when Asia's populace will reach their breaking point. Cancer villages and peasant riots versus rampant car ownership and urbanization have no clear-cut victor emerging. By some green metrics, the People's Republic is actually further ahead than more industrialized peers grappling with what they've destroyed with new fuel standards, driving restrictions, public transit, energy-efficiency, etc. Los Angeles itself required almost fifty years to get its full emissions-capping act together.

○

OUTSIDERS CURIOUS HOW THE Olympics affected China's interior soul would do well to forget about grand political theses of old and gaze 125 miles to the east. Who shed tears for the inhabitants of Tangshan after the crowds flew home from Beijing with their trinkets? The answer: not many.

The capital of the ham and egg Hebei Province had lived the effects of the pre-Games, antismog roundup, and lived it in their throats. Major polluters given the boot from Beijing had to land someplace. So, many came here. With them, Tangshan's past as an agricultural community and resort town gave way to a smokehouse ambience that Linfen's asthmatics would recognize. Among other industrial refugees driving pilings in Tangshan was steelmaker Shougang Group. Ditto for the historic Beijing Coking Chemical Plant, whose chimneys had hiccupped chemicals for almost half a century, and from which some 10,000 workers drew paychecks. The China of Olympic pride preferred these iron hulks squirreled away, which was good news for Beijingers unaccustomed to hanging laundry outside without coal dust streaking it. Also pleased were Tangshan's politicians, for the city's red-hot growth later outpaced China's overall GDP.

Less enchanted, as usual, were locals who could only watch machine-works saunter into town without having been asked their opinion first. "No one cares about us," one factory worker bellyached. "We are just farmers. In Beijing they are all high-class royals." The plants generated jobs, sure, but over time also an atmospheric takedown. One woman adapted by teaching herself meteorology. Whitish haze, she figured out, meant the wind was blowing from chemical factories. Gray was from the steel mills. And the black stuff? Easy—coal and coking manufacturing. There were no "Beijing 2008" pins for her.

Or vistas for others. A portion of a Tangshan industrial park near Dongmazhuang village jumbled with cement, steel, and building-material plants was so grotesquely devoid of any natural blue or sunshine, so sopped in emissions, that it dumbfounded even the journeymen activists who photographed it during a holiday break. Their pictures of finger-like smokestacks towering above cylindrical vats and conveyor belts appeared produced either by reverse-image camerawork or a comet that'd drop-kicked the terrain on impact. No modern troposphere, they believed, should be kidnapped like this. In an industrial apocalypse taken to extreme, could whole swaths of China emulate Tangshan?

Who knows, but in the here-and-now it was a terrifying portent. "As the evening approached, white, yellow, and grey colored smoke [pervades] the sky above the entire industrial park," the visitors wrote. They watched sheets of grit and dust sweeping low on the winds, raking "passersby who lowered their heads and shielded their faces from harm." Not even their inured spirits could "imagine" how life here was tolerable when all those steely pipes puffed simultaneously during normal operations.

The gag-worthy truth: Some Olympic legacies were far from the metal stands.

CHAPTER 12:

TWEETS FOR THE WHEEZY

W<small>HO EXACTLY DID THESE</small> Americans think they were—an imperial truth patrol, meddlers of the Zuckerberg age? In summer 2009, China's government was seething at US Embassy personnel in Beijing over the most delicate of topics. There'd never, in fact, been a bilateral contretemps like it. The spat had nothing to do with the treatment of the berobed Dali Lama, clashing views about how to neutralize pariah, missile-firing North Korea, or even state-sanctioned computer hacking. It was an unassuming piece of equipment spitting out numbers that had royally vexed the Ministry of Foreign Affairs. One representative voiced his displeasure over the contraption with finger-wagging bombast about the future of the "relationship" like a pushed-to-the-brink spouse.

A Twitter account had economic superpowers throwing each other the stink eye.

Ever since the Olympics, the American Embassy in Beijing had been posting real-time, hourly readings of PM-2.5 collected by a Met One Instruments Inc. machine wired up on the roof of its former compound. The State Department would later claim nothing provocative had been intended by the updates, whose technical elements had been meticulously planned. It was purely informational, a courtesy for embassy personnel and Americans traveling or living in the People's Republic. Beijing's Environmental Protection Bureau only uploaded daily averages of PM-10 from the previous twenty-four hours and then forecast conditions for the next day. From American eyes, those updates contained little value to the health-conscious, so it set up @BeijingAir as a more definitive source. *Hash tag this, hash tag that.* Interestingly, @BeijingAir hadn't piqued its resident city until *TIME* spotlighted it in June 2009—after a blurry curtain of smog prompted daytime drivers to toggle on their headlights.

The account's popularity blew up afterward despite the government's ban on Twitter, Facebook, and other Western social media it deemed unworthy. Young Chinese software writers, it seems, had discovered holes in censors Great Firewall. People could outfox it by tapping into alternative servers accessible through special apps. With a few keystrokes, they could now read an independent assessment of their air quality. Green Beagle, one of China's estimated 500 environmental NGOs, quickly parlayed @BeijingAir's notoriety. The group began equipping members and volunteers with small, hand-held P.M.-2.5 monitors to create a citizen air-quality database for Beijing's far-flung quarters. Doubt government data? Just click their links to expose a local particulate trail.

None of this industriousness sat well inside the Great Hall of the People. According to American diplomatic cables later released by *Wikileaks*, US officials were "summoned" to the Ministry of Foreign Affairs on July 7, 2009 to "listen to the Chinese government's litany of complaints about the feed's purpose and reach. Wang Shuai of the Ministry's US Affairs office, the leaked cables said, accepted the American premise that it was maintained for US citizens, but remained "unhappy" that the Chinese public could access it. The Embassy's postings, Wang stressed, were "not fair" to Beijing's Environmental Protection Authority Bureau, which he reiterated should be the exclusive voice on the atmosphere. Furthermore, categorizing city pollution as "unhealthy" based on US standards for PM 2.5 diminished China's hard-won achievements. "Insulting"—that's what it was. How, he asked, would Washington react if the Chinese Embassy there followed suit in D.C.?

But the invective wasn't over. Not even close. @BeijingAir, Wang said, had generated undesired "press fuss." More importantly, it had sowed enough confusion within the public to enflame "social consequences." Wang explained that he'd "hate to see" American-Sino environmental cooperation or the nations' broader relationship adversely "affected by this issue." Outside of the few who heard these private tantrums, nobody much appreciated the loathing the Ministry harbored for the Embassy's little blue Twitter bird.

Fumebanks that rejiggered @BeijingAir into survival reading became the site's ultimate ratings booster. From January 18 to 20, more than one-third of the eighty-six cities reporting PM-10 were smogged up. In Beijing, people were almost picking the crud out of their teeth. Less than a month later, on February 13, 2010, Beijing's PM-2.5 may have crested to its highest level ever. The first day of spring offered no letup when a honking sandstorm blew in from

Inner Mongolia, pelleting Beijing with yellow dust. Folks posing in front of Tiananmen Square donned sunglasses, facemasks, or used their palms to cover their mouths. On March 20, pollution needles in Beijing, Datong and Hohhot displayed APIs suspiciously stuck at shield-yourself, 500-index levels. Technical gobbledygook seemed almost futile describing the punch it delivered. Only citizen meteorologists could appreciate the broader picture: climate change was a handmaiden in their distress. High-pressure weather systems that typically gusted breezy, cold air—known in the Far East as the "Siberian High"—were losing strength as the Earth warmed. When winds stagnated, all that industrial and tailpipe filth just loitered over big cities, particularly communities encircled by mountains, bouncing and reacting off each other like a microscopic video game. Haze thickened, sunlight dulled – and the people grimaced. "It's not so much a vicious circle as vicious pretzel, or even knot," observed writer Didi Kirsten Tatlow.

Dark skies fisted again over the capital on November 18, 2010. Schools nixed outdoor activities. The elderly and souls with respiratory ailments were scooted indoors. In watching its own index break 500, the US Embassy believed the adjective "hazardous" next to the readings failed to convey the danger outdoors. @BeijingAir needed to say it more plainly, so it characterized levels as "crazy bad." Thousands viewed it online. Soon realizing how that tag would rub salt into the wounds that China's Ministry of Foreign Affairs was licking, the Embassy promptly deleted the phrase, clarifying it as "incorrect" terminology. American diplomats pledged to revise the terminology. The "crazy bad" slang the Embassy hoisted just once for 500+ readings was sanitized, softened into the more politically correct "Beyond Index."

China's umbrage with perceived American interference was unsalved by the lightning-fast clarification. For crusty old-timers, it was the West once again impinging on Asian sovereignty only now in cyberspace. What ethical torque did Washington even have? Since September 2008, China had surpassed Japan to become Uncle Sam's largest single foreign creditor, owning 1.3 trillion dollars in US debt. (Some calculate with intermediaries' money included, it could be 3.5 trillion dollars.) America needed to worry about reversing its Great Recession and national debt before it rudely barged in on others affairs.

Six months after the attack that instigated the "crazy bad" phraseology, two senior Chinese officials would still not relent about the site's existence. At a news conference, they ripped into the US, without mentioning it specifically, by stressing protocol breaches. "According to the Vienna Convention on Diplomatic Relations...foreign diplomats are required to respect and follow local laws and cannot interfere in internal affairs," Deputy Environment Minister Wu Xiaoqing told reporters. "China's air quality monitoring and information release involve the public interest and are up to the government." Parsing the legalities was a breeze: stop meddling! Make no mistake here: Official rationales aside, the Embassy could've avoided the dust-up by e-mailing pollution alerts to interested Americans instead of employing Twitter, which had become so central in developing-world upheavals. It was intended to provoke and enlighten.

Chinese NGOs enthusiastic about @BeijingAir bounded into the squall. To them, the Foreign Ministry's umbrage was a red herring. "What needs saving is the country's air quality, not the government's face," piped Greenpeace's Zhou Rong. The Embassy feed continued updating conditions through the back-and-forth. So did new Twitter accounts established at US consulates in Shanghai and Guangzhou, reporting dangerous smog levels with "just-the-facts" data. In @BeijingAir, Hu and other Chinese leaders had met an adversary not knock-kneed toward them. Everybody knew that if revolution visited China, it'd be digitally streamed. "I've never seen an initiative of the US government have such an immediate, dramatic impact on the country," remarked Gary Locke, then US ambassador to China, about the Twitter feed.

Erase it from the debate, and facts remained unchanged. Hu and his fellow growthsmogogists still had their feet stuck in a quicksand of constricted power. If citizens recognized the air was rotten just from breathing it, officials were probably sitting on more explosive data they'd be unable to explain with propaganda and promises. Yet blunting remorseless pollution was impossible absent measureable cleanup goals and specific avenues of attack, especially with local city halls often antagonistic to crackdowns on the factories keeping their coffers flush.

Weary-eyed Greenpeace activists appreciated every iota of this. The organization had combed through the websites of twenty-eight major eastern Chinese cities required to have legally binding action blueprints to restore their skies under the national Air Pollution Prevention and Control Law. What Greenpeace uncovered was a joke. As of 2010, the group concluded that not a single city with substandard air had a cleanup plan ready. Some had cobbled together piecemeal programs under different names involving the phase-out of high-polluting vehicles, coal caps, release of PM-2.5 data and such. Still, none—places like Shanghai, Wuxi, Changzhou, Tangshan, Tianjin, Shijiazhuang, Handan, and Baoding—had outlined specific targets. Only Beijing had circled

2030 with a comprehensible regimen to reach national standards. The Twitter feeds weren't going anywhere.

Again, Southern California was there to teach. For all its regulatory triumphs against human- and crop-dusting smog, the mega-region itself had no comprehensive strategy to meet federal standards until 1988, and then only after being sued aggressively by environmentalists. It still flubs some federal health targets today, despite mostly pristine mountain views.

◼

THREE YEARS DOWNSTREAM OF the pomp for the 2008 Olympics, China, environmentally speaking, was ripping apart at the seams. Street riots, the World Bank report, diseased factory towns, the Twitter brouhaha. Western companies that had previously attracted little flak for transferring their manufacturing to the Far East soon started being yanked into the crosshairs, too. And none took a public beating like Apple Inc., one of the world's most dominant and beloved technology companies. In the US, crowds routinely snaked around the block overnight to acquire new model iPads, iPhones, Macs, and other trademark devices. How Chinese production of them affected their environs—never a splashy controversy before—now elbowed to the head of the line.

In January 2011, three Chinese NGOs, among them the venerable IPE, issued the blistering report that Silicon Valley likely would've preferred not to hear. In *The Other Side of Apple* were case studies plumbing the dangerous conditions endured by workers at some of Apple's Asian subcontractors (or suppliers). Employees at Lian Jian Technology, a company manufacturing

Apple touchscreens in Suzhou, for example, had developed peripheral nerve damage in 2008. In wiping the screens, they'd evidently been forced to substitute an alcohol-based solvent with a toxic liquid called n-hexane that evaporated quicker, thus speeding assembly lines. In Shenzen, a fast-growing community in southeastern China affectionately nicknamed "iPod City" for its Apple-contracts, the drama was life-and-death. A dozen apparently demoralized workers at Foxconn Technology–Apple's largest Chinese supplier–leapt from building rooftops, killing ten of them during the first half of 2010. Foxconn, whose other customers reportedly include Nintendo, Samsung, and Hewlett-Packard, had a hand in forty percent of consumer electronics worldwide. The company with a 230,000 person workforce denied many of the allegations.

But the activists had peeled back an open scab crusting since the WTO. Bundles of China's low-wage factory jobs were America's formerly well-paid ones. Globalization had refereed it. A month after another sweatshop-esque incident involviing Foxconn, in February 2011, President Barack Obama and Apple CEO and cofounder Steve Jobs were face to face at a Northern California dinner. Obama had a question for Apple's chief. Could the company return to America some manufacturing from abroad, where almost all of the one hundred million tablets, phones, and other gadgets Apple sold that year were fabricated? The American middle class sure could have used the boost. While median US incomes had climbed succulently during the nineties, they'd fallen back in real dollars (to around 52,000 dollars per year) to where they'd been in 1989 when the first Bush occupied the White House. Jobs, whose pancreatic cancer would kill him by that October, refused to deceive the president. "Those jobs," he memorably told Obama, "aren't coming back." It wasn't only cheap salaries and disregarded environmental rules that'd kept them overseas, or the decline of American labor unions and surge in robotics. It was China's modular flexibility, supply chains, and sensational factory scale-up speed. It could take a US plant nine months to hire an engineer; in China, it required just fifteen days.

A *New York Times* exposé later expanded on the theme of exploited Apple's workers in the "factory of the world" by depicting what it was like to toil in them. Among other abuses it uncovered, Apple's suppliers sometimes required their workforces to labor excessive hours, sleep in crowded dorms, perform calisthenics for mistakes, and write confessions if late. One reason for the harsh treatment, the paper said, resulted from the hard bargains that Apple (which posted 108 billion dollars in 2011 sales), negotiated with suppliers. Something had to give, and it did. Breadcrumb margins compelled certain subcontractors to hunt for any savings they could shave on the factory floor. When in 2011 a pair of explosions ripped through iPad plants, killing four people and injuring seventy-seven, not even Apple's most diehard customers could ignore it. "What's morally repugnant in one country is accepted business practice in another, and companies take advantage of that," Nicholas Ashford, an occupational health expert, told the *Times*. Other multinationals were criticized, as well. Alarming working conditions, the *Times* said, existed in the Chinese supply chains of multinationals Sony, Toshiba, IBM, Dell, Motorola, and Nokia.

Keeping the pressure on Apple from its first report, the Institute and four other NGOs followed up seven months later with a second examination. This time the subject was how nine company suppliers had pocked the air, land and water around their factories. *The Other Side of Apple II* accused subcontractors of acting like, well, other Chinese factories. They'd installed hidden discharge pipes, released heavy metals. "Apple," the report sermonized, "has already made a choice: to stand on the wrong side, to take advantage of the loopholes in developing countries' environmental management systems…[to]…grab their own super profits, at the expense of the environment and communities." Activists now snarled that the era was over. They weren't so intimidated anymore chasing a retail colossus from another country.

One of the Apple suppliers the NGOs probed was the Kaedar Electronics Company plant in Kunshan near Shanghai, which manufactured laptop casings. Kaedar had discharged excessive, untreated wastewater reminiscent of some cancer villages. Nearby, the Kunshan Unimicron Electronics Company, which made printed circuit boards, had also racked up violations. Since 2006, the NGOs contended, fouled water, spray-coating vapors, and acid-gas emissions had minced people's health. The activists' sleuthing hooked the interest of Kunshan's Municipal Environmental Protection Bureau. After completing its own inquiry, the bureau determined that both factories were in general compliance, but made them retrofit in waste filters since they were so close to homes. Residents still carped about poisonous gases.

The transfixing scene that unfolded next rendered everything predating it bloodless. A woman who'd had her stomach removed during a cancer treatment filled a plastic bottle with fetid water from the stream, clutching it front of her. Ten other women joined Zhu Guifen. Simultaneously, they dropped to their knees, some of them steepling their fingers in front of the NGO's camera. "We beg you, help us!" they whinnied. "Help us ordinary people."

They seemed to need it. Nine people from one section of nearby Tongxin with less than sixty inhabitants had contracted or died of cancer since 2007, records showed.

Feeling bullied, Apple initially refused to confirm if the named plants were even its suppliers. "Apple is committed to driving the highest standards of social responsibility throughout our supply base," a representative said in typical corporate-speak. Obviously, there was work to do. A 2010 audit of 127 of its Chinese facilities concluded that while eighty-nine percent were in compliance with Apple's wastewater-control requirements, roughly a quarter did not meet its criteria for emissions-management, environmental permits, or reporting.

From all this, an organic question squiggled to the fore: where was Al Gore when you needed him? Shouldn't he have been weighing in on the mortal damage surrounding cheap, grunt manufacturing as Bill Clinton's ex-wingman? The green technology he'd wanted attached to the underbelly of China's industrialization with Western assistance was mostly non-existent. The Nobel Prize-, Oscar-winning eco-stud didn't even harness his celebrity, at least noticeably, to address the Asian controversies closer to him that most Americans realized. Gore had been an Apple board member since 2003, providing him an insider's view with a boatload of credibility to explain what outsiders didn't comprehend. *Bloomberg* valued his Apple stock options at about forty-six million dollars. Perhaps others treasured his relative silence.

Disturbing as it was, something positive rippled from the Apple coverage. Consumers with a selective blind spot for the ecological legacy of foreign-made products had been jolted. People fanatical about buying eggs from only companies that raised cage-free chickens and merchandise synthesized with recycled-materials had new victims to consider: human ones. Between American policy and globalization's love affair with cheap manufacturing, we had exported our past—noxious smog, inhumane assembly lines—someplace where we didn't have to watch it repeated. Worldwide dependence on China's discount wares was the enabler of a sort of Asian plantation society serving the West. Now, everybody knew. They just have to act. If we go to compassionate lengths for condemned animals that we intend to eat, shouldn't we ponder stamping insignias on foreign-made products, whether they're drill guns or dolls, averring that they were fabricated with techniques that harmed neither Mother Nature nor its workers? Moral umbrage at "blood diamonds" is already having its effect. Intel Corp., for example, is overhauling its supply chain so microprocessors only contain "conflict-free" minerals whose sales don't benefit murderous despots, militias and forced labor in places like the Democratic Republic of Congo. With billions of dollars in buying-power behind them, couldn't folks consuming Asian goods demand an eco-version of that? Couldn't the UN—or better yet, the WTO—commission a little symbol on product packaging, if only for our conscience? "It is easy to point a finger at unscrupulous industries and government officials willing to look the other way, but some responsibility for China's unhealthy environment originates outside the country's borders," preached an Earth Policy Institute study about cancer and disease. One thing's for sure: Chinese NGOs haven't relented coercing and cajoling multinationals into better practices. Offered public information by these organizations on how to green their facilities, Nokia, Philips, Alcatel, Vodafone, and Siemens were among the lead groups to take advantage.

China's textile industry, which weaves hundreds of billions of dollars of garments a year as the planet's biggest apparel manufacturer, itself has taken a drubbing from domestic eco-campaigners. Of thirty-nine major industries discharging wastewater, textile makers release the fourth most, or approximately 2.5 billion tons yearly. Zhejiang province's Shaoxing County may be the kingpin of fabrics-production, clustering more than 9,000 textile mills and about one-third of China's printing and dyeing capacity. Greenpeace asserts that hazardous chemicals from the trade have infected waterways there with compounds as novel to hear—chlorinated anilines, nitrobenzene—as they can be biological IEDs.

Nurturing a culture of corporate responsibility is one of activists' new tactics, rather than merely stressing "gotcha" revelations. Today, IPE tracks approximately 15,000 state-monitored polluters responsible for about two-thirds of China's air and water contamination; a digital map aided by Sina Weibo posters helped locate 4,000 of them. With technical data on their screens, advocates have grown ingenious at persuading companies to acquiesce to change. Should factories assume they could pull a fast one, IPE has developed a smartphone app that displays, where available, industrial emissions color-coded to peg whether a plant is in compliance. At one spot check, the watchdogs found that 370 major industrial companies were disgorging excessive plumes. Shaming them is much more legitimate with hard data the ideologues can't wish away. Query Apple. The company has ordered a series of workplace-improvements since *The Other Side of Apple* white paper, including agreeing in summer 2014 to eliminate n-hexane and benzene at some of its Chinese operations.

The focus of late has been cajoling minds and twisting arms to create greater transparency about environmental cause-and-effect, said Ma Jun, who founded IPE in 2006. Ma, a former journalist for the *South China Post,* has long sweated for an information revolution, going after not only companies, but also needling the government to reveal statistics it either buried or simply left uncollected. "The idea," the balding, soften-spoken Ma quipped in Beijing, "is to get all data on monitoring and discharges and make it public." To that end, his organization has published a stream of reports and maps detailing pollution sources and levels nationwide. Others like Greenpeace have followed suit. In its 2012 report "Toxic Threads: Putting Pollution on Parade," Greenpeace staged photographs of stone-faced, heroin-chic fashion models, one in a Calvin Klein shirt, posing next to foamy water, a dye plant, and other putrid locales of the People's Republic. Here, the West was implicated again. Forty-eight apparel brands outsourced contracts to dirty factories, Asian environmental groups charged in a study. Presented with the evidence, two-thirds of the companies declined to reform themselves. More receptive to disciplining their suppliers were Levi's, Nike, Adidas, Gap, Burberry, Walmart, H&H, and Esquel. They understood that even if regulators ignored them, the information-savvy NGOs wouldn't.

◙

IF GREENPEACE AND IPE were more self-possessed, ordinary folks with little experience challenging the status quo had learned gobs since Huaxi's 2005 "peasant revolt." Survey those in Dalian, an ancient fishing village scarred by centuries of war. In the summer of 2011, pandemonium clenched the seaport city of 6 million in northeast China close to the North Korea border. A storm had propelled waves through a dyke protecting the Fujia Chemical Plant, which produced the chemical PX. Residents of Xiamen had successfully blocked it from being made in their city during that 2007 uprising. PX production, though, had already arrived in Dalian, panicking folks with a nightmare image: a river of toxic goo caused by a tidal surge coursing through the streets, the Grim Reaper in a skiff not far behind.

Nobody here was accustomed to this type of hubbub, for Dalian had spent the last years counting its money. In the nineties, a magnetic, ambitious politician became mayor. Bo Xilai, you see, had a mission. He aspired to create a manufacturing/shipping/ logistics stronghold here on par with Rotterdam. By the time Bo departed for the Politburo, the former journalism student had reinvented the town. There was European architecture, pretty female police officers, seaside walkways, and robust industry, most notably a 2.5 billion dollar Intel semiconductor/wafer fabrication plant. Netherlands, watch out. Bo counterbalanced these adornments with a nationalistic passion for citizens to remember who they were. They should sing patriotic ditties and live their communist principles. Appealing to young and old, the can-do Bo was handicapped as a future premier.

Bo might've realized that promise, too, except that his enemies, some of them wealthier than him, decided to purge him on bribery and abuse of power charges in a 2013 show trial that mesmerized the country. Juicy yarns about political intrigue, his wife's poisoning of an English businessman, party privilege, and money handshakes made for China's own *National Enquirer* scandal. Pollution had a bit role, too. A young billionaire who'd earned his fortune in Dalian redevelopment projects before investing in traditionally fumy petrochemical plants allegedly repaid Bo for his influence by showering Bo's family with first-class trips, tuition for a Harvard-bound son, a villa in Cannes, and other gifts worth over three million dollars. For these misdeeds, Bo received a life sentence. "It was a typical relationship between a politician and a businessman—they traded money and power," one reporter explained. Perhaps, but there was nothing average about Bo, nor passive about his town's beef with PX.

Authorities safety reassurances about the chemical factory only gave most Dalians cold comfort. Local activists flocked to Sina Weibo and instant messaging systems. "Take a stroll," they implored everyone. Cyber-cops trying to stymie Web searches for keywords like "Dalian" and "PX" had moved too sluggishly. An estimated 12,000 demonstrators who packed themselves in front of a government office stiffened against a "wall of riot police" in a generally nonviolent standoff. People waved banners saying, "Fujia, get out!" A man in a gas mask wore a T-shirt that read, "Brother wants to live a few more years." Officials had all done this to themselves. They'd green lighted Fujia Chemical to begin full-scale production in 2009 without the required sign-offs.

What had unexpectedly ignited in Huaxi over an obscure pesticide company had blossomed into a wheeling carousel of Chinese unwilling to breathe and ingest contamination for the sake of jobs or national bragging rights. More and more, as well, the Communist Party leadership was permitting the nation's media to cover uprisings with remarkable candor, as if it had no choice. Provided the riots were contained, they'd allow people to rage. All bets were off for agitators presenting a wider threat. An American doctor in Beijing who'd recommended that everybody wear facemasks learned what happens when the gatekeepers decided a Pandora's box had opened. *The Global Times*, a Communist Party mouthpiece, sought payback against him in an editorial. The paper quoted a conveniently anonymous physician from Peking University, who blasted the doctor for creating "trouble out of nothing, as we've had polluted air for a long time, and we shouldn't be living with an American standard."

Double standards were more acceptable if you were in with the right crowd. Two hundred high-end air purifiers that cost as much as 2,000 dollars apiece hummed inside President Hu's office, the Great Hall of the People, and the Zhongnanhai, the special estate for the party's senior leadership and their kin. A ranking economic official promoting the Broad Group machine in a company testimonial refused to travel without one in his hotel room or car. "Breathing clean air," said Long Yongtu, "is a basic human need." The Politburo supposedly became believers in the equipment when they eyed its soot-grimed filters. News that party elders during 2011 were guaranteed purified air—to go with premiere healthcare, food, education for their children, and other perks—pin-wheeled bitterness and loathing through the hoi polloi. One Sina Weibo poster encapsulated it: "They don't have to eat gutter oil or drink poisoned milk powder and now they're protected from filthy air."

Protected, sure. But spared completely? Not really. Smog can't be outrun, hidden under the asphalt, propagandized, or otherwise commanded to retreat into a bottle. It's an equal-opportunity harassing creature indifferent about whether its victim is a thumb-sucking toddler, a desperate farmer, an asthmatic office worker, a cavalier Politburo member, or just about any sentient organism. "Of all the challenges facing Chinese policy makers, air pollution is uniquely communal," the prestigious medical journal *The Lancet* editorialized. "Even in a society of stark divisions and increasing inequality in housing, health care, and education, everyone still breathes the same air when they step outside."

Class warfare, as these comments illustrate, is on a low boil in Asia. Just as Americans decried the rise of the one-percenters— those making near the 400,000 dollars per year range—Chinese netizens have simmered about the clubby intersection of politics, affluence, and inside deals. The revelation that some of the tiptop men running the country and their kin have secretly parked billions of dollars they accumulated by different means in offshore companies and trusts reinforced the perception of two Chinas. Among many others, relatives of Wen Jiabao and Deng Xiaoping sent money abroad in this legal, if scorned practice, according to leaked documents obtained by the International Consortium of Investigative Journalists. Of course, firms like UBS, PricewaterhouseCoopers, and Western banks played middleman.

"Princelings" are what friends and family of those cashing in on their leadership connections are dubbed. Fascinatingly, some even have responsibilities influencing air and water quality. "China's corruption-plagued oil industry…is a big player in the offshore world," the consortium wrote. It named executives from Petro-China and the National Offshore Oil Corp. for squirreling funds overseas. Shi Zhengrong, formerly China's wealthiest man as the founder of Suntech, did so as well—until his debt-bedraggled solar company declared bankruptcy. Where was the princelings' wealth largely housed? the British Virgin Islands and Samoa, naturally.

Back in the capital, Xi's regime has pursued both "tigers" (elite officials) and "flies" (the unconnected) in an antigraft housecleaning unprecedented in decades. And it's pursued it even as Xi's own family has liquidated hundreds of millions of dollars in assets to inoculate themselves (and him) from unwanted notoriety, if not accusations of hypocritical nepotism. Besides Bo, two energy-industry tigers were on the path to being euthanized. Liu Han, a Sichuan mining tycoon, was sentenced in spring 2014 after being convicted with his brother of spearheading a mafia-esque racket that ordered nine murders and fed itself on extortion, assault, and gambling. It was part of an epic criminal gang. Lurid as his case was, it withered in political relevance with the once-secret investigation and detention of Zhou Yongkang, a former domestic security chief and retired Standing Committee member. Zhou's son and two in-laws, *The New York Times* reported, had amassed 160 million dollars, a good hunk of that peeled from the "oil and gas sector that was Mr. Zhou's political fiefdom, where he could shape decisions and promotions." If you're not getting the sense that a five-story-high stumbling block to China's ecological restoration are oligarchs duking it out amongst each other, we have some fine, Afghanistan garden-land to tantalize you into buying.

On a related note, California has also socked away the People's Republic's investment bucks. Some 2.6 billion dollars has wended its way, mostly in real estate transactions for hotels, condominiums, and office space in downtown Los Angeles. North of the city in deserted Lancaster, BYD, a multibillion-dollar Chinese conglomerate already selling low-emission cars worldwide, is managing an electric-bus factory on the grounds of an obsolete recreational-vehicle plant. Besides production of its so-called "eBus," BYD operates a nearby facility developing battery packs for wind turbines, solar panels, and SUVs. Whether any princeling funds trickled to the West Coast is unknown. One of the company's names, just the same, is worth a snort: Greenland Corp.

◘

FROM A CLIMATE THAT sometimes felt like magma was steaming nearby, celebrity names in 2011 made their voices heard for airshed cleanup. Real estate magnate Pan Shiyi, whose luxury developments peppered Beijing, veered into cyberspace. On a Sina Weibo account with millions of followers, he lobbied for improved monitoring, asking people in a poll sure to have ruffled government feathers to vote whether PM-2.5 readings should be released; ninety percent responded "Yes." Following his lead were fellow developer Ren Zhiqiang, actress Yao Chen, and the man who'd spearheaded Google China, Lee Kai-fu. A highly watched video parodying the Olympics embodied scoffers' view. The "Smoggy Capital [*sic*]," it said, "Welcomes you, with particles in the air."

People might've have been saying "blue skies my foot" at the official announcement that 2011 had begat 286 Blue Sky days, almost triple 1998's number. For many Chinese nationals, the US Embassy's Twitter feed was still the best arbiter of the sludge overhead. The yawning disparities between what the government regarded as healthy air and the rest of the world had a Kabuki Theater sensibility. It was there in the manipulated air quality indices, and pollution monitors shamelessly tinkered with or moved from smoggy locales to sprinkler-fed parks. It was there in lung x-rays.

The next year, popular discontent must've sounded like fingernails on a chalkboard for the party: shrill. Residents in Shifang brawled with police in July over a future 1.6 billion dollar copper refinery that drew barrels of newspaper ink. Beijing had been helping the modest city in the central Chengdu province amass a manufacturing base following the killer 2008 earthquake that left nearly 90,000 dead or missing and millions homeless. Signs around the factory zone there hyped a "low carbon, environmentally friendly" future, where denizens should "follow the party's lead to development." But Shifang's populace wasn't bowing down to Sichuan Hongda, one of China's foremost lead and zinc manufacturers. Executives claimed their refinery was government-approved and engineered to the highest tolerances, no matter the public outcry. A Reuters correspondent offered a more pejorative view, sketching a "grim-looking collection of buildings," around large slag heaps and "a stark, moon-like landscape [in] contrast with the verdant fields nearby."

Here as elsewhere, it was the same old story. Shifang's residents hammered local officials for not disclosing more about the project, including byproduct emissions arsenic and mercury. On a Sunday evening, thousands of people, including high schoolers, swarmed into the shady public plaza and exchanged blows with riot police. After some uploaded photos and videos of them brandishing tear gas and batons, local authorities rebuked citizens not to employ the Web or cell phones to further organize. In the riot's wake, the city inaugurated China's maiden air pollution hospital. "We should not fear smog," the facility's banner reads. "It's preventable and curable."

Inspirational message definitely, but is it really preventable given the linchpin economic priorities it underscores? If the

Politburo adapts a more liberalized philosophy toward the environment and workplace protection, the built-in expenses to achieve them may translate into higher consumer prices, and that could profoundly weaken China's capacity to undercut higher-priced competitors. In a perverted way, Western discount shoppers have depended on that tradeoff since the WTO just as the men of the Standing Committee have. No-name people are torn over this dichotomy. One need only return to Chengdu, which also hosts a six billion dollar petrochemical facility operated by the state's China National Petroleum Corp. that many locals never desired. Once censors learned of a planned demonstration to rage against the city-sized facility, they texted citizens to stay inside and, later, show up for work for Saturday. "My home was destroyed for the plant," one woman told a *Marketplace* journalist before he was chased away. "The sky here is always polluted now." Years before, a father who abandoned triathlons after the air darkened heard Gore speak in Beijing as Gore promoted *An Inconvenient Truth*. "I asked [him] what we can, as normal people, do to help China's environment," recalled Jin Lei. "He said, 'You are representatives of China's younger generation, and you must have faith that things can change.'"

Eyeballing it all from the capital, China's growthsmogogists must've been appreciative at least that the multitudes weren't clutching signs (or Molotov Cocktails) outside their windows. Only a few time zones to the west, half the Middle East was in sweltering revolt. People were tossing off the yokes of ruthless dictatorships perpetrated for decades by one-sided laws, payoffs, intimidation, and state murder. A Tunisian street vendor who lit himself on fire to protest his harassment had unwittingly ignited a regional tinderbox. Egypt's Hosni Mubarak was deposed.

Muammar Gaddafi's government was toppled, the strongman himself murdered by rebels. Protests and change roiled Lebanon, Yemen, Kuwait, Sudan, Algeria, and elsewhere. In Syria, a civil war would take 190,000 lives, some families gassed with chemical weapons. For those in charge in Beijing, extra cigarettes must've been puffed, contingency plans dashed off. Social order had to be maintained in case anybody tried franchising a branch of the Arab Spring to the Far East.

Fall 2012 wasn't exactly becalming for them. There was that nine day long fracas between residents and cops in Yinggehai over the coal-plant/receiving harbor. As blood ran there, the port city of Ningbo witnessed days of defiance turn violent over the future 8.9 billion dollar expansion of a Sinopec-controlled petrochemical operation. Protesters on tenterhooks about what its production of PX and ethylene augured for their health chucked bricks and water bottles, clamoring for the plant move to near Shanghai. "It is said that this project would bring a large increase in GDP—which may be a good thing for the city," one demonstrator observed with middle-class pragmatism. "But we believe it will pollute... We aren't so concerned about how much money the project brings because we are already satisfied with the current economic situation." Days after the skirmish, city officials announced the project had been scuttled pending additional "scientific debate."

The city hall in one village where residents were too cowed to rebel in November 2012 utilized a goon squad to keep its status as a cancer village hush-hush. Houwanggezhuang was a flyspeck hamlet about forty miles northeast of Beijing. A chemical factory there manufacturing polymer polyacrylamides for food packaging, among other uses, had discharged a pungent stink that people whiffed at night. Twenty-five of Houwanggezhuang's estimated 1,000 citizens had died from cancer, which many pinned on plant venting and water releases that blackened the river. So as not to be clubbed by hooligans employed by town officials, citizens could only whisper what they knew to outsiders. Ironically, their muffled words coincided with a speech by outgoing President Hu that devoted inordinate attention to environmental cleanup and its "vital importance to the people's well-being and China's future." Houwanggezhuang's ornery leaders seemed more concerned with protecting the town's industry. Reporters investigating the disease outbreak there, a *Daily Telegraph* correspondent among them, quickly discovered the town gestalt when men in red armbands reading "Security Patrol Volunteers" surrounded them. The volunteers tried ripping away a camera before expelling the journalists to the village outskirts. More strapping thugs next appeared and encircled one of the foreigner's cars. "Just leave now or you might be beaten and bitten by dogs," the ringleader snorted. They got away.

Evidently, the boiling pot of revolts had stirred impressions where they counted. During the November 2012 Communist Party Congress, where the next generation of officialdom was inducted, the government said it would henceforth require that new industrial projects include analyses of their risk to social stability, plus allow for public input. As Minister of Environmental Protection Zhou Shengxian expounded, nobody was surprised that the citizenry was up in arms. "I think it is inevitable that when a society is developed to a certain level, certain phenomena will naturally arise. For China…we are now in a sensitive period especially in terms of environmental issues. At the same time we are beginning to see a phenomenon called 'not in my backyard.'"

Spcaking about the NIMBY protests, he added: "What we need to do is to earnestly learn from these lessons."

Preferably, those lessons would come from someplace other than @BeijingAir.

Who was the public to believe? Like Los Angeles, it had taken China the better part of a generation to identify the genes arrayed on its smog chromosomes. Unlike its pan-Pacific counterpart, the best, accessible distillation of them was not necessarily stamped with a government crest, but that of an NGO, in this case the IPEs. Its sub-radar report, "A Road Map to Blue Skies," quantified as never before the effluents that China's industrial tentacles were whipping upwards. The volume was more than previously cited. Pirouetting into the atmosphere during one test year (2007) was roughly 13.2 million tons of PM-2.5, 31.6 million tons of sulfur dioxide, 23.2 million tons of nitrogen oxide, 16.5 million tons of carbon monoxide, and 9.8 million tons of volatile organic compounds, for a total of 94.3 million tons. Had black and organic carbon and ammonia been lumped in, the total would've flirted with the one hundred million ton per year mark. And that would've excluded a multitude of other contaminants, some even more lethal. What the IPE documented, the populace sensed.

To put a tragi-comic bow on 2012, the West's yo-yoing attention span with China's ecological mildew was stirred just as American athletes were boarding jets for the Summer Games in London. Nike had made the uniforms in which Team USA members would compete. But designer Ralph Lauren, under contract with the USOC, had farmed out to a Chinese clothing company the order for the blazers, berets, and pants showcased in the Opening Ceremony. "It is not just a label," bristled New York Congressman Steve Israel. "Today, there are 600,000 vacant manufacturing jobs in this country and the Olympic committee is outsourcing… That is not just outrageous. It's just plain dumb. It's self defeating."

Someone should've alerted a certain spy agency about "Buy American" before it was too late. When the CIA decided to try to scare Muslim children from idolizing Osama bin Laden by creating a lookalike doll with a peel-away red face resembling a demon, it didn't solicit Mattel Inc. for the job. It reached out to a former executive at toymaker Hasbro Inc. who'd worked on the popular G.I. Joe line. To China he took the concept, where a disputed number of prototype bin Laden figurines were quietly produced by a factory, possibly in Dongguan, according to the *The Washington Post*. Some in 2006 were shipped on a freighter to Pakistan. While the CIA scuttled wider dissemination of the twelve-inch-high replicas, the anecdote highlighted a reality maddening for some. Whether the merchandise was commercially intended or counter-insurgency driven, the People's Republic could knock it out lickety-split and ask what's next.

CHAPTER 13:

"GREYJING'S" LAST STRAW

THE FUMEBANK THAT CRIPPLED Beijing for much of early 2013 was one for the books, variously colored slab-gray, green, or a brownish shade of sweet and sour soup. You just as easily ignored it as an outbreak of the shingles. PM-2.5 on January 12 scaled to a lung-wracking 886 μg/m3, the highest recording the US Embassy's air quality index had ever charted. The next day it averaged 535 μg/m3, twenty-one times greater than international standards recommend for daylong exposure. From the capital to Guiyang in the southwest 1,400 miles away, authorities canceled flights and sporting-events, cordoned off highways, and begged people to stay indoors to protect themselves from the spume of the factory of the world.

"One-third of China's territory was heavily polluted," remembered Fuquiang Yang, a senior adviser for Beijing's branch of the Natural Resources Defense Council. "Nobody [was] happy."

Over the next five days, folks gasping with asthma, bronchitis, pneumonia, and the like thronged emergency rooms. At Beijing Children's Hospital one January weekend, they accounted for half of all patients. "Airpocalypse," caterwauled *ABC World News* anchor Diane Sawyer; "The city that never breathes" was another's motto. Even *The Daily Show with Jon Stewart* fired a potshot with a segment called "Things May Be Bad, But at Least We Can't Chew Our Air." Adding to the misery that impeded traffic and gauzed the sun was a viscous fog clouding eastern and central China.

Only in the parallel universe of state thought-control were things looking peachy. "Beautiful China Begins to Breathe Healthily" headlined a *People's Daily* story that same month. In officials' lens, smog laced with fog was still just benign moisture. Lest people forget the pink luminescence of a smog-less sunrise, Beijing authorities replayed them on big rig-long, outdoor LED televisions that usually promote tourism in Tiananmen Square and elsewhere. Propagandists unloosed even sillier tactics. A journalist on state-owned *CCTV* ticked off smog's benefits, saying they pummeled rich and poor indiscriminately, inspired humor and sobriety, and encouraged the citizenry to learn atmospheric science. "Without this haze, would you know what PM-2.5 was?" Thousands of bloggers commented, many scathingly.

Similar cynicism greeted suggestions that the blighted air would afford the Chinese Army "a defensive advantage in military operations." Aerosolized particles, this theory went, would throw a monkey wrench into missile-guidance systems that required infrared rays, lasers, and human sight to plot coordinates. The flip side, some said, was that terrorists might exploit that same opaque battlefield to launch attacks under the noses of security cameras that the government so keenly installed around the nation as part of its "Skynet" system (yes, the same name from the *Terminator* movie set in pre-doomsday Los Angeles).

Overall, not seeing was believing in a city where visibility in spots was axed to one hundred feet or less. The aerosol gumbo of nitrates, carbon, particulate matter, sulfates, microbes, and more blotted out the sharp, architectural lines of the 600-plus-year-old palace fronting the Forbidden City, where dynastic emperors once resided. It swallowed bicyclists and school buses. It reduced to ghosts New-Money high-rises with avant-garde designs like Beijing's new *CCTV* headquarters, nicknamed "Big Underpants" because it straddles the road with towers rising from each side like legs trussed by a waistline-ish bridge.

A Dutch inventor-artist flabbergasted watching that skyscraper "gradually disappear into a white-grey haze" on a business trip, was galvanized enough to do something about the onslaught. Pretty soon, Daan Roosegaarde was developing an "electronic vacuum cleaner" whose buried copper coils generate an electrostatic charge that attracts grimy aerial particles. One compared the device undergoing further refinements to a "giant hula hoop." An EPA research scientist and university professor himself riffed off artificial rainmaking, circulating a schematic to eradicate PM-2.5 by installing sprinklers atop high-rise buildings to douse the air with custom-made water droplets. Despite the shortcomings—water scarcity, overhumidification, cost—Yu Shaocai hailed his concoction as technically feasible. Suddenly, everyone was spitballing quick fixes and pilot projects for the misadventures of atmospheric chemistry. In northwest China, water cannons aping surface-to-air artillery spurt tap water 2,000 feet skyward. A batch of cities, Nanjing and Wuhan among them, plan to employ high-rise buildings as wind corridors upwind of factories to capture industrial plumes before they disperse. If history is any guide, whacky, geo-engineering type schemes often entertain the media before redoubled public effort puts the heat on regulators for concrete improvement. Think we're too incredulous of outsider genius? When armchair inventors decades back suggested billowing away Southern California smog by mechanical means, a cantankerous scientist yelled *whoa!*

A single, contaminant fumebank measuring 13,500 square miles was of such enormous weight (as in 250 *million* tons) that just banishing it for one day, he noted, would deplete the power churned out by a dozen Hoover Dam hydroelectric generating stations.

Elsewhere in Beijing 2013, electronic freeway signs became eerie buoys silhouetted against the chemical drizzle. From satellite elevation, one of the globe's mega-cities was imperceptible. Older Californians in the Far East might've suffered flashbacks to smog-alert days from the seventies, when helicopters fitted with microphones sometimes hovered over public pools to order everybody indoors, and mothers threatened politicians—in one episode with a hatchet—to do something! Chinese authorities hesitant to resort to whirlybirds to spur citizens into defensive action tried their best anyway to rally them with an *all-for-one* ethos. "Recent atmospheric pollution has really sounded a warning to us," editorialized the party's *Global Times*. "If we continue this way of development instead of adjusting to it, the long-term damage will be serious."

Will be? Average, working citizens were no long buying what the government was selling. Not after the recent months. China's flagship metropolis had crossed over into a prolonged, blinding soup that mocked feel-good statistics. Social disdain that snuck past the censors measured as high as the particulates, some of which drifted from the estimated 27 million tons of coal the capital burned annually. The climate was akin to "sulfur perfume," one writer said. Doctors, the joke went, prescribed shaky patients tailpipes to inhale to make them feel normal.

◘

PEOPLE IN THOSE UNREMITTING days caring for asthmatic or respiratory-ill children must've agonized over what defined "normal" anymore. At their homes, inhalers, sinus nasal washes, and painkillers sat nervously on counters. Physicians' numbers were cell phone contact favorites. Some parents kept their little ones at home during the worst days, or only sent them walking in facemasks to schools winnowed partly for the quality of their air purifiers. A pollution-gnarled school in the Hebei province had students practice kung fu aerobics, which supposedly helped the lungs detoxify; physicians were unsure if the movements did anything. For precaution, school trips and outdoor sports all over were postponed. Another blitz in late January kiboshed hundreds of flights, stranding many travelers with the "Beijing cough," only cured by not being in Beijing.

At Tiahe County's hospital in Anhui province east of Shanghai, we saw another side of the smog health-emergency. There, the medical director ushered Bill around, pointing out how doctors devised herbal remedies containing ginger, ephedra, white peony root, and other plants with techniques not splashed on WebMD. The dimly lit establishment without air conditioning was crowded with locals on a dripping hot summer day. Each of them waited their turn for acupuncture and other traditional remedies. Walking down hallways bustling with patients and staff, he peered into sparsely furnished community wards. Patients lay stripped of most clothing, some with heat pads covering various areas of their body. (Warming internal organs, so goes the theory, promotes circulation and immunity to infections and irritants from abraded conditions.) In other rooms, patients were flat with needles strategically inserted to boost lung and heart function. Bill's tour leader, a tall, aging doctor with an authoritative demeanor, explained that the hospital also has a more modern wing offering Western-style medicine. It's just that large numbers of the city's residents still favor ancient practices.

Without any magic remedies for the scratchy conditions that made some teeter like a "human vacuum cleaner," the government did what it knew. It reverted to the same civic padlocks as it had during its Olympics cold sweat. Fiats shuttered dozens of smoky factories and hundreds of construction sites in Beijing and in Hebei province. A third of the municipal workforce was forbidden from driving.

How dense with particles was the urban airshed? *Bloomberg* reported that at 194 µg/m3, Beijing's average PM-2.5 for the first twenty-nine days of January was filthier than the tobacco-fraught air inside sixteen US airport smoking lounges during 2012. (They averaged 167 µg/m3.) So horridly contaminated were China's skies that a fire ablaze in an abandoned furniture store in a city southeast of Shanghai roared for hours before anyone realized it. The Northeast, meanwhile, saw PM-2.5 of 1,000 µg/m3, a level proximate to forest fires. Pilots flying into the nation's ten busiest airports were told they had to be qualified to make landings using cockpit instruments when visibility fell below 1,315 feet. And it would.

Embarrassingly, these attacks occurred just as the government expected to be winning backslaps for its further evolution from the pollution-reporting Dark Ages. Starting New Year's Day, seventy-four of China's largest cities had begun posting hourly updates for ozone, sulfur dioxide, nitrogen dioxide, carbon monoxide, and, most importantly, PM-2.5. Any citizen with a keyboard could retrieve the numbers. Whether from groundswelling popular outrage or @BeijingAir's contrarian data, the Politburo had yielded. Speaking about urbanites' insistence on receiving PM-2.5 readings, Prime Minister Li Keqiang said leaders had to wake up. "It's an era of online information sharing; if you don't publish, the public will get the information from somewhere else. You fool nobody."

Realism bathed Keqiang's words. Just miles away, however, Beijing's information apparatus continued spoon-feeding citizens the kind of Pollyannaish statistics that it'd been programmed to spit out since the garish Red Army parades. Beijing officials on December 31, 2012, for example, bragged that the just-completed year represented the city's *fourteenth* straight one of improving air quality, with average concentrations of sulfur dioxide, nitrogen dioxide, and PM-10 all down from 2011. This, despite their subtle decision to cease reporting the number of Blue Sky days so out of synch with phlegmy reality. "Rather mysterious" is how a story in state media later described the causes of the murk, no buffoonery intended.

There was one secret that couldn't be maintained. Grassroots blowback over the pitted environment had supplanted land disputes as China's number one engine of social unrest, a retired-party political specialist acknowledged in March 2013. (An earlier poll surveying middle-class Chinese on quality-of-life concerns ranked smog behind wealth-gap inequality, housing prices, food safety, and corruption.) "If you want to build a plant, and if the plant may cause cancer, how can people remain calm?" asked Chen Jiping. Perhaps to soften his remark, he claimed the number of "mass [protest] incidents" had plummeted, though Chinese statistics are as malleable as its factory plastics.

Police officers whirling in tailpipe fumes seemed about the only ones catching a break. Authorities in Jinan, an industrial city in Shandong province, made history in early 2013 when they granted traffic cops permission to don facemasks on smoggy shifts. Before, many had contracted sore throats, colds, and eye irritations. Elsewhere around China, their colleagues pined for the Ministry of Public Security to snip the antimask red tape allowing them to do the same. Shanghai, home to about 2.5 million registered vehicles, innovated its own solution. The city distributed to traffic police in one district U-shaped filters for their nostrils, classifying the mushroom-esque plugs "invisible masks." It beat jamming cigarette butts up your nose as a homemade solution that some practiced, or expecting that eating broccoli by the bowlful shielded you from smog-triggered illness as some believed.

Eco-entrepreneurs, meanwhile, never smiled brighter, assuming you could see their grin. A cottage industry catering to China's multitudes found its wings during the bedlam from above. Masks sold at clips not seen since the 2003 SARS epidemic. Bargain cloth versions preferred by young people came festooned with Panda bears, Darth Vader, flowers, polka dots, elephants, cult heroes, Pokémon, and other cutesy designs belying the urban spume they were trying to sieve. A Shanghai mask-maker crowed he'd sold a million units since the summer. Bicyclist messengers requiring heartier protection from tailpipe blasts fancied neoprene covers rigged with military-grade-looking exhalation valves. Likewise, purifiers of all shapes and sizes flew off shelves, cheapies going for as little as fifteen dollars. The champagne version, an aesthetically designed, wood-trimmed beaut, cost 6,000 dollars. They sucked grit mainly for China's hoity-toity, including its Communist Party. Foreign makers like Swiss outfit IQAir and domestic brands such as Yadu and Midea were enjoying the dawn of a potentially billion-dollar market. At the Shanghai Fairmont, guests wavering over the best option can test out air-filter masks in luxury pouches the hotel provides as a courtesy. Leave the coughing to them.

A new sight in town must've made Chinese propagandists long for a Monte Carlo vacation. Puffing up for the first time across Beijing were enormous, synthetic domes the *Los Angeles Times* characterized as "a cross between the Biosphere and an oversized wedding tent." The International School of Beijing installed a pair of the rib-roofed enclosures held up by pressured air and sealed tight as a drum over tennis courts and other outdoor athletic areas. Students were now free to exercise regardless of weather or fumebanks. Ones spanning 54,000 square feet could fetch one million dollars. Broadwell Technologies out of Shenzen and a Southern California company that customarily served hospitals and other institutions banded together on them. "This is a product only for China," the head of Broadwell said, apparently deadpan. "You don't have pollution this bad in California." Civic boosters in one southwestern province exploited the moment with a droll, getaway promotion. "Fresh Fujian, take a deep breath," read the ad for clean-skies tourism there. Within a few months of its solicitation, photos appeared of wrinkly seniors, kids, and others from Zhenghou in Henan province with transparent masks around their faces inhaling "fresh mountain air via sealed bags." Half come-hither promotion, half sociology of the desperate, 2,000 cans of pure, blue sky oxygen collected from a cliff were emptied by takers within twenty minutes.

All the same, some merchandise was more political taunt than commercial venture. During the Beijingers so-called "winter of discontent," Chen Guangbiao, a mid-forties recycling tycoon, philanthropist, and self-promoter, reintroduced an item the dimension of a Coca-Cola can. Not only was the vivacious Chen one of Asia's richest men, he was also a skilled environmental huckster. Eighty cents would get customers a container full of nothing. Chen's fresh air in a can, available in Post-Industrial Taiwan or Pristine Tibet scents, had his caricature emblazoned on it and the message "Be a good person, have a good heart, do good things" on the bottom. He predicted sales of one hundred million dollars in its rollout year. (A half century earlier, some Californians had tripped on the same kitschy concept, hawking "Smog in a Can" reflective of a demoralized citizenry.) Grandstander and all, Chen beseeched China's rulers not to "chase GDP growth" at the expense of future generations. This was his second well-promoted stunt, having already smashed electric scooters to protest lead contamination.

More flagrant profiteering was in the offing. Also in 2013, perfume-cosmetics giant Dior unveiled a skincare lotion designed to smooth out pollution effects for concerned Chinese women. Dior publicized its One Essential line with environmental hipness; apps explained ozone and toxins in beauty-thrashing terms, as gorgeous women strolled Parisian streets. "Smog and sandstorms repeatedly infringe on the skin; among these, the greatest danger is PM-2.5," one come-on in Beijing read. The pitch also might've said there was nothing new under the dark sun. In Los Angeles, where the brown-air epidemic catalyzed murders, spiritual gloom, and mafia rumors, columnists once suggested that ladies counter smog-swollen eyes by dabbing on an astringent derived from witch hazel. This wasn't black magic. It was a shrub whose anti-inflammatory properties were also mixed into hemorrhoid ointments. On the heels of Dior's new product oozed something more consequential than skin cream. IBM, already in the People's Republic helping to manage China's electrical grid, disclosed that it was partnering with Beijing to develop pinpoint smog forecasts and emission tracking by harnessing supercomputers to take on the heavy calculations. Irving Krick, a tousle-haired, piano-playing meteorologist celebrated for accurately predicting the weather for World War II's D-Day Invasion, challenged California in 1949 to do the same with rudimentary technology. Sixty-five yeas later, why shouldn't an All-American company be a savior (for profit) in the Far East?

Giggle as you might, but accoutrements to outlive China's envelopment signaled a new state of thinking about existence in its aerial sarcophagus. Was this how it'd be from now on—a few, clear days followed by a grouping of intolerable, gray ones that made government stats look ten degrees of absurd? "PM-2.5 does not simply emerge form smokestacks and tailpipes; many of these particles are produced in the atmosphere by reactions between other pollutants—namely [sulfur dioxide], mono-nitrogen oxides, and volatile organic compounds—in a complex interplay with sunlight, humidity, and temperature," one writer explained during Beijing's season of pain. "The process is not unlike baking a cake, with mankind providing many ingredients and the weather acting as an unpredictable chef," (or a wicked one).

The point? Smog can be a Zelig, a chemical quick-change artist capable of frustrating the best of intentions. In five major Chinese cities, large amounts of nitric oxide spit out by cars, trucks, and other fossil fuel sources have caused secondary chain reactions that nobody desired. This matters greatly, since parallel efforts to simultaneously reduce air pollution and greenhouse gases are not always mutually reinforcing. Black carbon, a main ingredient in soot, for example, aggravates climate change and droughts. China disgorges about thirty percent of the stuff globally from contained combustion. Yet writing regulations to curb it by upgrading diesel engines or phasing out fossil fuel home stoves is fraught with unintended consequences. Why? Sulfur particles act as atmospheric cooling agents, so policies that target them have the paradoxical effect of ramping up other vapors, including carbon dioxide and, scarily, methane. The latter should almost be a four-letter word. Originating from landfills, coal mines, rice paddies, leaky gas, and other places, methane is twenty times more potent as a greenhouse gas than carbon dioxide. Recent studies show it can be more than eighty times as powerful a warming agency than carbon dioxide. Methane, ozone, black carbon, and hydrofluorocarbons—all so-called "short-lived climate pollutants" because their atmospheric lifetimes last only days to fifteen years—generate as much as forty-five percent of the gases microwaving the planet's temperatures. Some experts, nonetheless, opine it's cheaper to fight climate change by attacking smog ingredients.

Weary of endless sieges, more than a few Chinese began taking stances they probably never would've before. Pre-Internet public silence was history. In its place was a dispersed cacophony of voices insistent on remedies and openness from the men behind the curtain. The yearning was there on blogs and message boards, in private chats, even general circulation newspapers the party puppeteers to meter grassroots anger. In January alone, there were 2.5 million micro-blog posts containing the word "smog." More than 200 students from Beijing No. 4 High School signed a petition seeking tighter smog regulations and emergency measures. Even former NBA big-man Yao Ming was photographed grimacing skywards, where no one wanted to dunk anything.

Interviews of native Chinese in foreign media reflected generational views. "If Beijing's air is as bad as you say, how come we survive?" a street vendor asked. A woman who refused to strap a facemask on because it was unflattering swore by pear-infused water to safeguard her lungs. The head of the Beilun district south of Shanghai, where seventy-two factories had closed and 1.6 billion dollars spent addressing industrial waste, expressed annoyance that might've been deemed treasonous a decade earlier. Hua Wei had a cogent response for how to deal with dirty projects. "We should," he said, "use our iron fists."

No question, Beijing's smog circus was unlocking the imaginations of a stifled people. A pair of grad students from China and the US, one attending Carnegie Mellon, the other Harvard, put a resourceful twist on an ancient Chinese art. The duo's goal was to engage everyone in citizen-driven science. Tabbing their idea "Float Beijing," the college kids engineered kites fitted with LED lights and sensors that sniffed the skies for hydrocarbons and carbon monoxide. Depending on the air quality, the smart-kites lit up green for healthy, pink for dangerous, with categories in between. A master Beijing kite builder and local enthusiasts of the sport advised them. Municipal authorities that heard it about sent underlings to inspect the gear. As much as they probably wanted to confiscate the materials, they didn't for reasons unknown, classifying it less clever protest than "public art." Another fringe invention, this one innovated by a design firm, was protection for the millennial crowd. Sensors embedded in particle filters of facemasks uploaded chemical readings to an app linked to a computer network. In this way, people could check air quality by neighborhood rather than depend on government postings. Some daring artists were less mesmerized by technology than crafting provocative social commentary. A mannequin propped up in a gas mask; a photograph of a little girl with an oxygen tube that transforms into a balloon; a silk tablecloth "stenciled" by leaving it outdoors; muddy snow recreated into human organs on display. In the younger generations distant from Mao, pollution could be right-brain inspiration.

◘

CHINA'S GREAT SMOG OF 2013, the first prolific haze of the wired era, gave futurists grist to speculate about full-blown war precipitated by a nation downwind of an enemy reckless with its emissions. One day, might a country bomb another's coal-plant or fumy chemical factory where in the past it would've targeted a missile base or garrison? It wasn't as farfetched as it sounded. Japan, fresh from accusing Chinese jets of tracking its helicopters with weapons-guiding radar in a tit-for-tat over disputed airspace, in February suggested that PM-2.5 from China had blown eastward over the Korean peninsula to drape its island nation. Tokyo politicians wanted the windblown particulates gone—*like now.* They sprang forward with initiatives to dispatch physicians to

China to examine Japanese nationals, fashion an alert system, and more. The Chinese responded with sharp tongues, not empathy. One official contended that Japan's decision to stop using atomic energy while ramping up coal use and waste incineration following the Fukushima nuclear power plant meltdown meant "one cannot criticize only China" for what's happened. Discharges from Japanese companies operating in China, another argued, were its own wellspring of boomeranging pollution.

Washington had its own skin in the game here against an increasingly militarized, claim-staking adversary. Beijing in November 2013 made waves when it declared an "Air Defense Identification Zone" over the East China Sea that includes Japanese-run islands. China's Coast Guard has also thrown its weight around, disrupting Philippine ships ferrying soldiers to a disputed shoal. In response, the U.S. has periodically sent B-52s over China's protected vectors, knowing that Chinese and Japanese fighters were playing chicken elsewhere. Why would the Politburo roll the dice on confrontation? Macho power protection and raw territorialism: energy, or rather energy that doesn't emanate from the black stone. That's why it spent one billion dollars on a deep-sea, oil-drilling platform in Vietnamese waters. A nation is only as strong as it's access to fuel. Much of China's aerial jockeying, hence, is interwoven with its energy ambitions.

Geopolitical recriminations like these had little purchase on the mainland, where some contemplated whether Asia's lush career opportunities were worth the potential health detriments. The doubts were especially pervasive among the 600,000 foreigners and expatriates living in China's smog footholds, though corporate headhunters trying to lure people there or convince them to stay had no respite, either. At Chambers of Commerce, executives practically battled laryngitis answering questions about the subject. A Ford Motor Company executive was directed in writing by her pulmonologist to bail after four hospital stints for asthma she had contracted. Nestle with accent, Sony Corp. of Japan, and other multinationals tried the mitigation route to lock its talent in place: they simply gave masks to employees, equipped offices with filters, and even retained experts to coach people how to endure the unholy, plumes. When expats listed why they were jetting off, "the litany of reasons usually starts with air quality" one human resources expert admitted. A doctor specializing in air quality at Beijing Unified Family Hospital claimed he knew of "a lot of parents" deciding against renewing their employment contracts out of jitters for their kids wellbeing. So ubiquitous was this issue, so conveniently topical, that a Russian man arrested for trying to smuggle a pair of exotic birds sewn into his trousers for a flight from Guangzhou airport to Singapore had a ready-made argument for the secreted critters. "I was trying to protect them from smog," Nahum Pokrovskii told customs officials dismayed by the bulbous protrusion near his zipper. Those still sitting on the fence could not have been reassured reading a Deutsche Bank report around this time. Without a sea change in regulatory policy governing coal-burning and automobile purchases, it said, China's air quality could deteriorate an astronomical seventy percent by 2025. Bluntly stated, it'd be "unbearable."

To sweeten deals for their employees in Beijing, some companies tossed in "hardship" allowances. Coca-Cola Co., for instance, aimed to keep its expats in the country—and off the soonest jetliner out—with stipends reported to be fifteen percent above base salary. The State Department itself dangled bonuses for diplomats willing to relocate to Beijing; higher amounts were available for personnel who'd move to consulates belted by even more grotesque air. Some Chinese nationals in the US, predictably, were hesitant to return to places sautéed in chemicals like Beijing and Shanghai. Compatriots just wanted to maintain their family intact. In a case of matrimony versus the troposphere, a Beijing husband petitioned for divorce after his son fell ill from the city's airshed and his wife took the boy to tropical Hainan for better breathing. "Smog 'buried' my son's health, and it has [now] buried my marriage," the man said. Hong Kong, the Westernized island that China took over from England in 1997, was in no position to gloat. It'd consistently blown through clean-air targets since 1987, enshrouding itself in roadside pollutants higher than London, Sydney, and New York. In 2013, nearly 3,300 died there needlessly from singed air in the city that translates as "fragrant harbor." A thirty-five percent uptick in private-car registrations was one culprit. All those Mercedes-Benz E-class models scooting around, the region's top 2012 seller, don't run on water. Others, mainly educated Chinese millennials, were opting to leave big cities gripped by Western-style vanity for village life, where "luxury is sunshine, good air, and water." There was no getting around the issue. When US Ambassador Gary Locke announced in November 2013 that he was resigning, he practically needed to take a polygraph to shoot down social media rumors that smog had driven him home.

Who could've chided anyone for skedaddling after what was discovered that winter floating in the Huangpu River, one of Shanghai's major waterways. There were dead pigs and piglets, more than 16,000 in all. One-liners about extra "pork chop soup" and farm animals committing suicide to avoid breathing China Inc. dissipated with every repulsive photograph of decomposing carcasses washed ashore or netted out of viscous waters. The incident soon renewed public apprehension about national food safety and water contamination. Beijing's torpid, uneven handling also drew comparisons with how it dealt with pollution overall. Quipped one Sina Weibo user: "A sluggish response, a lack of disclosure of official data, and muddled information has done nothing to quell our doubts." Eyed as the source of the dumping were farmers skittish about selling dead and diseased animals to black market dealers anymore after a harsh court ruling. None of that made people relax.

Some agricultural experts about then perspired less over water-bloated swine and more about toxic air starting to resemble a nuclear winter in its shadowy disruption of farmland. Contaminants sticking to greenhouse surfaces were reducing sunlight down to half of normal, which taxed crops ability to convert light into the chemical energy they need to survive. Too much smog equated to too little photosynthesis. Limp, sickly plants required two months to grow, rather than the customary twenty days, tests indicated. Keep this up, one professor forecast, and the results could be cataclysmic for China's food supply. Like much of California in 2014, whole latitudes of the People's Republic, including Henan and Inner Mongolia, are roasting in record heat and drought. Climate change is no scaremongering hypothesis here. It's the death knell for barley, rice, and the like. They could all be stubbornly more difficult to keep alive in warmer temperatures of the future, since heat increases the amount of ground-level ozone produced when other vapors are present. Scientists dread that new famines will loom, with all kinds of repercussions for global food security. Some experts have even revised upwards their previous estimates of smog destruction to soybeans—a loss they'd once blamed on scorching temperatures. "Now," said He Dongxian, "almost every farm is caught in a smog panic... Our overseas colleagues were shocked by this phenomenon because in their countries nothing like this had ever happened." Perhaps, but West Coast historians could appreciate the ghostly echo. Air pollution by 1963 had decimated three quarters of the Los Angeles area's farmland—think lettuce, spinach, beets, tomatoes, etc.—along with gladiolus and other locally grown flowers that the leaf-attaching, silvery glaze from above killed by impairing nutrient intake. The Inland Empire's breadbasket never recovered. Subdivisions splatter the old fields now.

The acidic troposphere was creating new respiratory memories across the Pacific. In the Far East for a friend's wedding in spring 2013, California journalist Justin Chapman watched "a thick layer of filth" dog him wherever he traveled. Nothing prepared him for a boat ride on a lake in Hangzhou, where the craggy splendor poets romanticized for ages blended with a "gross," sallow-gray atmosphere that flamed the sun red. Not once over three weeks in four different cities did he glimpse blue when he peered up. Home in Los Angeles, America's smoggiest city by ozone count, was "a breath of fresh air," Chapman sighed. The Ladies Professional Golf Association also got caught up in what Chapman did, and then promptly dug itself a hole. At its first tournament in China, where the golf market has taken off, the Association delayed a tee-time ninety minutes to allow smog the US Embassy termed "hazardous" to lighten. Afterwards golfers, some of them in facemasks, were allowed to proceed in a decision that swiftly drew derision. At the China Open tennis finals in the capital around then, some bleary spectators sympathized. They tugged shirts over their faces for impromptu protection.

WHO a short time later confirmed what everybody already knew: Smog causes lung cancer just like exposure to arsenic, asbestos, and cigarette smoke. It killed a million Chinese annually, the organization estimated. An eight-year-old girl in Jiangsu province from a family of non-smokers and no genetic legacy to the disease in late 2013 was shockingly diagnosed with it. Doctors blamed particulate matter, though one of them was later ordered not to speak about it. Nationwide, the disease has soared almost fivefold since Deng's reforms.

Indicting air pollution for the spike in lung disease rates, though, is muddled by nicotine facts: The Chinese (mostly men) puff a third of the globe's cigarettes. Aside from being the number one consumer of smokes, the country produces more of them than anyone else, or about 1.7 trillion of them per year. (China's state-owned tobacco monopoly is a bigger earner, in fact, than the world's three largest manufacturers, Philip Morris International Inc. included.) All those cigarettes, many epidemiologists believe, is why tobacco is the predominant cause of lung cancer in China. As in some US cities, authorities have banned smoking in restaurants and other public places. To some extent, Chinese officials have also parlayed tobacco's harmful toll on the body to dilute public anxiety about smog. A University of Texas cancer researcher experienced that up close attending a big conference on the disease. "Ten years ago, it was sensitive to talk about smoking because the tobacco industry was so important to the Chinese economy," said Wei Zhang. "Now it feels safe to talk about smoking. But for pollution, people are not prepared."

◘

CONSIDERING ALL THAT, THE men inside the Great Hall of the People must've been stupefied in the wake of the public-health haymaker researchers from the University of Washington, fellow cooperating universities, an institute, and WHO lobbed at them in spring 2013. The previous year, *The Lancet* had published those experts' *Global Burden of Disease, Injuries, and Risk Factors Study*, which tabulated that "ambient particulate matter pollution" in 2010 was the seventh-leading risk factor of death worldwide. About 3.2 million yearly mortalities were attributable to it. But when some of those same specialists broke out numbers for the People's Republic, announcing them at a Beijing forum in late March 2013—a month state media acknowledged as the country's smoggiest in fifty-two years—the results were positively numbing. Outdoor air pollution in 2010, they asserted, contributed to the yearly deaths of 1.2 million Chinese, who sacrificed a combined twenty-five million healthy years by dying prematurely. This bumped smog up to the nation's fourth highest risk factor for early death behind poor diet, high blood pressure, and smoking. The other shoe had dropped.

It was easily the highest smog death-count in history—almost quadruple what the World Bank estimated about China in its benchmark 2007 analysis—and forty percent of the global total. (India lost 620,000 needlessly to outdoor air pollution in 2010, the newly refined statistics determined.) Expressed differently, only 100,000 more people perished annually from tuberculosis worldwide than from the air in China 2.0. With 3,288 mortalities every twenty-four hours, China lost more each calendar day to its chemistry-lab skies than the US did on 9/11 to Osama Bin Laden's jihadists. Western media ran wild with the numbers. How many Chinese were aware of the ghoulish tabulation was indeterminable. "Untrustworthy" was one adjective government brass reserved for the study. An April 15, 2013 Xinhua piece about a Global Burden of Disease symposium made not a single reference to the 1.2 million figure. Former Health Minister Chen Zhu subsequently estimated smog prematurely killed 350,000 to 500,000 yearly. Yes, that was the bureaucratic spin, at least for domestic consumption. But this wasn't just Asia's tragedy anymore, not after WHO revisited its own statistics. In spring 2014, it announced its belief that indoor and outdoor pollution was taking down twice its previous estimate. In 2012, venomous skies were responsible for the disappearance of seven million people yearly. Roll that number around in your mind. One of eight global deaths was tied to recidivistic smog. Every time you blinked, epidemiologists and company were discovering the undercounted dead required multiplication tables.

Whether by coincidence or cunning, the Chinese Academy of Environmental Planning just then interpreted 2010 from an economic slant. During that year, pollution and eco-damage equaled 3.5 percent of GDP, or 230 billion dollars. Pessimists who suspected the valuation from the MEP division was lowballed only need revisit Hu's quashed Green GDP calculation in the mid-2000s, when China's economy was smaller. Variations in how the statistics were compiled were fuzzy except for one common thread line: both lacked complete data. Going it alone, Greenpeace activists unholstered their own financial numbers measuring pollution costs solely on needless deaths. In 2010, they set Beijing back 328 million dollars, Shanghai back 420 million dollars. Trying to collect Chinese government data about remediation, chronic illness, and lost productivity, the NGO realized, was a fool's errand.

None of this research altered the consensus: graveyards across the Far East could be littered with bodies if trends continued. Urban air pollution come 2050 was on track to overtake fouled water and lack of sanitation as the planet's "top environmental cause of mortality," an earlier report by the Organization of Economic Cooperation and Development (OECD) cautioned The People's Republic and India stood to lose most. No need to wait to glimpse that future, either. It was here already. From Mongolia to India, fine particulate matter in 284 out of 300 cities across greater Asia surpassed WHO guidelines, Clean Air Asia, a regional coalition of air quality management groups, harped. Most of the complying cities were in wealthier Japan, too.

More and more, experts appreciated, location mattered. In another headline-grabber in a year full of them, there was one last unsettling fact: Chinese who lived south of a pollution-demarcation line on average enjoyed lifespans that were five-and-a-half years longer than the half-billion in the North. The differences between what each side breathed were poisonous ones. People above that line were simply exposed to heavier concentrations of downwind coal fumes spread by electricity generation and industrial smokestacks than their neighbors, according to researchers from MIT and Peking University. They'd weighed health and pollution data from 1981 to 2001, using the Huai River that runs parallel to the massive Yangtze and Yellow rivers as a control-point. A morose rule of thumb crystallized with the study, which appeared in the *National Academy of Sciences Journal*. Every additional 100 µg/m3 of particulate matter above the average levels in the south, in general, stripped three years off one's life.

China's history, its fusty entwinement with coal and fixation with social order, had interrupted its present. For decades beginning with Chairman Mao, the government had given away coal for boilers to help folks in chillier regions produce heat during winter. Natural gas keeping people from freezing was abundant in other countries, not theirs. All the same, the MEP disparaged the lifespan study as unconvincing. Of that, no one was surprised.

CHAPTER 14:

DETROIT EAST

TALL AND SOLID, BRUCE Jin pulls up to a plain, squat building in the outskirts of Changzhou. In front are tightly packed lines of small electric cars—red, blue, and green—that his company, Ample International, Inc., makes and sells.

We walk from the parking lot into a large garage past banks of tools and equipment used to make the cars that are in various stages of assembly. Jin leads me (Bill) and others to a conference room on a sunny Saturday morning. There, we share fruit and tea and we listen to Jin proudly explain his dream. He wants Ample to churn out 30,000 electric cars a year at a price that's in reach of China's growing middle class. The cars, which retail for 7,000 dollars each, are by no means worthy of a freeway in Los Angeles or Beijing. But when I later get in the seat to test drive one, it's smooth and peppy on city streets. That's exactly how Jin envisions them being driven. The cars, which can go almost a hundred miles on a single charge, would be perfect, Jin thinks, for non-freeway driving in Chinese cities, or in suburban and rural cities in the US. The environmental icing on the cake is that not only are there no tailpipes to spew emissions, but they could run on renewable energy, if only China would ever feed enough solar and wind power into its grid.

Until then, the middle-aged Jin and several young Chinese engineers he's hired—educated in the US at Stanford, Columbia University, and the University of California—are happy to work toward positioning Ample to cash in on an eventual green turn in China's economy. They're not alone. Even in this small industrial corner of Changzhou are a host of other companies staking their futures on green economics. Small sized, just like Jin's firm, they share not only his goal but also a joint laboratory to hold costs down as they fashion and test new products meant to create a sustainable way of living.

Ample and the others in this industrial park lie in Jiangsu Province, where government officials envision creating an "eco-civilization." To do that, Jiangsu's built a network of air and water pollution monitors, stepped up enforcement of environmental standards, and even required industries handling chemicals to develop emergency response plans in case of leaks. The move seems to be paying off, at least in terms of attracting businesses. Hundreds of companies that produce pollution controls, water recycling equipment, electric batteries, and other components used in non-polluting electric cars and equipment have located in the province near Shanghai. Ironically, Jin complains that although he's invested here, he can't sell his cars here. First, he needs to get a certificate from the provincial government, which in the summer of 2013 had not yet acted. It seems Jin's small company may not be important enough to get to the head of the line. That's why to advance his case, the energy- and determination-filled Jin came with us the night before to a dinner with provincial and municipal officials. It's there that he got his first face-to-face meeting as a Lazy Susan turned slowly and platters of fish, beef, noodles, and vegetables went round. Jin spoke up to ask about the certificate. The officials listened politely, but by the end of dinner made no commitment.

As we exited the government center on a warm Friday night, officials drove out of the parking garage and whirred off in their silver and white sport utility vehicles. They too, it seems, are caught up in China's newfound infatuation with the traditional gas-guzzler. The trend is telltale. In 2010, dealerships there sold 825,000 sporty utility vehicles (425 of them Hummers), sorties worth of Audis, BMWs, Mercedes, and Rolls Royces, and all of 200 Priuses. In the former Middle Kingdom, German brands—Mercedes, Audis, Volkswagens—are the prestige rides of choice, seemingly the bigger the better, rather than the small, sporty roadsters that whip along Italy's Autostrada or European expressways. Whatever the hood-ornament, the People's Republic is now the planet's number one automobile market. In 2013, its citizens bought some 20 million cars, roughly 5 million more than Americans. Citizens once prohibited from owning extravagant goods today can pick from Cadillac XTS, Ford Lincolns, slick, chrome German sedans, SUVs, and other expensive, big-engine vehicles that developed countries revel in as insignias of affluence. By 2020, China should hopscotch the US to become the top luxury-automobile market, a McKinsey & Company study forecast. How Jin's modest, non-polluting electric car built for the everyman will fit in remains unclear.

Far Eastern gas station operators couldn't be more delirious. In the fifties, US carmakers drooled over future profits to be wrung in flourishing, consumeristic America. Sixty years later, with the US mostly out of the freeway-building game and discouraging fossil fuels, the automobile-industrial complex is gleefully rubbing its hands about recreating Detroit in Asia. While I was there in the summer of 2013, both Mercedes and Volkswagen announced plant openings, expanding upon already existing operations in China. No surprise then that at last count, 5.4 million cars travel Beijing's highways, roughly a one-third spike since 2009.

Wired in to all this, General Motors aspires to pump out 5 million vehicles annually there by decade's end. Already it boasts a dozen joint-venture operations, two wholly owned foreign concerns, and 55,000 plus employees that hawk and service passenger and commercial models like Baojun, Jiefang, Wuling, Buick, and Chevrolet. Ford, the second largest American carmaker, is going gangbusters in the Far East, too, erecting a 500 million dollar engine plant in Chongqing and bulking up its Xiaolan assembly facility. Homegrown companies themselves have rushed off the sidelines. Geely, one of China's most prosperous automakers, now owns Volvo. Manufacturing sites for them in Chengdu and in the northeast constitute part of the six billion dollars Geely has invested in the Scandinavian-styled vehicles. It's understandable. Should some predictions hold, the Chinese could purchase 35 million autos in 2022, more than projected demand in the US and Europe combined. So tremendous is the appetite for what these companies are offering in Beijing that past lotteries designed to limit skyrocketing car ownership barely slowed the torrent.

Unless zero-emission vehicles become all the rage, or widespread driving restrictions actually work, healing the nation's airshed will be delayed indefinitely as palls of photochemical smog dogpile onto coal-based pollution. In Beijing, automobiles disgorge about a quarter of the capital's fine particulates. The changeover just from the nineties is astonishing, when most cars revving by belonged to government suits or state-owned companies. Some experts today conjecture that China's current fleet of 90 million passenger automobiles could mushroom into 400 million by 2030. (Car hungry as the Chinese have grown, only thirty-one in 1,000 own a set of wheels, compared to 424 out of 1,000 in the US.) Should the world turn its back on that ratio, it's at its ozone risk. Rest assured, too, foreign automakers will zealously don environmental clothing to close Far Eastern deals. Nissan, Volvo, and their competitors are installing "internal purifiers" in their new models to keep smog outside the windows; an Infiniti will supposedly perfume one's ride with a "fresh, leafy odor" to make drivers feel closer to nature. Others, including the Bill-Gates supported startup, EcoMotors Inc., and sundry component-makers are scrambling to assist carmakers pass stern, new Chinese emission limits, particularly for diesel gasoline thick with sulfur. Their know-how with transmissions, exhaust-treatment, fuel injection, and turbo charging could be worth its weight in gold as so many ex bike-riders slip behind a mechanical wheel. No one should be dazed learning that a unit controlled by France's Peugeot SA has its own fingers in the auto-market pie.

So, where are all those Chinese driving? For the half-billion-plus citizens expected to be in cities by 2030, and the millions of new vehicles gliding out of showrooms with them, the implications of a freewheeling lifestyle could be suffocating, if for no other reason than that urban residents on average consume three times the energy than those who hew to more rustic lifestyles, according to the World Bank. Then there's the commuter schedule. Urbanites, for instance, thrilled to be able to afford an apartment in a "superblock model" development common today might lose some of that brio when they negotiate the logistics. Often, they must take a four-to-eight-lane highway for a snarled drive to work into smoggy, cheek-to-jowl cities. In their off time, it's back onto that same pavement into town if they want to shop, dine, find a hospital, or hit a theater, because no one connected the superblocks with middle-class amenities.

All this zipping back and forth underscores why some superblocks are energy hogs, munching three times as much as other neighborhoods. To us, these paradoxes make China's supposed eco-restoration such captivating watching: the collision between the Peoples Republic's fading, Soviet-style, *pollute-at-will* urban planning and an economy light years ahead of where it was. Some suburban city halls, including many deep in debt, aren't shrieking for a less gridlocked, exhaust spewing layout; they rely on land sales for a fifth of their budget, and with demand high can fetch good prices for shoddy parcels. Developers making a bundle aren't kvetching, either. Nor are the car dealerships. President Li, if words matter, may actually be the loudest advocate for a greener, more efficient suburbia, promising that China will embed "a new type of urbanization." Whether he can do so is a crapshoot in a regimental, patronage-paying culture. But what choice does he have?

For Liu, the cancer village researcher, it's the wrong choices the upper echelon, with its live-for-the-moment zeitgeist, that's the shadow player in China's ecological unraveling. "High-end luxurious goods," he wrote, "are readily available, and...shopping habits and changing tastes are reshaping global trade flows of flashy cars, gold, elephant ivory, and dried seahorses. Availability of these...and the possibility of migration to a more developed country push for a never-ending demand for wealth, and China's elite are firm supporters of the 'grow-first' development policy." A cynic might tweak Liu's excoriation to read, "grow first, shop now, and restore later." Scan the terrain. Over in Lanzhou in central Gansu province, the country's preeminent construction company was flattening dozens of mountains, at a cost of 2.2 billion dollars, to carve out a new, 500 square mile urban district on the outskirts of a city already tagged one of China's most contaminated. Establishment officials have defended the titanic grading as a necessary evil of progress that will "make things better than before." Numerous mountain-leveling projects are underway, Chinese researchers say, because an upwardly mobile citizenry will eventually oversaturate flatland cities. You just don't want to tally the bill from all the bulldozing unless you earn a living reversing landside-causing soil erosion and headwater flooding.

New trucks, too, have poured into the People's Republic faster than e-waste. So starved was the nation for them that sales of heavy-duty models rocketed 800 percent between 2000 and 2007. In a revealing traffic jam only globalization could choreograph, ten thousand trucks bearing coal from Inner Mongolia once created gridlock that stretched for seventy-five miles, or roughly the distance between the Italian cities Milan and Genoa. Whether from small cars, flatbeds or big rigs, uncombusted fuel is gelling China's atmosphere with particles that once had Los Angeles politicians white-knuckled contemplating evacuations in the worst corners of the city. After Californians bought by the millions automobiles with catalytic converters, steely capsules which transform tailpipe-exhaust containing hydrocarbons, nitrogen oxides, and carbon monoxide into benign compounds via chemical reaction, some of that panic receded with noticeable airshed clearing. China's gasoline, however, has done its skies few favors. The damage yellowy sulfur inflicts on those emission-killing devices allows palpable amounts of vehicle fumes to leak upward. A few whiffs, and you know.

Asian smog-fighters have discovered something else: the cumulative effects of multiaxle vehicles on air quality exceed the weight they exert on the pavement. Little, in fact, epitomized the atmospheric downside of China's manufacturing sinew than its estimated ten million trucks, which by the mid-2000s constituted one out of every four vehicles on its streets, roads, and backcountry highways. With their mileage demands, they are a prime reason that China continues to be the earth's number three oil consumer, sucking over 9.4 million barrels a day, double Japan's rate and about half the world-leading US's. That volume would be less perturbing if the diesel fuel typically propelling China's fleet wasn't so insidiously polluting. Its sulfur content has been estimated at 130 times above what most American trucks burn. Eighty percent of the nation's vehicular particulate matter, in fact, barrels out of their tailpipes. Overall, the big rigs, tankers and the like are the leading generator of street-level pollution swirling at people's door.

Until recently, China's truck fuel standards dragged behind those of the West, its industrial oligarchs frozen in the past. Beijing's lobbying and arm-twisting to impel them to upgrade their refineries to distill lower sulfur fuel was unable to move the checker. For years, state-owned super-polluters like Sinopec and PetroChina effectively swung their political clubs, vetoing plant makeovers. The environmental machinery needed for them, they caterwauled, could lighten their coffers by 800 million dollars.

Consequently, the People's Republic, in its byzantine power struggle pitting healthier air against oil revenues, is at war with itself.

On the consumer side is a surging middle class that craves all the gas it can use but without smog in its gullet. On the opposite flank are government industries that have been pumping oil and producing electrical juice well before Deng's tenure. Caught in between are regulators savvy enough to know the oligarchs at Sinopec and elsewhere out-muscle them. "The Chinese economy is brutally competitive," stressed Andrews, the eco-statistician. "At the Ministry of Environmental Protection and the Beijing Environmental Protection Bureau, there are great people working there. Like the US and other countries, they're interested in improving the environment. But they have no real authority." Playing Solomon, the government has kept gasoline prices lower than they'd be on the open market for commuters while deferring brinksmanship with Sinopec and PetroChina to require them to do what they've resisted so far.

◼

MORE THAN JUST CHINA'S gasoline has frustrated Jin, who's still looking for the green lining in the environmental talk emanating from capitals on both sides of the Pacific. When I meet him months later in Los Angeles, he'd yet to hear back from his own province on whether he can sell his sporty little electric models there. Business for his dedicated and hopeful team of engineers who are trying to fashion a new sustainable way of living remains limited. Their goal of making and selling 30,000 electric cars a year still seems like a distant dream.

CHAPTER 15:

DRIFT & DECLINE

THE EASTERN INVADERS SNUCK into US airspace five months before Al Qaeda turned jetliners into missiles that surreal, crystal-blue day in September 2001. The experts who spied their movement could hardly believe the ominous shadow darkening the land. The tiny raiders first lit up satellites over Inner Mongolia bundled inside of an enormous, white cloud. Mottling it was brown grime forming a neatly twirled coil, almost reminiscent of Princess Leia's braids in *Star Wars*. Riding the atmospheric vortex, the plume chugged south, dilating every second. The ground-hugging tip of the cloud hoovered up so much dust, grit, dirt, and tailpipe-factory pollution that when it swept through Beijing, it threw a tarp around the sun that plunged the capital into daylight dimness. Next the mass blew east, over the Yellow Sea and Korea and above Russia's Kamchatka Peninsula. From there it winged across Japan and toward Alaska, before arcing southward on the same general trajectory that city-killing, Soviet nuclear missiles bound for the American West Coast might've flown in World War III.

Within days, Asia's trespassing compounds made shore in the Northwest on a continental flutter that'd carry it through Maine, before dying off in the Atlantic Ocean near Africa. While the atmosphere diluted the majority of what originally lifted off in the Far East, the estimated 55,000 tons, in fact, still represented two-and-a-half times the dust sources America by itself produces on an average day. It was the "most remarkable" image one noted researcher said he'd ever witnessed. Had it not been for the gut-wrenching visuals of the World Trade Center towers imploding or other smoky ruins on 9-11, the strange cloud might've unnerved more Americans about what was penetrating their sovereign skies. This wasn't your grandfather's Depression-era dust cloud from his youth in Oklahoma. No, this one was airmailed primarily from Chinese desert lands, on winds able to lift up airy, Asian soil no longer held down by a sealing layer of lichens, bacteria, and mosses. Chronic overuse and natural erosion had stripped away that protective barrier.

High in the air, that tawny dust devil was joined by some of the manufacturing-generated smog the West had exported to the Far East along with a host of exotic compounds. Americans were literally breathing China Inc. on a molecular level. In each gulp was coal of some variety and tailpipe spume. In it were microscopic particles leaked from sneakers, tablets, handsaws, sweaters, geriatric diapers, baby booties, and whatnot, many of them wares that American companies farmed overseas for productions savings. Our choices were lashing back at us.

Dan Jaffe, a world-renowned atmospheric chemist on Transpacific drift at the University of Washington-Bothell, might've labeled the wayfaring blob his personal validation. Ever since the eighties, he'd been engrossed by the notion of

Chinese dust piggybacking on the Jet Stream. A 1994 computer model had hinted at it. But colleagues were dubious that particles could traverse such distances. Be serious, they said. Jaffe's self-described "Eureka!" moment three years later dispelled some of their incredulity. Air samples drawn from a 1,500 foot mountain at Cheeka Peak on Washington's Olympic Peninsula—what Jaffe chuckled was "basically a big hill"—corroborated that the chemical payload was no abstraction. Mostly, it settled higher up, at elevations 6,000 to 20,000 feet. In it were sulfur, black carbon, and nitrogen oxide—all tariff-free.

The next year brought a double confirmation for Jaffe. A honking plume of Asian soil and industrial flotsam weighing some 140 million tons—the equivalent mass of dozens of Nimitz-class US aircraft carriers when it formed—gallivanted east toward Oregon, dappling the sky milky white. Along with dust were "measurable quantities" of arsenic, copper, lead, and zinc. Whether anyone as a result went to the hospital or morgue wasn't reported, but the cloud held the equivalent of forty percent of EPA-allowed fine particulates for the time. Emergency-room visits and death rates are known to swell when particulates soar.

As a youngster growing up in Boston, Jaffe had been baffled when his grandfather took him fishing in New England in the seventies and the old-timers told him that acid rain from industry in Indiana and Ohio had killed the fish. Science had trouble then explaining aerial drift with much precision. Not anymore. "What's changed dramatically is that in the early nineties, we were essentially blind," Jaffe said. "Satellite data was limited." Today's computers, wind tunnels, and digital imaging underscore that "we need to do more if we are all going to survive on this planet," he added. "With seven billion people, can we all live the classic

American lifestyle?" If what was skipping along the troposphere in "The Pacific Dust Express" was any indication, the answer was self-evident.

Two years before the 2008 Beijing Olympics, Steven Cliff, (another star of the field at the University of California, Davis) and his colleagues visited a mountaintop test site they'd prepared north of San Francisco. Chemical fingerprinting revealed it contained particulate matter from East Asia's coal-fueled power plants, diesel trucks, and smelters. The specks had slingshot across the Pacific in less time than it took to mail a letter between continents. Earlier that year, a viscous swirl of coal-stewed pollutants sprinkled Lake Tahoe in California's Sierra Nevada mountain range. Astounded scientists claimed they were the darkest particles they'd seen outside of congested, urban sites.

Evidence mounted from there like receipts from a US Black Friday sale. Inland from the San Francisco Bay Area, a 2010 National Oceanic and Atmospheric Administration (NOAA) analysis concluded that more than three-quarters of the ozone fouling sections of California's Sacramento Valley was of Chinese origin. The butterfly effect had developed enormous, veined wings. South of there, as much as a quarter of the ozone blotting Los Angeles' air on certain days whipped from the People's Republic. Under a few scenarios, it someday could account for one-third of ozone in California, which still exceeds federal health standards even after a seventy-year campaign. "The ozone on the West Coast in a few years will be controlled not by California and Oregon," a NOAA official forecasted. "It will be controlled by China" in seasonal dust storms and in prevailing winds gusting through the troposphere year-round. Don't expect the rest of America to be granted any pulmonary clemency, either. Should climate change continue to raise the planet's thermostat, the US by 2050 could experience a seventy percent upsurge in days with unhealthful air, especially from ozone, the National Center for Atmospheric Research now predicts.

The cloud of dust described in "The Pacific Dust Express" was becoming a meteorological species capable of blowing minds. One drift was bound up in ribbons as deep as the Grand Canyon and wider than the Amazon as it sailed on prevailing winds. Jaffe and fellow researchers who trekked into the thin air of the Cascade Mountains in Central Oregon pegged Chinese ozone at fifty parts per billion, which was not far off the EPA limit of eighty parts per billion for the tasteless, furtively-poisonous gas. Intermixed with it there on Mount Bachelor, a Northwest skier's paradise, were dots of black carbon, particulate matter, mercury, and even PAHs linked to smoky e-waste and metal processing. They all posed risk of disease. Asian plumes, as such, have joined other nations regurgitating their aerial waste into foreigners' lives. For years, US smog has cruised across the Atlantic to infiltrate Europe. African dust has spritzed over Miami and southern cities. Puffy smoke from big wildfires in Canada and the third world has hazed vast distances downwind. In the troposphere what goes up spreads around.

Like its economy, China's role here is not to be underestimated. Its deserts—among them the Gobi, the largest in Asia, and the Taklimakan, the earth's biggest sand-dune desert—are virtual dust launching pads. Mother Nature has reacted scornfully. Desert dust storms on average flared once a year in the Beijing area winding back to 1200. Today, with so much wispy sand and weather patterns shaken by climate change and smog, they can belt the capital twenty times annually. Initially, scientists presumed Chinese dust and detritus were only hefted by these storms. As the 2000s wore on, Jaffe and others came to realize their hypothesis was wrong. If conditions were ripe with the uplifting of air via convection over heated ground, "we are transporting [compounds] all the time," Jaffe said. An implacable plume, in other words. Envision the future if China's car-buying binge accelerates. More of its nitrogen oxide emissions, which climbed fifty-five percent between 2001 and 2006, will wing to US shores. More particulate matter from Chinese tailpipes, already generating ten percent of the US average, will arrive, let alone enough ozone to swamp the horizon.

Either way, Americans better accustom themselves to the airborne incursions from the Far East, an EPA-sponsored study by the National Research Council determined. Hard as it is to separate from domestic sources, foreign ozone is probably already corroding US farmland, ecosystems, and health. Particulate matter lofted by dust storms, biomass burning, and such is less of a worry, isolated events notwithstanding. Foreign sources only contribute a "negligible" amount of the pollutant. East Asian mercury, though, is another story, a more lethal one, since the chemical is light enough to inflict damage over great distances. Once released skyward, it undergoes changes, fusing with other biosphere chemicals into variations capable of penetrating the food chain. Mercury is not like other effluents. In upper atmospheric winds it's truly "a global pollutant," experts stress. Soil, oceans, lakes, ice, and snow soak it up. A UN analysis estimated that China generated forty-two percent of worldwide emissions of mercury, mostly from coal combustion, metal processing, and waste incineration. India was the penultimate source at twenty percent, with North America chipping in about nine percent.

Scientists since Newton have regarded the mysterious heavy metal as a "forbidden fruit." In liquid form, it's been nicknamed "quicksilver" for its proclivity to ball into small, silvery globs repelled by any mass it touches. Best to limit your time around the neurotoxin; in humans, the potential carcinogen assaults the kidneys, liver, and the nervous and endocrine systems alike. Exposures don't have to be prolonged to invite illness either. Same as lead, mercury is especially virulent for young children and fetuses by suppressing their cognitive function later in life.

The EPA under the Obama Administration has cracked down on coal power plants emitting it in the US, and others sure wish China would follow suit. Its mercury has freckled the atmosphere around Mount Fuji and other sections of Japan, a hypersensitive topic for the country. (Mercury dumped into Minamata Bay some sixty years ago by a chemical company killed hundreds, rendered thousands deformed, and traumatized Japan's culture.) Today, trace amounts of the stuff linked to dark smoke from Chinese plants in cities like Datong and Linfen regularly cross the sea to parachute into Oregon's Willamette River, sometimes at "dangerously high levels," studies indicate. China as of 2007 was one of only two nations (with Kyrgyzstan) still excavating virgin mercury from the earth, mining it in spots thought to contain half the world's supply. Why the effort? Chinese factories utilize the silvery material as catalysts to fabricate polyvinyl chloride (PVC) plastic from coal and in battery production. Unfortunately.

By the time winds parachute it into America, some of the mercury has transformed to a gaseous variety that dissolves in water. From there, it's fully capable of stealing into the ecosystem. Tiny microbes shape it into methylmercury that organisms absorb, equipping it to migrate from plants to small animals to fish, fish that are later consumed by bears, marine mammals, birds, and finally, people. Mercury levels, whether from volcanic eruptions, oceans, other naturally occurring, or man-made sources, have edged up since 2005, a UN assessment concluded. Somewhere between 1,010 and 4,070 tons of it speckle the atmosphere yearly. The UN blamed Asia for generating most of the anthropogenic emissions of it, with China responsible for seventy-five percent of what floats out of the general vicinity.

What's changed from decades earlier? Coal: Whole mountain ranges of the dusty, dark gold the People's Republic shovels into electricity plants, steel mills, oil-refineries, boilers, and whatnot. In each scoopful are minute amounts of mercury that escape when that ancient fuel is burned. As much as fourteen percent of the mercury trashing America's Great Lakes Basin was born in China. Sometimes it just wreaks havoc closer. Researchers from the Universities of Hawaii and Michigan recognized that when they dissected swordfish and tuna in the northern Pacific. Samples contained high levels of the metal they linked forensically to Chinese coal-fired electricity makes. For reasons involving isotopes and microbes, the deeper the susceptible fish's habitat, the more mercury infecting it. International efforts to prod China to renounce the compound have stalled, largely because its breakneck industry depends on it for fifty types of uses.

Other uplifted Asian pollutants are barging into our lives by stoking climatic changes edging nearer every second. Picture atmospheric turbo-charger. Effluents are intensifying worldwide weather patterns through the Pacific storm track that generate typhoons and tropical cyclones. Deep, convective clouds associated with extreme storm activity have surged twenty to fifty percent just since the late eighties, Texas A&M scientists believe.

For the first time, a definitive connection has been established between emissions and weather. Prior research had linked Amazonian rainforest wildfires with furious storms and hazy city skies with intense lightning. But that hypothesis is now scientific canon. Asian pollution is brewing more frenetic storms and larger clouds.

Besides pounding local areas, disrupted storm patterns are also tampering with global air and heat circulation. The turbulent atmosphere, climatologists suggest, may be what's propelling industrial contaminants and hotter temperatures northward— and with sufficient firepower to hasten melting of the Arctic ice caps, which then raises sea levels. Indeed, the majority of global warming the planet has experienced has hemmed around the poles, according to the Intergovernmental Panel on Climate Change, the leading international body on the subject. A 2014 analysis by Texas A&M and NASA's Jet Propulsion Laboratory not only confirmed that but also noted their disturbance on the US. "Huge amounts of aerosols from Asia go as high as six miles in the atmosphere and these have an unmistakable impact on cloud formations and weather," said Texas A&M scientist R. Saravanan. Brace yourself for more.

Already, California's Sierra Nevada Mountains are experiencing extra rain and snow from the Pacific Express' chemical bomblets. Researchers deciphering a pair of 2009 winter storms whose clouds held equal amounts of water vapor observed that one produced forty percent more moisture than the other. In examining ground samples afterwards, they identified a plethora of dust, probably from Saharan, Chinese, and Mongolian deserts, in the wetter of the two systems. It "was a bit of a scientific epiphany," explained Marty Ralph, an NOAA research meteorologist. "I came into this very skeptical and have come to where I am now, coauthoring a paper saying aerosols can have a significant impact." Those immense tons of sands and particulate matter act like a weather whisperer. Deeper into the twenty-first century, dry areas will become more desiccated. Wetter regions, especially those filmed by Asian drift, will get wetter.

Our flattened planet is nothing if not relentlessly karmic on dizzying levels. Emission researchers led by Peking University concluded that in the 2006 test year alone, more than a third of China's discharges of sulfur dioxide and a quarter of its nitrogen oxide and carbon monoxide were generated during the production of exported goods. Equally disturbing, a fifth of those emissions from exports, plus black carbon, were directly connected to merchandise shipped to the United States. (Black carbon, tied to heart and lung ailments and cancer, is a special worry since it doesn't wash away with rain.) Then there's good, old greenhouse gases to mull. In 2005 alone, a third of China's carbon dioxide emissions originated from the foreign goods they pumped out to make our shopping experiences pleasurable. Expressed mathematically, that's 1.7 billion tons, which dwarfs the estimated 230 million tons the nation released in 1987. If those same products had been manufactured in the American cities where they were consumed, their pollution levels could be one-fifth higher in a worse case. Nobody is safe in the hot box of globalization.

China's chemical drift even wafts over the heads of Asian tourists spending more-per-tourist than any other visiting nationality in America. Coach wallets, Tommy Hilfiger shirts, cheap vitamins: they covet it all. The high rollers aren't sitting on their wallets either. They've secured deals for American pork manufacturers, bought up properties from San Francisco to New Jersey, purchased AMC Theatres, and snagged golf courses, including a set of links turfed over a former landfill in the Southern California's heavily Asian Gabriel Valley. One Chinese contingent was willing to fork out 1.2 billion dollars to buy the Los Angeles Dodgers, a Major League Baseball team whose older players remembered plenty about playing in the city's mystifying air.

Pollution bedfellows strewed the earth.

○

WHILE CHINESE ONCOLOGISTS RACED to treat a new generation of cancer and respiratory disease patients ill from breathing air laden with poisons, US economists were preoccupied with an outbreak of American pink slips. The facts were as clear as the unemployment lines were long. Between 2001, when China joined the WTO, and 2008, marked by the Beijing Summer Games, 2.4 million manufacturing company jobs disappeared in America. They were effectively shifted to China, according to an Economic Policy Institute report in 2010. There was, however, a countervailing effect that eased the blow on the American working-class. Cheap Asian imports had become the welfare for Americans that no one talked about openly. They kept families who were struggling to pay their bills afloat, offering them affordable necessities and the ability to still enjoy a few luxuries, albeit at the expense of stable, decent-paying American jobs that would've given them more spending power in the first place.

Eureka, California, in the heart of the misty Redwood Empire along the north coast of the state, is emblematic of this seeming job-loss/low-price-lifestyle paradox. There, an area called Samoa rests on a sandy spit separating the Pacific Ocean from Humboldt Bay. On it, Bob Simpson's Freshwater Tissue Co. once aimed to do great things at the old Samoa mill. A hopeful and idealistic entrepreneur, Simpson wanted to mass-produce eco-friendly toilet paper with forest residuals—unusable detritus left after logging and milling wood—instead of fresh wood. Instead of creating a small green revolution, he learned the hard way that in a globalized world, some businesses are best to avoid it.

Paper-making, to be sure, is an energy-intensive activity tricky to manage depending on your country's flag. A 2013 study by the World Resources Institute determined that energy alone accounts for almost nine percent of the total cost of generating pulp and paper. Environmental compliance can thin margins, as well. Limiting mercury emissions when chemical plants make caustic soda needed for making paper is one weighty expense. Applying chlorine to bleach wood pulp white is another contaminating activity, since it produces dioxin that then is discharged into waterways. Mills heating caldrons of water, chemicals, and lumber also release formaldehyde, ammonia, and other toxins. Because pulp and paper mills are energy hogs, they need electricity-generators, boilers, and turbines that emit fumes. Add it up and paper-making is the third largest industrial source of greenhouse gases.

The Samoa pulp mill, as you'd expect from these burdens, had no shortage of run-ins with California environmental agencies monitoring air and water pollution before Freshwater came along. Louisiana Pacific, which owned the plant for twenty-eight of its forty-three years, spent 175 million dollars to comply with environmental standards, cutting pollution by two-thirds. Even with all those zeroes, the plant in its last full year of operation in 2007 still pumped eighty-six tons of undesirable elements into the coastal city's skies and 1,203 tons a year of pollutants into its waters. When Freshwater acquired it in 2009, the company planned to spend another fifty million dollars for environmental controls to further limit the mill's pollution footprint. That money was to be one piece of a larger 400 million dollar investment to modernize and modify its property after it closed under the old management in 2008.

None of it was to be. Freshwater owner Simpson banked too heavily on Uncle Sam for the rebirth. He must've thought he was in China where the government seems to be in the business of subsidizing Chinese paper factories, particularly at the provincial level. He'd intended on borrowing much of his capital from the US Department of Energy under the federal economic stimulus plan Congress enacted after the Great Recession hit in 2008, the worst economic downturn since the Great Depression of the thirties. But the project didn't qualify for a loan. It was a crushing blow for Simpson and unemployed workers hoping to return to their careers. Left with only bad options, Simpson in 2010 had to abandon his plans to reopen the factory. Had it been successful, the company would have hired 2,015 workers at a "family wage." Many workers easily could've earned twenty dollars an hour, or more. Globalization helped stomp Simpson's dream like a bug.

Humboldt County, majestic and relaxingly natural as it may be, is today like a California version of Appalachia. About three-quarters of its population are white and display signs of rural poverty that visitors notice in a jiffy. The average household income at 37,000 dollars annually is 20,000 dollars less than the state average. Five years after the 2008 downturn, unemployment there is still above ten percent. In Eureka, its biggest city, unkempt vagrants roam the streets panhandling. Commerce in its old downtown is nil. Even the newer shopping mall on the south end of town is struggling, with vacancies and a deserted parking lot on Saturday afternoon. Timber can no longer sustain the place. Mills and related companies, many sagging under the weight of regulations to protect the Redwoods and keep the air and rivers pristine, have gone silent. Resource activists believe it's for the better, yet beneath the surface bitterness percolates about severing traditional employment in forestry products and fishing. The sinking standard of living has driven many residents to trade in their saws for horticultural equipment to grow high-grade, medical marijuana legalized by state law.

But there's another reason besides environmental rules for the economic plight of the former paper mill workers, and so many others in Humboldt County. Right there in the fine print on paper product wrappers in the dollar stores that abound in this depressed northwest corner of California is a clue as to why this is happening. Increasingly, the aisles trafficked by bargain shoppers living on slim household budgets are lined with paper merchandise from China. Indeed, the Humboldt mill began slipping toward disuse just as China elevated itself to second place behind the rule-laden US for the world's top paper-maker. In fact, in its final years of operation, the Samoa mill sent its raw pulp product to Asia, sailing on ships that were about the only reason to keep Eureka's port open. That China was a top paper producer was strange since the nation contained no significant forests anymore, or other natural resource advantages relative to competitors. Then again, perhaps those are overblown. The sector did enjoy thirty-three billion dollars in government subsidies between 2001 and 2009. Twenty-five billion dollars in public handouts went to cover the cost of pulp, the majority of which was imported, including from places like Samoa before its mill closed. Three billion helped pay for coal and another 778 million dollars for electricity, most of it coal-fired. All that money, too, went for a production method out of sync with the Communist Party's green proclamations. Paper mills in the US or Europe, for instance, burn on average 0.9 to 1.2 tons of coal and consume about thirty-five to fifty tons of water per ton of pulp; Chinese plants, by comparison, use 1.4 tons of coal and 103 tons of water. In other words, subsidies for inefficient use of resources burden China and the globe with more pollution than really needed to make paper, in the digital age no less. That's undercut people like Simpson, mill workers in Eureka, and other US companies in communities scattered across the nation.

So even if America is still the number one paper-maker, it's hollow sustenance, and probably fleeting. The US is now dependent on China for the very same product. It imported less than one billion dollars of it in 2001. Eight years later it was 2.5 billion dollars. The flood of paper towels, tissue paper, computer paper, cardboard, and other products from Asia might as well have been a steamrolling pink-slip dispenser. A cascade of mill closures and layoffs nationwide, including at Samoa, ruined the livelihoods of 50,000 workers. And so it goes for many at formerly rock solid, blue-collar jobs at energy-zapping, high-emissions factories.

Joining the out-of-work pulp and paper makers losing their jobs to China were 158,000 workers in the metal products industry, 59,000 in rubber and plastics, and 22,000 in chemical production. The computer and electronics fields had no immunity either. They surrendered 628,000 positions to People's Republic factories. In teetering American factory towns bracketed in rust and defeat, trade policy and the globalization it unleashed was the disease. American manufacturing nosedived between 2000 and the end of the decade. Gone were a whopping six million paychecks, casualties of automation, overseas production, and changing markets, as Department of Labor figures illustrate. Jobs too pricey to maintain in countries with occupational safety protections, unions, healthcare provisions, and environmental stewardship disappeared, were robotized, or sent abroad. They've been replaced in the US with low-wage jobs, according to research by Public Citizen's Global Trade Watch, a non-profit that Ralph Nader helped form. Ironically, the McJobs have created the illusion that the economy has emerged from globalization, unscathed since the total number of American jobs has not changed much. Don't believe it.

In a world where every cent matters, China stands supremely attractive. Foreign manufacturers eager to strengthen their profit margins or merely frantic to survive view Asia's production horsepower as an option they'd be insane to turn down. On average, Chinese factory employees earned seventeen dollars an hour less than in the US. In a typical forty-hour week that translated into a 680 dollar difference per worker! While the popular notion remains that the Rust Belt states were pummeled worst by job losses, other areas lost too. Alabama and Georgia shed employment in computers, electronics, furniture, and textiles, as did the high-tech industry in Northern California hamstrung by environmental red tape, taxes, and labor costs. In Massachusetts, one industrial district alone waved farewell to about 17,000 jobs to China since the millennium began. Oregon, home of Nike

Corp., has taken a beating itself over shifting jobs to the Far East; some 21,000 positions are now in China. North Carolina furniture makers and Vermont manufacturers of snowboards and snowshoes could hum that same bleak song.

Hence, America in the post-WTO marketplace was papered in welfare applications and dependence on Walmart, Target, and other big-box retailers staking their business on selling discounted Chinese merchandise to families often living paycheck-to-paycheck. Their sales aisles cloaked a sour truth of an emasculated middle class. Since 1989, the median US household income is almost the same amount in real dollars. So without cheap Asian labor and their adaptable production networks, those same families might've discovered that the iPhones, jeans, plastic dinosaurs, hoodies, and sheets they covet would be priced out of their affordability range. China, meanwhile, is on the receiving end of "exported pollution"—pollution no longer brewed in the West—from discharge pipes, boilers, diesel tailpipes, and other chemical-launching delivery vehicles part and parcel of its manufacturing "miracle." Free trade winners and losers are getting harder to distinguish.

At the same time, layoffs in high-paid American jobs smote by cheap foreign imports have been like a two-for-one deal in some corporate headquarters stateside. For companies like Walmart, it's been an empire-builder. The multinational has added surplus workers to the labor force, causing wage stagnation, allowing it to not only hire for less, but also propagate the number of down-sized customers who can't afford to shop elsewhere, according to Public Citizen's Global Trade Watch group. Walmart was perfectly suited to meet the growing American appetite for low prices by remaking China into a titanic company assembly line. Roughly

30,000 Chinese factories whip out seventy percent of everything on its shelves. Every second of every day, 300 people are buying something at Walmart's approximate 9,000 stores worldwide.

But operating in China was getting hairier, as environmentalists pressed Walmart to decontaminate its operations. When the retailer announced in 2005 that it intended to be the greenest corporation on Earth, reducing its carbon footprint at stores and distribution centers by one fifth, executives pledged that their Chinese suppliers would all comply with the country's environmental and labor standards. So far, it's been a tough slog. Plants supplying Walmart in China, for instance, missed energy efficiency targets at ninety-one out of 200 sites that, theoretically speaking, should've curtailed harmful vapors bubbling from coal-fired power plants. Knowing whether Walmart's goals have been realized is further muddied by deals cut among Chinese manufacturers. As *Mother Jones* reported, the corporation's best "five-star" plants may cross every regulatory "t" concerning fair employee treatment and safe working conditions. A network of thousands of "shadow factories" they frequently subcontract orders to—places that are nestled away or run out of somebody's home, vexing company auditors—can behave as they please. Every ounce of waste has a story

When you knit together all these threads, it's little wonder that idealistic entrepreneurs like Bob Simpson in Eureka have little chance at succeeding. The deck has been stacked against them by agreements their own government has codified in the fevers and hypocrisies of the post-WTO world.

Simpson's frustration, along with the ranks of the unemployed in Humboldt County and places like it across the US, exemplifies how nothing came for free on either side of the Pacific under the

Clinton-Gore free trade scheme. Panglossian rhetoric from US politicos and Communist suits alike, the Somoa mill still stands idle, while this growth-smog axis of politicians talking green continues to blow smoke in the faces of US and Chinese citizens alike.

CHAPTER 16:

RINGING THE BELL

HIGH ATOP A HOTEL overlooking the city of Taihe, a middle-aged man in navy blue slacks and a patterned polo shirt is the center of attention. He circulates around a table with thirty guests, getting each to rise for a toast. His official title is "activities director" for the city's mayor, but he shall go unnamed for reasons soon to become evident. Loud and jovial, the fellow bellows with enthusiasm as he moves from guest to guest to lift and drink successive glasses of wine and bottles of beer. As he gets the party going, waitresses bustle in and out of the dining room carrying trays. They keep a Lazy Susan on the circular table filled with platters of fish, pork, beef, vegetables, and noodles, bowls of soup and salad, baskets of fruit, and trays of dessert. They pour wine and beer after setting down the food, keeping the glasses before each guest brimming with libation.

As dinner winds down, they come again, this time carrying bottles and filling shot glasses for all with strong multigrain liquor known as Moutai. The activities director then rises, proposes a toast, and downs the liquor in one gulp. People laugh with approval. Next, he comes to each American, raising additional toasts of Moutai and challenging each to a drinking contest. Eventually, an American businessman takes up the challenge and rises to stand next to the activities director in front of a tray full of Tsingtao beers and a bottle of Moutai. In rapid sequence, the two drink four shots of Moutai, washing each down with a whole bottle of beer. It whips the crowd up into a frenzy. People applaud and hoot with each drink. The Americans chant, "U-S-A!, U-S-A!" The suspense of the college frat-like contest reaches a climax as the activities director pours a fifth shot for each, which he and his contestant quickly down. Finally, they lift their beers, but as they chug, the activities director can't get it down. The foamy beer flows down his face onto his shirt and pants, forming a bubbly puddle on the carpet as it washes over his black loafers. The crowd roars. The US businessman has won.

But the day's work isn't done yet for the activities director. He still has additional duties ahead. Indeed, the fun is just beginning. Next he leads the group to the hotel's private karaoke bar. Waitresses bring trays with open bottles of beer, plus more Moutai. Staggering, but still standing, the activities director grabs the microphone in one hand, a beer in the other, and begins singing and dancing to the music, dizzily whirling around the karaoke bar. Then the American business man takes the floor to sing. As the guests listen and sip their beer, a group of young women who work at the hotel filter into the room to circulate and invite the men in the party to dance.

The revelry sparkled that night in a hotel owned by Chinese entrepreneur Haiquan Liu, who as we noted earlier gets full attention when he calls city hall. Fortyish, neatly groomed in snappy sport-clothes and a gold bracelet, he seems to enjoy himself that evening, but exudes reserve in sharp contrast to the frivolity and enthusiasm of the activities director. Mr. Liu remains sober, knowing his limits, so he can keep his mind on the business empire he's built, known as the Anhui Jinggong Group, CO., LTD. Mr. Liu started as a carpenter when young, but from humble beginnings today has become emblematic of China's glorious new wealth. Aside from the twenty-five story hotel, he owns a cement plant, the local hospital, and a real estate development company that's literally rebuilding almost the entire city of Taihe in Anhui Province, east of Shanghai. He's also interested in investing in green technology, seeing it as another potential moneymaker. This is what's brought the Americans here. And before the uproarious evening ends, he tells the American businessman who's come to China seeking to gain an investor to help outfit a factory for making emissions-free commercial lawn and gardening equipment that he likes him. That's important to the businessman because he cannot make the commercial electric lawn and gardening equipment for maintaining parks, golf courses, and athletic fields in the US at a price that's competitive with conventional gasoline-powered equipment that pollutes the air. The best place to do that is here in China. That's why, aside from amusement, the antics of the activities director have served as a test of character and the businessman has proven himself hard as nails, a man in the mold of Deng Xiaoping. That's what Chinese investors like Liu like to see.

Aside from his wealth, what's abundantly clear as the evening and next day unfold is that Mr. Liu, as he's known around Taihe, is the real power in this Chinese city. Some even refer to Taihe as Mr.

Liu's city. And Mr. Liu's influence is typical in cities and provinces across China, where industrialists and business tycoons often call the shots. It's evident here. Not only was the mayor, along with top aides and the activities director, there at dinner, but the next morning at 7:30 a.m. the mayor and other city officials were back for a ceremony honoring the American guests and to accompany Liu on a tour of his city, with the local newspaper and TV station in tow. Not surprisingly, the previous night's activities director was in no shape to make it, but instead wound up checking into Mr. Liu's hospital for alcohol poisoning in the wee hours. It turns out, though, it was all part of his job. That's because activities directors in China are charged with the job of "drinking, singing, and dancing" to lubricate deals between government and business. And that makes them a metaphor for a nation. While drink destroys their health, the air pollution that stems from the deals they help lubricate under free trade agreements destroys the health of millions unless business suddenly takes a major green turn.

◘

IN ANCIENT TIMES, WHEN faced with unfairness, commoners would go to city hall and ring a large bell to get an audience with officials to air their grievances. Today, the bells are but tourist attractions, but the people still figuratively ring them with protests and comments on social media about pollution. China's Communist Party leaders hear their complaints, just like their feudal predecessors, though often grudgingly. Meanwhile, just like in the days of Emperor Qin, and even before, spies monitor events and track public opinion. Ministers operate with overlapping functions to check their power. And informal meetings with patrons and elites—like Mr. Liu in Taihe—dominate decision-making, though hearings are held in which people can sound off. Together, all of these techniques have one overarching goal: to ensure the power structure maintains social stability and deters bloggers, green activists, ethnic minorities, wily anarchists, and others who'd change the system. Especially since the 2008 Olympics, the party has channeled its attention on public dissatisfaction with pollution, evident in fevered, street protests over poisoned air, land, and water. While concerned about the health effects, top party echelons mostly seem to fear that public dissatisfaction over the environment could undermine their power and China's social stability. Some sages speculate it could ignite riots, or even revolution.

Dissatisfaction seems wide, evident even in casual conversation. In a train station in Xi'an, for instance, a young music teacher dressed in stylish blue jeans and a lightweight blouse in the heat of summer dreams of moving from her home in coal-fume-blasted Shaanxi Province to the Maldives. While waiting in the crowded station, she explains that in large part it's because of their natural beauty and blue skies. A student on her way from Taiyuan in Shanxi back to college in Toronto complains about smog. As she holds her iPhone in one hand and nurses an iced coffee in another while riding the bullet train on the way into Beijing, she says she wants to settle in Los Angeles, not only to be near Hollywood's glamour, but because she hears it's a much cleater environment than that of her home. As she explains, visibility suddenly drops to next to nothing as trees, power poles, and farm buildings fade into a fog-like haze that's grey and eerie. Asked about whether it's fog, she replies, "Oh no. That's the air pollution." Days before, Changzhou factory manager Richard Wang griped that even in summer—typically the cleanest time of year—Beijing's besieged by atrocious smog. Wang, thirtyish and studious looking in his wire-rimmed glasses, complains that many government officials don't seem serious about solving the air pollution problem, but instead try to brush it under the rug. In this way, Wang and the others are all softly ringing the bell, expressing their grief over the nation's smoky skies.

And government at all levels can't help but hear the rising clang, perhaps because officials realize their own necks are on the line, not to mention that the bureaucrats breathe the same air. A board member of the Southern California's smog-control agency who frequently visits China to confer with officials notices in the summer of 2013 a distinct attitude shift from what he encountered in 2008. Then government managers and politicians told Michael Cacciotti economic growth was number one and pollution just wasn't a big deal. Now, they're quick to concede the blurry smog and explain what they're doing about it. The new mindset is evident as Li Ping, Heifei Municipal People's Government deputy-secretary, boasts about the city's hybrid buses and compressed natural gas taxicab fleet, not to mention the subway the city of 7.5 million is building. By all measures, Chinese air pollution and greenhouse gases would be more acute than they are today if folks like Li and those at the national level were not doing things the US has hardly begun to tackle in the EPA's forty-three year existence. The contrast between America and China over land-use, transportation, living spaces, and consumption cannot be sharper, all of which matters in determining the extent to which smog will continue to dominate China.

Unlike the US, traditional single-family homes are a rarity in the People's Republic. People live in apartments and condominiums, most outfitted with solar water heaters. A good-sized apartment housing a family of three, plus a grandparent or two, usually does not exceed 1,000 square feet. Singles and couples with one child or no kids can reside in units as small as 250 to 300 square feet. The eco-implications compared to American suburbs, where stucco McMansions tower, are obvious. There's less energy use per household, less space to store material possessions, which keeps a lid on consumption.

Arguably China's one-child per family policy, instituted by Deng Xiaoping, has been a formidable pro-environment policy, acting like a draw-string tying off popular demands for more spacious housing and more of everything else. It's been meted out at times with despotic brutality, including forced sterilizations and abortions. The one-child restriction, which stems from China's history of famines, may also curse its superpower dreams. As the century advances, China's graying population could lack enough working-age people to keep its GDP sizzling. This alone is causing China to now ease the restriction on family size as it seeks to keep economic growth going strong.

Despite population control, automobile sales have gone through the roof in recent years with rising prosperity. Yet, China is unlikely to ever match the per-capita level of auto ownership that long ago made America a car-strewn country studded with gas stations, tire dealerships, and greasy repair shops. Despite McKinsey's projection, it appears there just isn't the room in its crowded cities, nor are the masses likely to afford car ownership even as incomes rise. Rather, the millions mainly ride electric scooters that stores sell everywhere, peddle old-fashioned bicycles, and travel on trains, subways, and buses. Beijing by itself has four major intercity train stations the size of Grand Central or Penn

Station in New York and five long distance bus depots compared to one train station and one bus station in downtown Los Angeles. At rush hour in Beijing, train packers manage passenger loading and unloading from crammed rail cars. As Chinese towns grow and redevelop, construction cranes dot skylines to build high-rise apartment complexes at a pace not seen elsewhere in the world. Train stations pop up next to them like freeway onramps in US suburbs. Electric bullet trains whoosh at 200 MPH, making them a faster way to move between cities than flying, especially when you count traveling, parking, and waiting at airports.

Besides, a gallon of gas tops five dollars plus drivers going between cities or from downtown to the airport pay stiff tolls for the privilege. Not only does the People's Republic host the largest network of toll roads anywhere, according to the World Bank, many of its metropolises require car owners to take alternate transit during the week. Consequently, there's surprisingly little traffic between population centers compared to the congestion that ails the I-5 between Los Angeles and the San Francisco Bay Area or along Interstate 95 from Washington to New York. Instead, China's inter-city trains and buses are routinely packed to the gills.

By 2020, it's likely the construction boom will end, as China completes modernizing housing and transportation. Cement and steel plants that spew out greenhouse gases and air pollution will slow. Remaining discharges will circle around coal-fired power plants electrifying cities and industries until alternative energy can take over, provided the world can wait that long. Meanwhile, energy efficiency standards for appliances, new buildings, and industrial operations that shaved the energy intensity of a unit of GDP about twenty percent since 2005 should cut it another twenty percent by 2015, says David Fridley, a scientist with Lawrence Berkeley Laboratory who's worked on energy studies in China for more than thirty years.

Much of the progress has occurred at the local and provincial levels, where the differences can be just as great as between California, with its green dream for a carbonless future, and West Virginia, which still banks on coal. Shamed in the mid 2000s for its appearance on several most-polluted lists, Linfen put itself on an industrial detox program. It padlocked or relocated dirty plants. Illegal coalmines that once numbered nearly 400 were chopped by three-quarters. Villagers and hotels that traditionally burned coal converted to solar water heaters. Roads were paved. Coal truck payloads were tarped to prevent their cargo from spilling onto streets and being atomized into dust that free to blow in the wind. Government suits rated on how they upped GDP were also judged by their cleanup results. "Ten years ago, we didn't have blue skies," one resident said. "Now it has improved a lot," even if the remaining smog still blotches white shirts. Linfen's turnaround was illuminating. Hard choices can pay off.

Today, Linfen is cleaner, but still has a long way to go to achieve healthful air. As the train I (Bill) ride approaches the city in the morning dawn, it reminds me of an American rust belt city. The smell of sulfur hangs in the air. Lights from old looking industrial plants glow in the distance. Disembarking at the Linfen station, it's unlike others I've seen, old and drab instead of new and sparkling. Another contrast is that unlike the electric-powered bullet trains I've ridden, the train I've taken here still runs on diesel fuel. At the heart of the town outside the station are dreary Communist era government buildings around a concrete plaza. People here look decidedly less prosperous than in China's stylish coastal cities, and buildings are drab and run down. As I ride through Linfen, the air is grey. Coal trucks rumble along the main road, kicking up dust. Not far north of the city on the road to Taiyuan, the air becomes acrid and grey with coal smoke. Visibility drops so much that drivers turn on their lights in broad daylight and traffic signals are hard to see.

Clearly, Linfen and other communities across China have taken steps that are encouraging, but they've hardly stopped China's eco-crisis or its record greenhouses gases from growing. Nor have the recent flurry of standards, penalties, initiatives, and emissions caps announced since the smog-enveloping winter and fall of 2013. Next to the regulations credited with dramatically cleaning up the air in US cities, China's scattershot actions recall Los Angeles in the forties and fifties. Efforts have been uncoordinated, awkward, uneven, and reactive, more like a shotgun response to public concern than a crystallized battle plan. Where the two nations do agree is that they can solve smog without downshifting a gangbusters economy.

◘

PROMISES, PROMISES; CHINA'S RULING elite for years tried soothing the population with starchy bluster that it was escalating its war on smog, just hang tough. The ensuing credibility gap could've blown a hole in the Great Wall. Scattershot targets of old—to lop coal burning, elicit public feedback, cap specific gases—mostly tanked. The hamstrung past then seemed to be replaced in 2013 with resolute action. The growthsmogogists proclaimed they were going green, no fooling this time. You almost needed a scorecard to keep up with the government's initiatives, even if the

275 billion dollars it was earmarking over the next five years was less than half its stimulus program to combat the world's Great Recession in the late 2000s. Officials vowed to write new measures to curb nitrogen oxides coughed by automobiles and cement plants, bird-dog manufacturers, beef up rail lines and buses, and promote renewables. New regulations were slapped on industry and agriculture misting fine particulates. Smoky machinery and ramshackle factories would be modernized quicker. Just in case China's neighbors felt marginalized from the cleanup soiree, the government later agreed to participate with Korea and Japan (fierce territorial issues and all) in a novel, "concerted effort to reduce air pollution caused by particulates." The party even jumped on the global transparency train, requiring 15,000 factories, state-owned ones included, to post air- and water-emissions in real time.

Chomping for a role in the initiative mania, China's legal system widened its own tent. In summer 2014, the Supreme People's Court decreed that a special tribunal to eliminate "administrative interference from local governments," especially in public-interest suits, would be created. Nationwide, 134 "pilot environmental courts" would be expanded in tandem. But this wasn't just about adding new dockets. The top justices also announced harsher penalties for fourteen types of eco-crimes. Among them were formations of toxic hotspots that spurred people to evacuate or were uncovered near schools, hospitals, and large residential tracts. One possible sentence for negligent polluters: state execution in a country that, until now anyway, led the planet in capital punishment.

Wherever you went, accountability was tiptoeing closer to the source. From now on, local city halls, not ministerial badges, bore added responsibility for checking off restorative goals. In a greener China, they'd be graded for the aerial char and other crud they pared, not just the big industry they enticed. Projects lacking environmental assessments would be spiked, their bank credit, electricity, and water hookups denied. Zeroing in on the worst haze-zones, the area around Beijing, Tianjin, and Hebei was ordered to stomp out a quarter of its PM-2.5 by 2017, while the capital itself outlawed coal in six of its main districts by 2020. Separate to that, a battery of cities were joining Beijing, Shanghai, and others restricting new vehicle purchases to chop tailpipe vapors and traffic before ozone canopied them. Beijing's dream: healthy air by 2030, with particulate matter squashed down to an "internationally recognized safe level." This new emphasis on local crackdowns was a Sinology dissertation waiting to be written. It suggested that the Politburo's cunning approach of "skillfully deflecting blame toward protectionist local officials and state-owned enterprises," as *Foreign Affairs* framed it, had exhausted its shelf life, that the central government had to act so with a steady hand at the tiller where it counted. Permitting "coal bosses" to run towns while officials spouted hollow rhetoric about "ecological civilizations" was merely a recipe to toxify public attitudes.

To achieve objectives like this in a nation where seventy-one out of seventy-four monitored cities flub minimal air-pollution standards, the environmental ministry has gone so far as to copycat the US military. The MEP now incorporates drones to spy overhead on incorrigible polluters who've foiled regulators before. The eleven unmanned aircraft, which employ thermal imaging and infrared lights and can cover seventy square miles in two hours of flight, may become the ministry's slyest inspectors. "The drones captured pictures of flames in the open air," an official enthused. The remote-control eyes-in-sky have also sniffed for criminal shortcuts at desulfurization and wastewater facilities. One day they could be retrofitted with parachutes enabling them to spray smog-dissolving agents, as if lords of the atmosphere. Technocrats on the ground continue to sharpen their cleavers, too. Emission scofflaws are being nailed with pricier fines than previous slap-on-the-wrist tactics. The Chinese subsidiary of American energy-gadget manufacturer Babcock & Wilcox Co. in July 2014 was dunned with a 97,000 dollar fine—one of the highest levies in memory—for open-air painting around its factory boilers. Speaking of the U.S., the People's Republic has emulated another one of its clean-air tactics in its push to decommission millions of older, dirty automobiles.

Some bureaucrats with attitudes about spilling delicate subjects weren't as willingly buying in. Under somebody's orders, they were still withholding statistics on soil contamination that fueled numerous food-safety scandals, most notoriously 10,000 tons of cadmium-laced rice that went to market in the Guangdong province. The data, recalcitrant officials snipped, was a "state secret." Either way, roughly 3.3 million hectares (or about 13,000 square miles) of the nation's farmland are thought to be too toxic for planting, the bulk of it in eastern and central China rejiggered by development. Hence, not everyone has received the party's message. Some big companies, in fact, just plugged their ears. During 2013, the year of the facemask, giant power-maker Huadian followed a prevalent tactic. It released sulfur dioxide without particle scrubbers capped over its smokestacks because it was more profitable to generate electricity that way. Then Huadian sold its juice at higher rates reserved for lower-emission sources by doctoring the paperwork. A criminal justice term was used for Chinese electricity companies pulling these mostly-unpunished shenanigans: "repeat offenders."

Feeble enforcement stems in part from lopping individuals out of the action. In America—home of the Clean Air and Water Acts—citizens and organizations can file lawsuits against government agencies refusing or unable to enforce standards. No such luck in the People's Republic. Folks can't target officials with legal action to protect themselves and their families from chemical onslaught. In theory, they are permitted to seek compensation when harmed by a single pollution incident, but few have done so triumphantly.

Standing back, were there new reasons for genuine optimism or more false hope? On the one hand, it's difficult to reconcile how China can tackle a disaster as severe as the Mariana Trench is deep. Its environmental agency has never even publicly outlined a systematic approach distilling what's needed to achieve righteously healthful air. Stunningly, it doesn't even have an exhaustive inventory of pollution sources. Deutsche Bank tried drafting its own blueprint to chip away at the mystery, yet in the end needed to resort to Chinese emissions estimates compiled by Greenpeace. For doubting Thomases, it's akin to a doctor touting a miracle surgery without first conducting a blood test.

All the same, as smog gumshoes from Los Angeles, we have some reason for bullishness. We just don't know how much. For instance, sulfur-cutting gasoline standards that Sinopec historically crabbed were too exorbitant to meet were approved recently. State-owned electricity providers that devoured about half the nation's coal themselves have agreed to dig into their corporate pockets for retrofits. All this, too, as scientists announced that atmospheric carbon dioxide had crossed the 400 parts-per-million threshold, a level that could ratchet up global warming like a neverending storm.

Across China, sacred cows were becoming fair game in the screw tightening. Big-city smog czars reimposed prohibitions on lighting fireworks, which many believe scare off evil spirits, during the New Year and other national celebrations. Electronic pyrotechnics could replace them. Though a poll in Shanghai reflected overwhelming support for a ban on the sky-painting incendiaries due to the sulfur dioxide and other chuff they release midair, it struck others as political decoy. "The fireworks last only a dozen days, but the country has long been plagued by smog," growled an East China Normal University professor. "Why should we change our traditions just because the government has failed to do its job during the rest of the year?" PM-2.5 at one Beijing air monitor on the first day of fireworks in 2013 was smokestack-esque, with particle pollution at 1,593 µg/m3 of air. Again, WHO's guideline recommends that 25 µg/m3 is a safe exposure level.

Harnessing small, public sacrifices are thus part of the remedy in China Inc., just as it was in Southern California when backyard incinerators were outlawed despite a tsunami of opposition about trampled liberties. "We want to promote a culture of individual responsibility, of doing little things that can help create better air quality," explained Green Zhejiang activist Chu Xumin. "So driving less, smoking less, fewer fireworks."

Operators of outdoor barbecue stands, another commoner's favorite, received no hall pass. Rolled out into the streets and alleyways at night along with impromptu set-ups of tables and chairs, the carts draw throngs of diners out for a smoky meal at an affordable price. But officials decided that public lungs trumped taste buds. In November 2013, inspectors resembling BBQ shock-troops descended on street vendors grilling spicy mutton and chicken kebabs to ensure they were licensed. Never before had the beloved treat, often paired with frosty Tsingtao beer on hot days, cultivated this attention. Five hundred "illegal" BBQ stands were targeted. Police reduced some to metal ribbons with torches while city wardens watched stonily. Likewise, a bus that metamorphosed into a rolling BBQ restaurant, seemingly to adapt to the new laws, blackened into a shell in spring 2014 when it mysteriously burst into flames. Before it did, the eatery-on-wheels had been raking in customers.

Maybe, as with the fireworks controversy, the harassment was cover from the intricacies of managing rampant vehicle exhaust and plant emissions without stymieing economic dynamism that recreated China into not just a phenomenon but also a brand. As the state-run *China Daily* said in May, those dastardly grills were implicated as a serious pollution scourge even if the paper cited no statistics. Soon, a contemptuous poster on Sina Weibo responded, "They'll ban farting in order to clean up the air." Again, Los Angeles nodded sympathetically. Regulators in the late eighties and early nineties pounced on emissions from hamburger joints and BBQ restaurants on the grounds their charbroiled aroma masked the health risk of their smoke. Just like in Asia, popular resistance flashed at the specter of rules seen more as public relations than meaty Blue Sky progress.

If nothing else, one sensed the ground shifting inside the heads of the People's Republic's biggest cheeses, Prime Minister Li Keqiang has been especially vocal, pledging "even greater resolve and more vigorous efforts" to shrink contamination. He told the World Bank he was "working day and night" with his team to fine-tune a plan for "clean, livable cities," later adding that his government will "resolutely declare war against pollution as we declared war against poverty." Just not exactly; proposed national reductions in steel and cement production and coal burning would only scalpel emissions by a few percentage points. Around then, the open secret of cancer villages was at last acknowledged, too, albeit in a bloodlessly indirect manner following years of strenuous avoidance. "Among [the cleanup plan's] contents," the *Beijing Times* reported, "is a clear demonstration that because of chemical poisoning, 'cancer villages' and other serious [threats] to social health have begun to emerge in many areas. Moreover, according to media person Deng Fei, those villages were spreading from the middle of eastern China to the west."

The torturous state language was sumptuous in its meaning. Deng was the young, spiky-haired journalist who'd posted on Google a map of those cancer villages in 2009, awaking the planet to their existence. Early in 2013, having now transformed himself into a crusading activist, he urged people on Sina Weibo to upload photographs of chemically-thrashed rivers. Officials peeved with his suggestion reportedly dispatched staffers in Beijing to halt the media from reporting about it.

No matter the media gags, there was no denying the green revolution blossoming everywhere was a people's referendum on the republic of chemicals that their government was often incapable of taming. In May, a thousand-plus citizens demonstrated in the southern city of Kunming, marching and hooting against a proposed refinery by the parent of state-owned PetroChina. Some protestors wore masks with the letters PX struck through. Roughly 1,500 miles to the east, huge crowds in Hangzhou near Shanghai shuffled their feet to oppose a planned waste incinerator with the usual after-effects: injuries, upended cars, populist turmoil and city hall demands for provocateurs to turn themselves in. Another symbol of a more engaged citizenry shimmied up the eco-flagpole in February 2014. A man from Hebei's provincial capital broke precedence by affixing his name on an unfamiliar document. In his public-interest-type lawsuit, Li Guxin indicted Shijiazhuang's Environmental Protection Bureau for failure to "perform its duty to control air pollution." Everything he'd done to shield himself—wearing a facemask, buying an air purifier, using a treadmill indoors when the atmosphere thickened—wasn't enough to stop him from coughing severely for months. Li sought 1,600 dollars in damages and government subsidies for public facemasks and filters. Whether a Chinese court would hear such a delicate case for "administrative compensation," likely to elicit other claims, was unknown. "The reason that I'm [doing this] is to let every citizen see that amid this haze, we're the real victims," Li was quoted as saying.

Whether it was Li's or Wang Hui's, the message was getting through to officialdom. Just the excitement slathered on a grinning Chinese President Xi as he promenaded around Beijing sans-facemask on a smoggy day in February 2014 telegraphed an appreciation for the *something-must-be-done-now* ethos. So what if it was probably a staged photo-op designed to produce the headline: "He Breathes the Same Air and Shares the Same Fate?" Empathy pays dividends.

Even with these positive optics, the party's ambivalent response on other environmental fronts has short-circuited transmission of an unequivocal signal to all of China's elite. People like Mr. Liu, for example. He still isn't sure that his investments in clean technology to sanitize air that you sometime need to mechanical lung to survive will pay off. Indeed, for him the net result has been *nada*. Four months after the drinking contest, Mr. Liu and the American businessman meet again, this time at a Mexican restaurant in Los Angeles. Mr. Liu is happy to see him, this time over tequila instead of Moutai. But despite their seeming friendship, the Chinese tycoon still hasn't invested in the green gardening equipment company, amid continuing government uncertainty on both sides of the Pacific on his nation's air pollution and the world's climate change dilemma. As long as government leaders support fossil fuel as much as or more than cleaner technologies, Mr. Liu prefers to keep his money on the sidelines when it comes to green investments. Instead, he's headed to Las Vegas the next morning where the odds are at least clear. Confucius would have lamented.

CHAPTER 17:

"MONEY IN THE GROUND"

ONE SPRING DAY IN 2013, Deng Ping and a few other scientists snuck onto the grounds of a major industrial plant in Inner Mongolia that turns coal into liquid fuel for vehicles. Night was giving way to dawn, so Deng, a small, young, college-educated woman, and her team rushed to avoid being spied by the plant's security guards. In the twilight of morning, the team grabbed samples of the energy station's milky-white wastewater. Their hunch was that the toxic chemicals being discharged to man-made lagoons, where they percolated downward into groundwater upon which local herders and farmers relied, were at levels above what Chinese law permitted. "We had to get samples really quickly," Deng recalled. But it wasn't "that scary. It's necessary for our work." Upon returning to Beijing, the group from Greenpeace and the Chinese Academy of Sciences analyzed the water they'd gathered. In it were ninety-nine volatile organic compounds, many carcinogenic like styrene and cresol, lab tests showed. Chemicals for which there were standards were found in concentrations up to 3.3 times the health limits. For other detected substances, frighteningly, there were no written thresholds.

Results in hand, the energized researchers published a report about the plant, owned by Shenhua Group, in Ordos in Inner Mongolia. They hoped revealing the contaminated water would pressure the government to force Shenhua, China's largest coal conglomerate, to clean up. But their biggest hope was that by showing Shenhua was befouling the environment, it would persuade Beijing to temper or abandon plans to build a series of potentially climate-wrecking coal bases. The bases are to convert the rock Marco Polo marveled at into electricity, synthetic natural gas for heating, gasoline, diesel fuel, and chemicals integral in plastics, medicines, dyes, and other products. They simply believed that China should have greener aspirations than continuing to rely on coal as the be-all end-all fuel. Sustainable alternatives, like wind and solar power, better energy efficiency— these should be the nation's future. For now, water contamination in desert-like Inner Mongolia was the most traumatic problem for locals around Shenhua's operation, so Deng and the others seized on that to argue against the coal bases.

Deng and company's report detailed how the dirty water flowed. They further disclosed how Shenhua's enormous water needs had lowered the natural water table so much that surface vegetation, including grass on which Mongols have grazed herds for thousands of years, had withered. No longer was it usable for agriculture and livestock. For all the stunning findings, the report got paltry news coverage except in what Deng called "five brave newspapers." China's masters appeared to pay almost no attention to what Deng and company had dug up. So, Shenhua continued to pursue tripling the size of its Ordos plant, as if nothing was wrong. But things would soon change, at least a bit.

◼

IN THE LATE EIGHTEEN-HUNDREDS, China sought English steam engines and foreign know-how to dramatically increase coal production. More than one hundred years later, China itself is a leading manufacturer of mining equipment, including powerful machines that cut coal with whirring blades in underground mines. Chinese mastery of extracting the fuel is so advanced that heightened capacity has lowered the price of the pervasive material, long the feedstock for electricity generation. You can't miss it. Throughout the land, there are 620 major coal power plants, according to the World Coal Association, representing about twenty-seven percent of the world's total of 2,300. Many have been erected in cookie-cutter fashion, quick to build and frequently high-polluting. And that's the rub. Low coal prices have motivated the industry and local governments to scurry to develop city-sized coal bases to turn the substance into profitable liquid fuel and sundry chemicals, but the globe may not be able to survive the devastating warming they could unleash.

China until recently has looked the other way on the savage ways of coal fumes. For decades, perhaps millennia, people have known that the fuel muddied the sky and made folks ill. For some more recently, there was no outrunning it. On March 16, 2010, a dust storm blew a large yellow cloud of coal ash containing sulfate and a variety of toxic metals, such as lead and arsenic, from ash piles in the western province of Gansu all the way to Beijing, where it darkened the sky. It then continued eastward, riding strong winds to envelope Korea and Japan. Roughly 270 million people were in its path. Such ash storms gust sixteen to nineteen times a year. China, the planet's heavy-weight coal-mining champ, has underground issues, as well.

Subterranean coalmine fires burn 10 million to 200 million metric tons of the stuff per year. The smoldering coal produces carbon dioxide, carbon monoxide, mercury, and other pollutants. Dutch scientists estimate that China's sixty-two documented coal fires may account for as much as two to three percent of global carbon dioxide emissions from fossil fuels. Sixteen of the fires are located in Inner Mongolia's Wude coalfield, China's largest. They rage 110–220 feet below ground, advancing about one hundred feet a year. "An underground coal fire is like a dragon," one official explained. "We can sense the dragon's tail—that is, the area already burned." Using satellites today, officials try to guess its path to "chop off its head."

If only a dragon killer could solve coal's aboveground dilemmas, especially its prime role generating sulfur-laced smog. In the Beijing region, home to more than one hundred million people when including Tianjin's forty-two million inhabitants, coal is the sheer lifeblood. Electricity makers, steel mills, and other industries devour half a billion tons of it a year in the giant metropolitan area. When experts bemoan fine-particle air pollution, they're really talking about the soot, sulfur, nitrogen oxides, and carbon released from burning the coal. Last winter when PM-2.5 levels were forty times greater than WHO recommendations in Beijing, not much could be done about it. Forty-five percent of the fine particles that regularly blanket the nation and can penetrate people's lungs are from coal use. It provides seventy percent of China's total energy needs. "Too much coal," lamented Fuqiang Yang, NRDC senior advisor on energy in Beijing, as he waved his hand across his face. For two months in Beijing in winter 2013 and one month in a third of the nation's land area where most of its population lives, everyone went outside wearing masks. The spell prompted the government to announce a cap on coal use in ten major cities in three major metropolitan areas of the nation: Beijing, Shanghai, and the Pearl River Delta around Shenzen and Hong Kong. But it didn't halt the march toward even greater reliance on the fuel to maximize the nation's drive for energy self-sufficiency.

China's rulers hyped their goal of capping and trimming back coal use between 2013 and 2017 along the nation's populous coast and some other areas in a plan of hazy detail and questionable practicality. In fact, by summer of 2014, the New York-based energy market information company PIRA Energy Group could find no evidence of diminished coal production in China, saying "definitive proof" of any dramatic turn away from the fossil fuel "remains elusive." But no such uncertainty surrounds another point. China is the king of greenhouse gases. In 2011 it released 8.7 billion tons of carbon dioxide from burning fossil fuels. Behind it was the US, which put out 5.5 billion tons that year. That means China produces twenty-seven percent of the worldwide total of 32.5 billion tons annually.

How could it not? China consumes forty-six percent of the coal burned worldwide. The 3.8 billion tons it gobbled in 2011 was almost as much as the rest of the planet. When the Great Helmsman, Mao Tse-Tung, died in 1976, the nation shoveled about 250 million tons per year into furnaces and the like. Since then, it's gone up by more than 1,400 percent. The International Energy Agency estimates that by 2017 it will burn half of all the coal burned in the world. Ironically, that's because the year the government outlined coal caps was the same one in which it pushed ahead with blueprints to erect 363 new coal-fired power plants nationwide. Voices of scientists concerned that the country might lack the water to run them and supply the mines were faint. Under the business-as-usual approach, China's carbon dioxide emissions will keep mounting until 2030 when it could be releasing 10 billion tons annually, according to projections by the Lawrence Berkeley National Laboratory. The bright side, if there is one, is that China's coal use and greenhouse gas emissions could peak a decade earlier by revving up energy efficiency, cleaner fuels, and renewables, the lab's analysis says. For Deng and fellow environmentalists, stopping the government's aggressive push to expand fossil fuels is their top priority.

But China just can't seem to get enough of the dirty fuel. Even as the world's preeminent coal producer, it imports fifteen percent of the material sold on the world market. For all the US's lecturing about global warming, its companies have been shipping coal to the People's Republic in taxpayer-subsidized deals. Power plants and steel mills along China's coast bring in overseas supplies when it can't be delivered to them fast enough from domestic sources or at competitive prices because of transportation bottlenecks. Natural Resources Defense Council Asia Director Barbara Finamore calls them "coal truck traffic jams." American coal exports to China coincide with tightening US regulatory screws to phase out coal electricity by strengthening emissions standards for mercury, other pollutants, and now greenhouse gases. California, for instance, is forcing its own utilities to do away with their out-of-state coal plants in Arizona, New Mexico, and Utah. There are no coal plants in California.

In response, US coal mining companies have doubled their yearly exports since 2007, from 60 million tons to more than 120 million tons. A quarter of those sales now go to China and other East Asian nations. Companies like Peabody Coal ship their product to China's coastal power plants out of Los Angeles, Seattle, British Columbia, and other West Coast ports, and are eyeing building new ones to cash in on the export business. The shipments have triggered protests in the Pacific Northwest and in the inland cities through which long, chugging trains would continually haul coal. In the big scheme of China's coal use, these are minor-league sales. It equals only about one percent of the coal used in the East Asian market, where China is the biggest importer, and just four percent of East Asia's total imports. But what is irksome to some in Congress is that the American public is effectively subsidizing the deals. Massachusetts Democratic Representative Edward Markey sure dislikes it. The federal government, he's pointed out, leases the coal development rights to mining companies for ninety percent of the Powder River Basin in Wyoming, where much of Asia's imports originate. Washington, however, has never charged companies more than one dollar and ten cents per ton of coal produced on these federal lands. Meanwhile, companies are selling the coal from federal land to nations like China for some twenty dollars a ton, compared to selling it for fourteen dollars a ton here. Upset by the differentials, Markey ordered an investigation by the Government Accountability Office into whether the government was collecting the required fair market value on its coal leases. And coal is just the start. Not only is the US taxpayer subsidizing Chinese coal, but China uses the coal to make steel, cement, paper, and other products that undercut US producers.

But the US coal industry's hopes may soon be dashed. China is busy following blueprints to construct fourteen hulking coal bases that in the name of the self-sufficiency and industrial efficiency championed by Deng Xiaoping will likely spell the end of coal imports. They are modeled, in part, after Shenhua's plant in Ordos. Five are for making liquid fuels, including gasoline for cars, synthetic natural gas, a wide range of chemicals, plus electricity to sate growing demand along China's populous eastern coast. The other nine bases are to mine coal for sixteen major adjoining coal-power production bases. Should all go right, 351,000 megawatts of power will be generated, equivalent to a third of the total US power-generating capacity today.

The forty billion dollar Shenhua project in Ningxia will span an area almost the size of sprawling Los Angeles when completed in 2020. There'll be mines, electricity stations, chemical-processing facilities, refinery towers, tanks, pipelines, power lines, heaters, smokestacks, rail tracks, and roads everywhere. Ningxia already has a plant to make methanol, a fuel additive, and another to make propylene, a chemical used in plastics. A liquid fuel conversion plant and other facilities are on the way. Building the base will necessitate the biggest cranes in the world to hoist components into place. Should Ningxia and all the other coal bases be fully built—and concerns about water scarcity may be the only thing standing in the way—they will span 11,438 square miles, an area larger than the state of Massachusetts. Ninety-eight separate coalfields with an estimated 690.8 billion tons of reserves will supply them. Greenpeace calculates the bases will constitute the single biggest new source of greenhouse gas emissions on Earth by 2020, pouring out 1.38 billion additional tons a year of greenhouse gas emissions. That alone will boost total world carbon emissions from fossil fuels by 4.2 percent from today's level. It will dwarf the impact of the Canadian Tar Sands and related Keystone XL Pipeline, emitting 3.2 times more carbon dioxide.

Then there's the growing coal base in Datong, in smog shrouded Shanxi Province. A recent *Fortune* profile of the complex by Richard Martin describes "miners masked in black grime" toiling in coal pits near a plethora of industrial plants that make power, chemicals, methanol to fuel cars, and even bricks from otherwise unusable mining waste. The area is blanketed in "fine black grit," Martin reports, in sharp contrast to the Datong Coal Mine Group's description of the operation. The company says it "beautifies the environment, clarifies the air, reduces pollution and…creates a clear, comfortable and beautiful working environment for the employees."

Today, China is well on the way to building out the coal bases, notes Chi-Jen Yang, research scientist at Duke University's Center on Global Change. The central government has so far approved nine plants to make synthetic natural gas out of coal on the various coal bases. Two are currently operating with the other seven now being built due to open over the next two years. Most are on the coal bases being built in Inner Mongolia and other areas to the west of China's big population centers near the coast. They will feed the gas to big cities, in hopes that substituting it for burning coal will cleanse the foul urban air. The research scientist believes that will just dig the world into a deeper hole on global warming. That's because the nine syngas plants alone will emit another half a billion tons of greenhouse gases a year themselves, boosting China's total carbon emissions by almost fourteen percent alone. Counting all the energy used to make the syngas out of coal, the product emits seven times as much greenhouse gas as conventional natural gas from a well. It pumps out up to eighty-two percent more than if you simply burned the coal to make electricity, according to a report by the Duke center. It doesn't stop there. Big Chinese energy companies are planning to build another thirty-one syngas production plants at the coal bases and other locations. If they're all built, it would boost China's contribution to melting ice caps, rising seas, and raging storms by almost a third alone, not to mention all the power-generating and liquid fuel- and chemical-making plants being built at the sprawling coal bases. The only development so far that may derail many of the planned coal-to-gas plants is the 400 billion dollar natural gas supply deal China penned in spring of 2014 to purchase gas from Russian fossil fuel titan Gazprom. However, it's no clean air panacea. Energy analysts estimate that once a pipeline is completed in 2018 to move the gas from Siberia to the People's Republic it will only meet about ten percent of China's still growing energy needs.

Keystone may have US and Canadian environmentalists hopping mad, but there's hardly been a whimper on the world stage about China's ambitions. Greenpeace has mustered the only significant effort. Breaking what Deng calls China's coal addiction, the heroin of fossil fuels, requires pick axing at the nature of Chinese culture—its authoritarian governing system, its deeply seated values of communitarianism, self-sufficiency, and hierarchal social order handed down by a lineage from the days of Confucius, and Emperor Qin, and then rejuvenated by Mao and Deng Xiaoping. In this milieu, the work of developing reasoned, scientific arguments and advocating them to influence policy is tolerated by the central government in Beijing, but ignored if at cross purposes with an established plan adopted by the self-preserving power structure. Inside Inner Mongolia, meanwhile, people at the local and provincial level are supposed to go along in the spirit of the greater public good. Dissension over tapping all that coal, a.k.a. "money in the ground," is not tolerated, Greenpeace's Deng observes. Protests are carefully controlled, threatening as they do vested interests of the rich and connected.

Fortunes have sprouted in China from the black mineral. Inspect the spoils. One major coal boss, the Liansheng Group's chairman Xing Libing, threw a seventy million dollar wedding for his daughter in Shanxi Province, the coal belt's heart. Chinese celebrities performed at the gala, for which Xing rented the local Ritz Carlton, Marriott, and Hilton hotels to house wedding guests he flew in on three chartered jets. The bride's dowry? Six Ferraris lined up outside the Ritz. Xing became fabulously wealthy by purchasing a state-owned coal mine for what the Chinese refer to as the "price of cabbage." Documents unturned by a Chinese investment advisor revealed that he bought a mine with 1.5 billion tons of coal at a cost of six cents a ton, turning him into an overnight sensation worth more than 1.6 billion dollars. In contrast, in the US members of Congress complain about US companies getting coal for one dollar and ten cents a ton.

You didn't need to attend the wedding to appreciate what was happening. Coal companies occupying the top rung of China's elite are now busy working with the government to evict Inner Mongolians from their lands to make the utmost use of the mineral and boost profits. When they do so, they don't have to trifle with what Americans call "due process," observes Barbara Freese, a US attorney and author of the book *Coal: A Human History*. Already, the line has been drawn. Mess with the blueprint and people will get hurt. Mongolia is a vast grassland area that lies inland from the Pacific Ocean and on the north side of China. Part of it, known as Inner Mongolia, is controlled by China and part is an autonomous nation, known as Mongolia, which lies further north. It's traditionally been home to nomadic herders, who have been at odds with sedentary Chinese farmers since before the days when Ghenghis Khan's son Kublai in the 1200s successfully invaded China and set up the Yuan Dynasty to rule over it. Emperor Qin, before then, built the Great Wall to protect against the Mongols. Not surprisingly, enmity continues to characterize the relationship between the two peoples.

Today, Mongolian activists opposing forcible eviction of herders from their native territory to exploit the black gold can attest to Chinese repression. They've suffered iron-knuckle treatment: beatings, murders, mass arrests, harsh prison sentences, and Internet censorship. While longstanding cultural and ethnic conflicts underlie the violence, in recent years government grabs of land then sold off to the energy companies are increasingly sparking protests and standoffs, according to Enghebatu Togochog, Southern Mongolia Human Rights Information Center director.

The touchstone incident involved bloody tire treads. In May 2011, the driver of a coal-truck ran over a Mongolian herder named Mergen as he tried to protect his grazing land from coal miners. His death ignited major protests that local police had to quell. Later in 2011, the coal truck driver was convicted of murder and executed, but only after another Mongolian herder, Zorigt, was similarly killed by an oil transport truck while defending grazing lands for his animals. Something extraordinary occurred afterward. People sympathetic with those who drew their last breath as they resisted being booted from ancient family land for the sake of modern coal rights and other Chinese aims decided they, like the man in the Huaxi revolt, could take it no longer. They had to take a stand.

In March 2013, they tried boarding a train to the capital to demonstrate against the expulsions at a meeting of the National People's Congress. It was at this gathering that China's congress selected Xi Jinping as the nation's new president. A hooting, large-scale protest would have embarrassed the new leader whose installation the world press was covering. So, the Mongolian protesters were detained before the train left the station. They were driven home, but only after police beat a group of them. Some were fighting expansion of a military training camp. Others wanted to halt evictions making way for the Yi Cheng Coal Mining Company. Everybody wanted the dead herders to be remembered heroically. A day later, a Chinese blogger who wrote about the incident, Yu Guofu, was threatened with arrest for being "antirevolutionary." His Internet posts were mysteriously taken down.

The soul of the People's Republic had spoken. Coal was thicker than blood. That August something even grislier occurred—and it was captured on film. Workers for the state-owned Railway Bureau No. 23 brutally beat to death a fifty-eight-year-old Mongolian herdsman named Bayanbaatar. He and others had been protesting construction of a road for trucks to haul coal to a rail spur, according to the Southern Mongolian Human Rights group. The railway laborers, one of them in a Polo shirt with the stub of a cigarette in his mouth, were angry. Just before Bayanbaatar died, they'd pounded other herders after threatening to fatally stab them. Bayanbaatar's son was badly injured in the confrontation to protect grazing lands for herders' animals

Tellingly, police did not arrest any of the attackers, even though they were caught in the act of beating people on film. They detained Bayanbaatar's family in a funeral parlor until a central government representative from Beijing arrived to negotiate a settlement. The agent offered 82,000 dollars to the family, which they initially refused. Justice was what they desired. Eventually, though, the family acquiesced after it was evident authorities would not charge the perpetrators.

The US State Department raised the topic of China's treatment of Mongolians at its annual Human Rights Dialogue meeting in 2013. It also asked about an activist imprisoned since 1995. "We highlighted some of the various ways in which Chinese citizens are speaking out more about their expectations of their government with respect to corruption, environmental degradation, worker and consumer safety, lack of rule of law, religious freedom, and other aspects of government policy," Uzra Zeya, an acting Assistant Secretary of State, told the press. But he refused to share China's reaction. Togochog was not hesitant about it, however, confiding that he learned from State Department officials that their Chinese counterparts responded with utter simplicity: the country had population pressures that required more resources. They compared the treatment of Mongolians to the way the US in the late eighteen-hundreds behaved in its own push for resources during westward expansion. The US Calvary slaughtered Native Americans or forced them onto reservations. "You did it," Togochog said the Chinese reportedly told the State Department. "Now, we're doing it." Bottom line: the Chinese suits reacted as they did with the Embassy's Twitter feed. Americans, they believed, should bug out of their internal affairs.

While thick-skin sorts might dismiss the suppression of the Mongolian herders as the heavy-handed work of cowboy-like local and provincial authorities similar to police brutality in the American South during the sixties civil rights storm, the buck doesn't stop there. It winds back to the Politburo in the Great Hall of the People. It's evident the central government is dealing with itself. Shenhua, which is at the heart of China's efforts to maximize the role of coal, is wholly owned by the People's Republic of China. The central government is really its board of directors. Shenhua acknowledges its entwinement, stating that its mission since 1995 has been to serve as "a backbone state-owned enterprise" under Beijing's thumb, with "coal as its foundation" to assist power-making, ports, rail, shipping, fuel conversions, and such. Shenhua's description of itself as "the largest and most advanced coal enterprise of China and the largest coal distributor of the world" is no self-worshipping gibberish. *Fortune* ranks it at 234 in its Fortune-500 index of the world's largest companies. In 2012, it produced 460 million tons of coal from its sixty-two mines. The company also owns the Ordos and Ningxia coal complexes, twenty-one subsidiaries, power plants with more than 63,000 megawatts of generating capacity, rail lines, ports, and eleven ships. It employs 211,500 people, dwarfing China's environmental protection workforce.

But the giant corporation displayed at least some scruples. After Greenpeace exposed the company's depletion of the water table in Ordos, and that it continues to contaminate what's left, the Shenhua began recycling some of the water the hulking coal project uses in Inner Mongolia and treating what it disposes of. Greenpeace found that even with these steps, water use will increase almost three times by the end of the decade as the plant is fully expanded. More hopeful, though also of questionable effectiveness, is that China's Ministry of Water Resources late in 2013 decided to assess the impacts of the coal bases on water supplies and limit their size if need be. It showed that the central government realizes the huge fossil energy projects threaten to use too much water and may need to be smaller than planned.

For researchers at the Lawrence Berkeley Laboratory the conclusion is obvious. "China has been, is, and will continue to be a coal-powered economy." The nation's coal supply, they note, holds more energy than Middle Eastern oil reserves. The world needs to watch it. China's headlong push to develop the coal bases resembles in some ways its construction of the Great Wall, an attempt to shield itself from outside marauders and events that could disrupt its social order. But when you tote up the global warming effect, maybe it's the world that should be building fences around what China wants to dig up.

EPILOGUE:

LOOKING FOR CONFUCIUS

THE TWENTY-FIRST CENTURY IS ticking down on the International Space Station, and maybe for the Earth's fate, too. Inside, astronauts squinting at civilization below are mortified at the fumy bedlam staring back at them. After a handful of orbits, the on-board antidepressants start going faster than the smuggled chocolate. Without experiments to distract them from flipping out about loved ones they can't always reach, it'd be a capsule of madness up here.

Onboard cameras zoom in to record ecological turmoil pole-to-pole. Rising sea levels swamping the coasts of Southern Asia and Pacific Island nations have created bulging columns of refugees—tens of millions in all—shambling inland bearing everything they can carry. Squalid tent camps overseen by the UN and relief groups teem with infectious diseases and ethnic-religious tensions that crackle like Baghdad in 2005. On Mainland China, an ascendant middle class that had cozied up to air conditioners and gas-guzzlers is earning blowback for adopting that western lifestyle. Monstrous fumes burped by myriad coal power plants rain perfidious fine particulates on urbanites. Residual banks of ozone and mercury flutter on winds toward North America, where they constantly trip cell phone alerts. Washington, and Beijing frequently aren't speaking over who's to blame.

Old and young alike sick with heat stroke, asthma, lung cancer, and heart disease pour into emergency rooms on both sides of the Pacific, straining even the biggest wards when the grey blanket stews for weeks on end or temperatures crack triple digits. (And here Americans circa 2014 reckoned they'd largely exterminated air pollution.) Of course, the US has to multitask. It's also grappling with climatic diaspora, relocating hundreds of thousands from Midwestern "Tornado Alleys" after the umpteenth high fatality twister. Don't ask Asia to weep. In Inner Mongolia, otherworldly-sized coal-bases the government believed was the answer to its problems have drained aquifers, wringing tawny rangeland into bone-dry desert. Herders ancestrally tied there have been bused to Chinese cities, welfare-dependent and under the paranoid eye of a Communist leadership that deep inside frets that a regime change is already underway. How could it not be? With near-daily "peasant" uprisings against toxic air, weary riot police are champing for raises (if they haven't already switched sides).

To the west, Africa is getting drilled. Sweltering temperatures aggravating food and water shortages have wilted crops in the fields, felled beasts of burden, and pretty much guaranteed hundreds more years of continental misery. Over Mexico, the astronauts in our hopefully fictional doomsday gulp at corkscrewing fires lit by starving masses looting towns. People of developed nations don't feel so first world anymore. Millions of chronically poor hang on monthly dilemmas whether to pay rent or gouging electricity bills as they try to keep from melting in unremitting heat. A devilish, pollution weather pattern dubbed the "urban heat-island effect" can make the outdoors an unbearable sauna. Showers now are basically an egg-timer experience; desalination and conservation can only reverse droughts so much.

Then there's Mother Nature's dethawed freezer atop the world. The Space Station's infrared trackers record methane clouds rising up from the desiccating tundra in Alaska, Canada, Russia, and Scandinavia. Greenland's glacial cover is mostly slush. Some former political elites and one-percenters have had to seal themselves into high-security, barbed wired compounds. Even so, it's impossible for them to fully escape the mega bandwidths of *how-could-you-have-let-this-happen*?

Just when the astronauts want to tug down the shades, something T-bones the Space Station. Houston can't help them; a downed electricity grid severed communications days ago. The well-trained crew doesn't panic. A fist-sized asteroid or piece of space junk might've struck them. When the astronauts take to the windows, they see they were mistaken about what collided with them. It's a world of better angels granting a planetary second chance.

Reflections from millions of solar panels glinting from the American West, former oil tyrannies of the Middle East, and China's hinterlands bathe them in golden light. Forests of wind-farms on gusty ridgelines in Europe, Latin America, and Asia spin their turbines beneath. City-dwellers asked to sacrifice for future generations have accepted the small-is-beautiful homily Jerry Brown used to preach. They've moved into denser quarters where natural gas buses and solar-powered trains serve them. Greenbelts lie where pavement once did. Fresh fruit and vegetables are no longer diesel-trucked into supermarkets. Urban farmers harvest them at the edge of town.

With traffic jams the exception and work-at-home common, the Space Station team draws straws to book window time. It might not be the Aurora Borealis, but the white incandescence from super energy-efficient LED lights that years ago replaced the orange-greenish glow of billions of energy-hog bulbs is mesmerizing to watch. A confirmation of survival deserved!

Nobody saw it coming, but leaders of the biggest countries had disassembled the status quo. They'd done it by dusting off the environmental Global Marshall Plan that Al Gore devised in the early nineties on the cusp of China's doubled-edged economic revival—the one that threw climate changes into overdrive, turned exported smog into a serial killer of millions per year, and knee-capped American manufacturing. They also rediscovered the wisdom of Confucius, driven into hiding by Mao's Red Guards during the Cultural Revolution but hardly extinguished. Today, a new flock in China is rediscovering what the ancient philosopher's early followers described as the true nature of their country and world, which under the legacy of the great master is seen as a rich heritage merely entrusted to the present generation by those yet to be born.

Inspired by these ideas, President Obama and President Xi had checked off the impossible. After a breezy 2013 meeting in Palm Springs, where Hollywood celebrities once fled to escape Los Angeles' smog, they followed up with an agreement to dramatically slash hydrofluorocarbons, a stepchild greenhouse gas. Sometime later they quarterbacked arguably the most important document since parchment was invented. Not wanting to be left out, the European Union, Russia, India, and Brazil signed on too. As polarizing as any war or civil right, especially to those dependent on the fossil fuel economy, revolutionizing the way humanity extracts the energy it requires had to be refashioned—and refashioned at the speedy clip that the US and Soviets once brought to the Space Race. History books tout the landmark agreements as the day the Earth refused to stand still. Our astronauts can't wait to land.

■

WE CAN SENSE THE eye rolls, the tongue clucking, and we don't blame you. The clashing futures presented herein echo strains of fanatical environmentalism meant to scare, if not quixotic delusion of Disney-esque vapidity. Here's the bloodcurdling reality, however. The dire scene that made the astronauts itchy for Prozac *was* grounded in science. The forecast we tried humanizing was compiled by a growing number of authoritative organizations, most notably the Nobel Prize-winning Intergovernmental Panel on Climate Change. Thousands of university professors in different fields worldwide who comprise the group have devoted their careers to fighting off global warming before it becomes a five-alarm fire. Had we all treated Earth like the fragile "spaceship" it is—recall the luminous blue orb the first genuine astronauts photographed—neither smog nor torrid climate change would be in our faces.

Southern California's bruising experience with an atmosphere unable to absorb the chemical uplift sealed our dependence on advancing technology so we could retain our car keys. All hail the catalytic converter! Spared from retooling how we lived, nobody should be surprised it's now Asia's turn in the smog chamber. The regulatory latticework and brink-pushing engineering that largely defanged the beast in America was shunted aside by multinational manufacturing. Ecologically, how did that work out? Wall Street and free trade enthusiasts watching a permanent fumebank encamp over the Far East still hummed about a New World Order where "isms" were out and opportunity was in. But maybe it was the political order most at fault, the one married to dead-end models promoting consumption as economic medication. Karma, like the atmosphere, never forgets.

Air pollution as the Grim Reaper, consequently, is back on the prowl when it should be scribbling out its will. During the twentieth century, smog killed between 25 million to 40 million people. Unless cheap rhetoric hardens into sincere action on smog alone, the People's Republic by itself stands to lose an estimated 120 million (roughly Japan's population) in this grand, new millennium, by one estimate. Being glass-half-full types, we'd like to sing what Freddie Mercury of the rock group Queen once belted out: "It's late but not too late." We'd love to accept Beijing's declared frontal attack on noxious air after 2013's wicked conditions as a transcendent moment.

But we can't lie.

Think of the world as a proverbial frog that hops into a pan of water set to boil. In his first minutes in the cauldron, our little amphibian friend, all pleasantly warm, can't believe his luck. Once the bubbling starts, it's too late for Mr. Rippet to return to his lily pad in a do-over. That could well be us today. Preeminent scientists who've spent decades analyzing how the world's carbon-centric economy has roiled traditional weather patterns recommend not betting the house that we'll reset them. In fact, there's only a two-out-of-three chance at preventing Earth's average temperature from rising by two degrees centigrade from preindustrial times— the fail-safe transom—if future worldwide annual emissions of carbon don't stay under 275 billion tons, the Climate Panel's 2013 draft assessment confirms. An impossible goal? Probably. Unless China quits pursuing business-as-usual and goes green by slowing its red-hot GDP, adapting a litany of energy reforms sure to incense entrenched interests, and requiring that a quarter of its cars are emissions-free electric models, the People's Republic by itself come 2050 will billow almost half that tonnage. The other essential step to uncock the climatological gun at our head is just as unlikely. The rest of the world must by then cease burning fossil fuel entirely, making gasoline practically a banned substance, like heroin or jumbo-sized sodas.

So what do we do? With no panacea imminent in either geo-engineering or suddenly inexhaustible energy like nuclear fusion, our destiny greatly rides not just on tapping into civilization's marvelous capacity for adaptation but also on limiting the gargantuan damage with a certain persuasion campaign. The needle must point eastward, too. China has to largely break up with coal, from which it extracts seventy percent of its energy needs, and transform how it electrifies the needs of an expectant citizenry. Doing so would start bending the arc of calamity back in our favor. But the nation's longtime union with the rock that entranced Marco Polo will probably drag on if party elders sign off on construction of fourteen immense bases to transmute coal into liquid fuels, synthetic natural gas, fertilizers, chemicals, and electricity at unparalleled levels. Whether the Politburo has the spine to turn away from the mineral still so plentiful and cheap in a dramatic way is the gazillion-dollar question. "There's no scenario we can conceive of that's rational where coal gets backed out," explains David Fridley, a Lawrence Berkeley Laboratory scientist who's been studying Chinese fuels for more than thirty years. "Coal is the foundation of their energy system."

History made it happen. The Opium Wars, occupations, and foreign exploitation that China suffered reinforced the wisdom of its quest for self-sufficiency. By snapping itself closed like a wounded oyster, environmental movements that swept through the industrialized West found little entryway into Mao's homeland. For decades, natural gas techniques, nuclear power plants, energy efficiency, and new ways of thinking bypassed the country like a missed bullet train. Over time, China realized it could enjoy the last laugh by inverting its former adversaries into dependents. You know the rest. We got affordable merchandise camouflaging an eroding standard of living. They got smog, toxins and heavy metals that galvanized thousands of snarling protests. The tables have flipped 180 degrees from the days of gunboat diplomacy that preceded Macartney's trade-mission debacle to Emperor Qianlong. Now Asia's tiger is threatening to ride those coal bases to further "greatness" that's not good for humanity hoping to make it to the year 2100.

Here's what your humble pollution sociologists would suggest, not that anyone asked. It's simple. President Xi needs to make eco-restoration as much his legacy as ridding the party of the endemic graft he so loathes. It's like destiny has been tapping its watch expecting him. Xi espouses a kind of Marxist-libertarianism, speaking dreamily of transferring power to the people when government stumbles. He might be Asia's Bill Clinton, what with that infectious smile and razor mind, a dislike of jargon, and a lanky, "portly" frame. Chew on his personal narrative as a potential game-changer. He studied chemical engineering, had a persecuted father, was party boss in pollution-decked Hebei, and married a famous folk singer that could engender quite the green following.

We realize the odds are stacked against him. Los Angeles can appreciate how much perspiration victory demands. Mickey Kantor, Clinton's ex-WTO trade negotiator, conjures memories about it whenever he sets down in opaque Beijing. His reaction: "Oh my God! This is a disaster. [Conversely], forty years ago in LA it was bad. Some thought [a cleanup] couldn't be done. But there was a commitment and drive. Momentum builds on itself. It pervades a society."

Chinese uninspired by California might find a more contemporary precedent for system change from an old hammer-and-sickle benefactor. You know, the land of Vladimir Putin today.

In late April 1986, a routine test at a candy-striped nuclear-power plant in the marshy Ukraine went awry. One of four reactors there—all designed without concrete containment shells—overheated, melting it down to the core. Explosions rocked Chernobyl with such seismic violence that it blew through the reactor's thin roof and into the sky a stream of radioactive gases, pulverized fuel rods, and graphite specks. An atomic fire smoldered for ten days. Hearing few details, the world was unsure what had happened. As flawed as the plant's design, the government's handling of it was worse, as winds lofted those particles hundreds of miles over populated Europe. Firefighters and helicopter pilots wore atrocious protective gear or none at all. Three days lapsed before the first evacuation. The Kremlin downplayed the burning wreckage to the media, yet inside the

Kremlin the symbolism wasn't lost. "The great glowing crater at Block 4," one observer quipped, "had revealed deep cracks in the state."

Mikhail Gorbachev, the Soviet's newly appointed general secretary, had only been the nation's majordomo for thirteen months when Chernobyl erupted. In those tumultuous first days, he was terrifically indecisive. So, the obscure agricultural economist with a Rorschach-like, purple birthmark on his round forehead took a step back before he took over. In the process, he appreciated what the "glowing crater" meant. Russia's political apparatus itself was so rotted out that it was near collapse. On July 3rd, when Gorbachev berated the country's nuclear industry, he might've been berating the entire Iron Curtain culture. "For thirty years you've been telling us that everything was safe. And you expected us to take it as the word of God." Where yes-men saw order, Gorbachev discerned a system "plagued by servility, bootlicking, window-dressing...persecution of critics, boasting, favoritism, and clannish management. Chernobyl happened and nobody was ready." Gorbachev could not stop dwelling on another existential question: if an atomic-energy accident like this could cause such destruction, imagine the annihilation of a nuclear exchange? In the aftermath, he was a changed man, accelerating his *perestroika* and *glasnost* campaigns and allowing the Soviet empire to dissolve. A few years later, in the unlikeliest of pairings, he and US President Ronald Reagan, the former B-list actor and General Electric spokesman, agreed to massive nuclear arms reductions that may have spared the world apocalypse.

Could Xi stand before his colleagues to deliver a fire-breathing speech like Gorbachev's, proclaiming that environmental restoration cannot wait for economic maturation? Might he intone his people to lead the virtuous path as taught by China's transcendent philosopher, Confucius? Or, will chaos force his hand after a million-person march in Tiananmen Square that tanks can't roll back? Or a toxic-air calamity that makes everyone forget the "great smog" of London in 1952? Or even an oil-well blowout that can't be stopped in a wintry, deep freeze? A Chinese initiative with hard, transparent targets to wean the nation off coal and usher in a worldwide Clean Air-Greenhouse Gas reduction protocol, Xi might thunder, could be the People's Republic's latest and greatest gift to mankind—its new dynasty. Here's what he might say: "When we rise, we will experience an epiphany as we discover this crisis is not really about politics at all. It is a moral and spiritual challenge. At stake is the survival of our civilization and the habitability of the earth. Or, as one eminent scientist put it, the pending question is whether the combination of an opposable thumb and a neocortex is a viable combination on this planet." If a Chinese president borrowed such impassioned rhetoric, he'd have to get the permission from its author: Al Gore, politician, visionary, businessman, and eco-mortal.

Until then, we've been to China and back. We've seen the growing fumebank of toxins aloft, swirling in the winds around the planet. We've witnessed the rising tides while leaders ignore the signs, too preoccupied counting votes and riches on both sides of the Pacific. To escape being boiled alive, we believe the people must figuratively rise, just like the slaves who sacked the Emperor Qin's tomb to dissolve his evil empire by smashing his Terracotta Army and seizing their chrome polished swords on the way out.

For it seems in the arc of history there are times when only dissolution offers hope.

REFERENCES

PREFACE

"Air Pollution in China." Factsanddetails.com, last visited February 20, 2014.

Brill, Emily. "Is the Air Quality in Beijing Worse Than Ground Zero's After 9/11?" *The Atlantic*, September 11, 2013.

Jacobs, Andrew and Ian Johnson, "Pollution Killed 7 Million People Worldwide in 2012, Report Finds," *The New York Times*, March 26, 2014.

Osnos, Evan. "Your Cheap Sweater's Real Cost," *Chicago Tribune*, December 16, 2006.

Plumer, Brad. "Will China Ever Get Its Pollution Problem Under Control?" *The Washington Post—Wonkblog*, March 11, 2013.

Watts, Jonathon. "China's 'Cancer Villages' Reveal the Dark Side of Economic Boom," *The Guardian*, June 6, 2010.

York, Anthony. "China Pollution May Hold Silver Lining for California," *Los Angeles Times*, April 10, 2013.

CHAPTER 1

"Air Pollution in China." *The Encyclopedia of Earth*, May 13, 2008.

"Chinese Protestors Clash with Police Over Power Plant." *The Associated Press/The Guardian*, October 22, 2012.

"Clashes Trigger Lockdown." Radio Free Asia, October 22, 2012.

Falkenheim, Victor C. "Hainan," *Encyclopedia Britannica* online, September 25, 2013.

Foyster, Gary. "Linfen, China: Ancient City to Apocalypse—Linfen, China, Asia," Bootsnall.com, April 8, 2007.

"How Does Target Compare to K-Mart and Wal-Mart When It Comes to Selling American-made Products?" *Manufacture This* blog, AmericanManufacturing. org, June 7, 2011.

Larsen, Janet. "Cancer Now Leading Cause of Death in China," Report, Earth Policy Institute, May 25, 2011.

Lim, Louisa. "Air Pollution Grows in Tandem with China's Economy," NPR, May 17, 2007.

"Protesters Beaten, Tear-gassed." Radio Free Asia, April 13, 2013.

Sidhu, Nancy D., Kimberly Ritter and Ferdinando Guerra. *Manufacturing: Still a Force in Southern California*, Los Angeles County Economic Development Corporation, Kyser Center for Economic Research, 2011.

"Six of the Earth's Most Polluted Cities Are in Asia." AsiaNews.it, October 19, 2006.

"Toxic: Linfen, China." *VICE* television show, August 5, 2008.

Von Braun, Margrit. "Top Ten Most Polluted Areas in the World," The Socrates Award Lecture, Blacksmith Institute, 2006

Wan, William. "Chinese Villagers Clash with Police in Protests Over Environmental Issues," *The Washington Post*, October 22, 2012.

Wong, Edward. "On China's Hainan Island, the Boom Is Deafening," *The New York Times*, March 30, 2010.

CHAPTER 2

Coal Museum of China. Narrated Private Tour, August 28, 2013.

China-US Joint Statement. Issued in Shanghai, February 28, 1972.

Cressey, George Babcok. *China's Geographic Foundations*, McGraw-Hill Book Co., 1934.

Buck, Pearl S. *China As I See It*. The John Day Co., 1970.

Burner, David. *Herbert Hoover: A Public Life*, Alfred A. Knopf, 1979.

"Confucius Forest." Ministry of Culture, People's Republic of China, 2003

Fairbank, John King. *The United States and China* (Harvard University Press, 1979).

Freese, Barbara. *Coal: A Human History*, Perseus Publishing, 2003.

Heston, Robert. "The Macartney Mission a British Embassy to China in 1793," *Humanities 360,* January 12, 2012.

Hoover, Herbert. *The Memoirs of Herbert Hoover,* The MacMillan Co., 1951.

Hsieh, Chiao-min. *Atlas of China,* McGraw-Hill Book Co., 1973.

Kissinger, Henry A. *On China,* (Penguin, 2011).

Li, Tianchen. "Confucian Ethics and the Environment," *The Bulletin of the Centre for East-West Cultural and Economic Studies,* January 1, 2003.

Lubow, Arthur. "Terra Cotta Soldiers on the March," *Smithsonian Magazine,* July 2009.

"Nixon's China Game." *The American Experience,* WGBH TV, 1999.

Palmer, Martin. "Can Confucianism Save China's Environment?," *South China Morning Post,* August 6, 2013.

Polo, Marco. *The Adventures of Marco Polo,* The John Day Co., 1948.

Roberts, J.A.G. *A Concise History of China,* Harvard University Press, 1999.

Siven, Nathan. *The Contemporary Atlas of China,* Houghton Mifflin Co., 1988.

Tang, Louise Su. *Cantonese Yankee,* Oak Garden Press, 2010.

The Museum of Qin Terra Cotta Warriors and Horses. Guided Tour, August 26, 2013.

Wright, Tim. *Coal Mining in China's Economy and Society 1895-1937,* Cambridge University Press, 2003.

CHAPTER 3

Birkakos, Jim. Phone Interview.

Cressey, George Babcok. *China's Geographic Foundations.*

Dikotter, Frank. *Mao's Great Famine,* Walker & Co., 2010.

Economy, Elizabeth C. *The River Runs Black: The Environmental Challenge To China's Future,* (Cornell University Press, 2004 & 2010 editions).

Fairbank, John King. *The United States and China.*

"Health for the Masses: China's 'Barefoot Doctors." NPR, November 4, 2005.

Kissinger, Henry A. *On China.*

Mao, Tse-Tung. *Quotations from Chairman Mao Tse-Tung,* art-bin.com/art/omaotoc.html.

Mao, Tse-Tung. *Selected Readings from the Works of Mao Tse-Tung,* Fore Languages Press, 1967.

Mao, Tse-Tung and Lin, Piao. *Post-Revolutionary Writings,* Anchor Books, 1972.

Yuan-Li, Wu. *Economic Development and the Use of Energy Resources in Communist China,* Hoover Institution on War, Revolution and Peace, 1963.

Schwartz. Harry, *China,* Antheneum, 1965.

Shapiro, Judith. *Mao's War Against Nature,* (Cambridge University Press, 2001).

Bureau of the Census. *U.S. Vital Statistics,* 1957.

Zhou, Xun. *The Great Famine in China, 1958-1962: A Documentary History,* Yale University Press, 2012.

CHAPTER 4

"Brave New World: China in the Red." *Frontline,* PBS, 1995.

"Deng Xiaoping: A Legend Who Recast China." *CCTV,* A Vanguard Cinema Release, 2005.

"Deng Xiaoping: Man of the Year." *TIME,* Jan. 6, 1986.

Deng Xiaoping. *Speeches and Writings* (Pergamon Press, 1984).

Evans, Richard. *Deng Xiaoping and the Making for Modern China,* Penguin Books, 1995.

Lam, Willy Wo-Lap. *The Era of Jiang Zemin,* (Prentice Hall, 1999).

Fenby, Jonathan. *Tiger Head Snake Tails, China Today, How It Got There and Where It Is Heading,* (Overlook, 2012).

Vogel, Ezra F. and Joanne J. Myers. "Deng Xiaoping and the Transformation of China," Carnegie Council for Ethics in International Affairs, March 21, 2013.

Tyler, Patrick. "Deng Xiaoping: A Political Wizard Who Put China on the Capitalist Road," On This Day, *The New York Times,* February 20, 1997.

CHAPTER 5

Albright, Madeleine K. "Revoking MFN Would Rupture U.S.-China Relationship," Testimony of Secretary of State Madeline Albright Before the U.S. Senate Committee on Finance, July 9, 1998.

Baucus, Max. "Statement of Senator Max Baucus on MFN for China," *Congressional Record,* May 18, 1994.

"Biography: Hillary Rodham Clinton." *The American Experience,* WGBH TV.

Buchanan, Pat. "Pat Buchanan on Free Trade," On The Issues, 2013.

"CARMA: Carbon Monitoring for Action." The Center for Global Development, 2014.

"China GDP." Trading Economics, 2013.

"China Most-Favored Nation (MFN) Status." Hearing Before the US Senate Committee on Finance, 1996.

Corsetti, Giancarlo, Paolo Peseti and Nouriel Roubini. "What Caused the Asian Currency and Financial Crisis?" Federal Reserve Bank of New York, April 1999.

"CO2 Emissions from Fossil Fuel Combustion: IEA Statistics." International Energy Agency, 2012.

Deng Xiaoping. *Speeches and Writings.*

"Ex-Im Bank Approves $792 Million in Sales to China." Export-Import Bank, Press Release, November 19, 1996.

Gephardt, Richard. "Fair Trade, Free People," *Vital Speeches of the Day,* May 27, 1997.

Gore, Al. *An Inconvenient Truth: The Planetary Emergency of Global Warming and What We Can Do About It,* Rodale Books, 2006.

Gore, Al. *Earth in the Balance: Ecology and the Human Spirit,* Houghton Mifflin Co., 1992.

Gore, Al. "Vice President Gore's Remarks at the U.S. China Environmental Forum, 1997," March 25, 2007, http://china.usc.edu/ShowArticle.aspx?articleID=534.

Hanley, Mary F. "A History of the President's Council on Environmental Quality During the Clinton Administration 1993-2001," The Clinton Administration History Project, Office of the President, 2000.

Hornblower, Sam. "Wal-Mart & China: A Joint Venture," *Frontline,* WGBH TV, November 23, 2004, .

Kantor, Mickey. Interview in downtown Los Angeles, January 22, 2014.

Knowlton, Brian. "Clinton Gives Strong Push to Admitting China to WTO," *The New York Times,* April 8, 1999.

Lam, Will Wo-Lap. *The Era of Jian Zemin.*

McMenomy, Chris D. "Clinton and the Process to Pass NAFTA: Making Sausage," National Defense University, Naval War College, 2002.

Miller, Emily. "Wal-Mart in Washington," *Frontline*, WGBH TV, Nov. 16, 2004.

Pregelj, Vladimir N. "Most-Favored-Nation Status of the People's Republic of China," *Congressional Research Service*, December 6, 1996.

"President Elect Bill Clinton Briefing." Clinton Presidential Library, 1992.

Rich, Bruce. *Foreclosing the Future*, Environmental Defense Fund, 2009.

"S 2467, GATT Implementing Legislation." Hearing Before the US Senate Committee on Commerce, Science, and Transportation, 1994.

Shapiro, Ira. "Testimony of U.S. Trade Representative General Counsel Ira Shapiro to the U.S. Senate Environment & Public Works Committee," 1994.

"The President's News Conference, March 29, 2000." The American Presidency Project at the University of California at Santa Barbara, http://presidency. ucsb.edu/ws/?pid=58305.

Warren, Elizabeth. "The Middle Class on the Precipice," *Harvard Magazine*, January/February 2006.

CHAPTER 6

"A Road Map to Blue Skies: China's Atmospheric Pollution Source Positioning Report (Draft)." Institute of Public & Environmental Affairs, December 2011.

Andrews, Steven Q. "Seeing Through the Smog: Understanding the Limits of Chinese Air Pollution Reporting," Journal Report, Woodrow Wilson International Center for Scholars, China Environment Series, 2008-2009.

Economy, Elizabeth C. *The River Runs Black.*

Fenby, Jonathan. *Tiger Head Snake Tails.*

Kahn, Joseph. "World Trade Organization Admits China, Amid Doubts," *The New York Times*, November 11, 2001.

Monastersky R. "Asian Pollution Drifts Over North America," *Science News*, December 12, 1998.

Mong, Adrienne. "Bathed in Smog: Beijing's Pollution Could Cut 5 Years Off Lifespan, Expert Says," NBC News—*Behind the Wall*, February 24, 2012.

"Particulate Matter (PM)—Health." US Environmental Protection Agency March 18, 2013.

Shapiro, Judith. *China's Environmental Challenges,* (Polity, 2012).

Wilkinson, Lua. "China's Asthma Problem Is Bad—and Growing Worse," *The Atlantic*, June 26, 2013.

Wong, Li Anne. "China Ousts U.S. As World's No. 1 Goods Trader," NBC News, January 10, 2014.

Yardley, Jim. "Beijing's Olympic Quest: Turn Smoggy Sky Blue," *The New York Times*, December 29, 2007.

CHAPTER 7

Bodeen, Christopher. "In 'e-waste' Heartland, a Toxic China," *The New York Times*, November 18, 2007.

"China's 'Cancer Villages' Heavily Polluted." *Washington Times,* August 16, 2009.

"China's 'Cancer Villages' Pay Heavy Price for Economic Progress." *Agence France Presse*, May 9, 2006.

"Countries of the World." Worldatlas.com, http://www.worldatlas.com/aatlas/populations/ctypopls.htm.

Economy, Elizabeth C. *The River Runs Black.*

Fenby, Jonathan. *Tiger Head Snake Tails.*

Feng, Kuishuang, Steven J. Davis, Laixiang Sun, Xin Li, Dabo Guan, Weidong Liu, Zhu Liu and Klaus Hubacek. "Outsourcing CO2 within China," Journal Report, Proceedings of the National Academy of Sciences of the United States of America, November 19, 2012.

"Following the Trail of Toxic e-waste." *60 Minutes*, November 9, 2008.

Ford, Peter. "Deng Fei Goes Beyond Journalism to Right Wrongs in China." *The Christian Science Monitor*, February 6, 2012.

Griffiths, Dan. "China's 'Cancer Villages' Pay Price." BBC News, January 17, 2007.

Goodman, Michael, Joshua S. Naiman, Dina Goodman and Judy S. LaKind. "Cancer Clusters in the USA," United States National Institutes of Health, April 21, 2012.

"Cancer Now Leading Cause of Death in China," Earth Policy Institute.

Liu, Jianguo and Jared Diamond. "China's Environment in a Globalizing World," *Nature* magazine, June 30, 2005.

Liu, Lee. "Made in China: Cancer Villages," *Environment* magazine, March/April 2010.

Lyn, Tan Ee. "China's 'Cancer Villages' Bear Witness to Economic Boom," Reuters, September 16, 2009.

"Recycling of e-waste In China May Expose Mothers, Infants To High Dioxin Levels." *Science Daily*/American Chemical Society October 23, 2007.

"Residents Near Chinese e-waste Site Face Greater Cancer Risk." *Science Daily*/Oregon State University, January 23, 2013.

Sanger, David E., David Barboza and Nicole Perlroth. "Chinese Army Unit Is Seen Tried to Hacking Against U.S.," *The New York Times*, February 18, 2013.

"Surveillance, Epidemiology, and End Results Program; SEER Stat Fact Sheets: All Cancer Sites." National Cancer Institute.

Stevenson, Thomas. "The Dirty Secret Behind Shanghai's Bluer Skies," Tealeafnation.com, December 6, 2012.

Watts, Jonathan. "China's 'Cancer Villages' Reveal Dark Side of Economic Boom," *The Guardian*, June 6, 2010.

Wee, Sui-Lee. "China Cancer Village Tests Law Against Pollution," Reuters, January 16, 2012.

"When It Comes to E-Waste, Be Afraid—Be Very Afraid." *Yahoo! News*, February 27, 2013.

CHAPTER 8

"A Road Map to Blue Skies." Institute of Public & Environmental Affairs.

"Air Pollution in China." Factsanddetails.com.

Andrews, Steven Q. *Seeing Through the Smog*.

Beech, Hannah. "China Rising: Environment: They Export Pollution Too," *TIME*, June 19, 2005.

"Big Bang Measures to Fight Air Pollution, Special Report—China Strategy."
Deutsche Bank Asset & Wealth Management, February 28, 2013.

Bienkowski, Brian, "China's Babies at Risk from Soot, Smog," Environmental
Health News, April 17, 2014.

Bradsher, Keith and David Barboza. "Pollution From Chinese Coal Casts a Global
Shadow," *The New York Times,* June 11, 2006.

"Cancer Now Leading Cause of Death in China." Earth Policy Institute, 2011.

"Cost of Pollution in China: Economic Estimates of Physical Damage." The World Bank
and What is Now China's Ministry of Environmental Protection February, 2007.

Economy, Elizabeth C. *The River Runs Black.*

Fenby, Jonathan. *Tiger Head Snake Tails.*

Gollom, Mark. "China's Costly Pollution Problem," CBC News, July 5, 2012.

Gu, Wei. "Time for China to Look Beyond Deng's Big Ideas," Reuters, Opinion,
June 7, 2012.

Huang, Yanzhong, "The Sick Man of Asia," *Foreign Affairs,* November/December 2011.

Kahn, Joseph and Jim Yardley. "As China Roars, Pollution Reaches Deadly
Extremes," *The New York Times,* August 26, 2007.

Larson, Christina. "Air Pollution, Birth Defects, and the Risk in China (and
Beyond)," *Bloomberg Businessweek,* March 28, 2013.

McGregor, Richard. "750,000 a Year Killed By Chinese Pollution," *Financial Times,*
July 2, 2007.

McNeill, J.R. *Something New Under the Sun: An Environmental History of the
Twentieth Century,* (W.W. Norton & Company, 2001).

Platt, Kevin Holden. "Chinese Air Pollution Deadliest in World, Report Says,"
National Geographic News, July 9, 2007.

"Profile: Hu Jintao, President of People's Republic of China," Xinhua, March 15, 2003.

Szczepanski, Kallie. "Hu Jintao," About.com Asian History.

"Waiting to Inhale: The State of Air Pollution in South China." US Diplomatic
Cables, Wikileaks.org, August 16, 2006.

Watts, Jonathan. "WikiLeaks Reveals China's Failure to Measure Dangerous Pollution," *The Guardian*, August 26, 2011.

"The East is Grey: China and the Environment." *The Economist*, August 10, 2013.

Wong, Edward. "In China, Breathing Becomes a Childhood Risk," *The New York Times*, April 22, 2013.

Zhang, Junfeng (Jim), Denise L. Mauzerall, Tong Zhu, Song Liang, Majid Ezzati and Justin V. Remais. "Environmental Health in China: Progress Towards Clean Air and Safe Water," *The Lancet*, March 27, 2010.

CHAPTER 9

Hao, Tang. "Xiamen PX: a Turning Point?" Chinadialogue.net, Opinion, January 16, 2008.

Jacobs, Chip and William J. Kelly. *Smogtown: the Lung-Burning History of Pollution in Los Angeles*, (Overlook/Penguin, 2008).

Kahn, Joseph. "In China, a Lake's Champion Imperils Himself," *The New York Times*, October 14, 2007.

Laifang, Li. "Around China: Villagers Win Fight Helping Build a 'Beautiful China,'" Xinhua, December 23, 2012.

"Material Safety Data Sheet p-Xylene MSDS." (about paraxylene/PX) Sciencelab.com.

McNeill, J.R. *Something New Under the Sun*.

Shapiro, Judith. *China's Environmental Challenges*.

"Successful Pollution Protest Shows China Takes Careful Line with Rising Middle Class." Associated Press/Fox News, October 29, 2012.

"The East is Grey." *The Economist*.

"The Impact of the 2008 Olympic Games on Human Rights and the Rule of Law in China." Hearing Before the Congressional-Executive Commission on China, United States Congress, US Government Printing Office February 27, 2008.

"The Long Story About Huaxi/Huankantou." *Phoenix Weekly* (Hong Kong), Translated on site EastSouthWestNorth, June 1, 2005.

"The Warriors of Qiugang: a Chinese Village Fights Back." Documentary (filmmakers Ruby Yang and Thomas Lennon), *Environment360*/Yale University January 10, 2010.

Tianjie, Ma. "Environmental Mass Incidents in Rural China: Examining Large-Scale Unrest in Dongyang, Zhejiang," Journal Report, Woodrow Wilson International Center for Scholars, China Environment Series 2008-2009.

Watts, Jonathan. "A Bloody Revolt in a Tiny Village Challenges the Rulers of China," *The Guardian*, April 15, 2005.

CHAPTER 10

"A Road Map to Blue Skies." Institute of Public & Environmental Affairs.

Anderlini, Jamil. "Beijing Confronts Pollution Dilemma," *Financial Times*, January 14, 2013.

Andrews, Steven Q. "Beijing's Sky Blues," Opinion, *The Wall Street Journal*, January 9, 2008.

Andrews, Steven Q. *Seeing Through the Smog*.

"China: Olympic-Sized Growth in Carbon Emissions." Worldwatch Institute, 2013.

Falkenheim, Victor C. "Inner Mongolia (Autonomous Region, China)." *Encyclopedia Britannica* online, March 27, 2013.

Fenby, Jonathan. *Tiger Head Snake Tails*.

"Global Sources of Local Pollution: an Assessment of Long-Range Transport of Key Air Pollutants To and From the United States." Journal Report, The National Academy of Sciences 2009.

"Jiangsu Province of China." Jiangsu.net.

"Cancer Now Leading Cause of Death in China," Earth Policy Institute.

Liu, Jianguo and Jared Diamond. "China's Environment in a Globalizing World," *Nature*.

"Ranking Eastern Chinese Cities by Their 'Clean Air' Actions." Greenpeace East Asia May 25, 2012.

Rogoway, Mike. "Intel Finds Asian Pollution Makes Computers Sick, Too," *The Oregonian*, October 19, 2013.

"Shandong Province." *People's Daily* (English).

"The East is Grey." *The Economist*.

Wong, Edward. "Outlasting Dynasties, Now Emerging from Soot," *The New York Times*, May 17, 2014.

Yardley, Jim. "Consultant Questions Beijing's Claim of Cleaner Air," *The New York Times*, January 10, 2008.

CHAPTER 11

"A Road Map to Blue Skies." Institute of Public & Environmental Affairs.

"Amy Yoder Begley." Mini-Profile, *Runners World*.

Andrews, Steven Q. *Seeing Through the Smog.*

"Association Between Changes in Air Pollution Levels During the Beijing Olympics and Biomarkers of Inflammation and Thrombosis in Healthy Young Adults." Journal Report, *Journal of the American Medical Association*, May 16, 2012.

Beech, Hannah. "China Rising: Environment: They Export Pollution Too," *TIME*.

"Beijing Ready and Calm at 10-day Countdown." *China Daily*/Xinhua, July 30, 2008.

"Beijing Steel Giant Building New Plant." SmasHits.com/Xinhua, March 12, 2007.

Buckley, Chris. "Beijing Olympic Water Scheme Drains Parched Farmers," Reuters, January 22, 2008.

Cha, Ariana Eunjung. "In Cleanup Effort, Beijing Moved Factories to Clog Air Elsewhere," *The Washington Post*, August 7, 2008.

Cha, Ariana Eunjung. "Olympic Teams Prepare for the Dirty Air in Beijing," *The Washington Post,* January 24, 2008.

"China City Traffic Cops Given 43 Years to Live." Reuters, August 7, 2007.

Cook, Theresa. "Clinton Calls on Bush to Boycott Olympic Opening Ceremony," ABC News, April 8, 2008.

Davis, Bob. "Most of Beijing's Olympic Pollution Cleanup Evaporated a Year Later," *The Wall Street Journal* (originally posted on China Realtime), March 29, 2011.

Demick, Barbara. "China Plans to Halt Rain for Olympics," *Los Angeles Times,* January 31, 2008.

Demick, Barbara. "Olympians Air a Gripe about Beijing: Fearing the Pollution, Some May Wear Masks Or Skip the Games," *Los Angeles Times*, March 12, 2008.

"Environmental Group Recognizes Beijing's Efforts to Clean Up Air." Xinhua, July 28, 2008.

Fan, Maureen. "Acting Beijing Mayor Named As City Rushes to Prepare for '08 Olympics," *The Washington Post*, December 1, 2007.

Fenby, Jonathan. *Tiger Head Snake Tails.*

Guilford, Gwynn. "China Creates 55 Billion Tons of Artificial Rain a Year—and It Plans to Quintuple That," *Quartz*, October 22, 2013.

Heifetz, Aaron. Phone Interview.

"Independent Environmental Assessment: Beijing 2008 Olympic Games." United Nations Environment Programme. Report, February 2009.

Jaslow, Ryan. "Reducing Air Pollution During 2008 Beijing Olympics Boosted Residents' Heart Health, Research Reveals," CBS News, May 16, 2012.

Kent, Jo Ling. "China Tells Bush to Butt Out," ABC News, August 7, 2008.

Langewiesche, William. "Stealing Weather," *Vanity Fair*, May 2008.

Lovett, Rick. "China's Olympic Pollution Efforts Paid Off, Expert Says," *National Geographic News*, August 15, 2008.

Macur, Juliet. "Cyclists Say Apology Is Too Little, Too Late," *The New York Times*, September 15, 2008.

Madrigal, Alexis. "Beijing Leads in Race for Most Polluted Olympics," *Wired*, August 7, 2008.

Mone, Gregory. "Can China Clean up Its Act in Time for the Olympics?" *Popular Science*, June 28, 2007.

Pasternack, Alex. "Beijing's Olympic Pollution Solution: Luck + Data Manipulation," *Treehugger*, June 22, 2009.

Powell, Bill. "Bush's Olympic Diplomacy Plan," *TIME*, August 8, 2008.

Reiss, Spencer. "Smog and Mirrors: China's Plan for a Green Olympics," *Wired*, July 24, 2007.

Riding, Alan. "Olympics; 2000 Olympics Go to Sydney in Surprise Setback for China," *The New York Times*, September 24, 1993.

Shipley, Amy. "Olympic Officials Want to Clear the Air," *The Washington Post*, March 18, 2008.

Spotts, Peter N. "Study: China's Olympic Effort to Curb Smog Had Little Effect," *Christian Science Monitor*, June 23, 2009.

"The Impact of the 2008 Olympic Games on Human Rights and the Rule of Law in China." US Government Printing Office.

Trinidad, Alison. "Beijing Olympics Experiment Links Air Pollution Exposure, Cardiovascular Disease," USC News, May 15, 2012.

Ueberroth, Peter. Phone Interview.

Vecsey, George. "Cycling in a Fog Near the Great Wall," *The New York Times*, August 9, 2008.

Wade, Stephen. "Rain Out: China Aims to Control Olympics Weather," *USA Today*, February 29, 2008.

Watt, Louise. "China Pollution: Cars Cause Major Air Problems in Chinese Cities," Associated Press/*The Huffington Post*, January 31, 2013.

Yardley, Jim. "Beijing's Olympic Quest: Turn Smoggy Sky Blue," *The New York Times*.

Zencey, Eric. "China's Infinite Growth Haze," *The Daly News*/Center for the Advancement of the Steady State Economy, April 9, 2013.

CHAPTER 12

"A Road Map to Blue Skies." Institute of Public & Environmental Affairs.

Alcorn, Ted. "China's Skies: A Complex Recipe for Pollution with No Quick Fix," *The Lancet*, June 8, 2013.

Anderlini, Jamil. "Beijing Confronts Pollution Dilemma," *Financial Times*.

Barr, Michael and Joy Y Zhang. "China's Green Warriors," *Global Public Square*— blog, CNN, October 11, 2013.

Blanchard, Ben. "China Pollution Protest Ends, But Suspicion of Government High," Reuters, July 8, 2012.

Blanchard, Ben. "China Says Only It Has Right to Monitor Air Pollution," Reuters, June 5, 2012.

Buckley, Chris, "China Says Zhou Yongkang, Former Security Chief, Is Under Investigation," *The New York Times*, July 29, 2014.

"Cancer Now Leading Cause of Death in China." Earth Policy Institute.

"Celebrities Pressure China Over Pollution Gauge." AFP, November 8, 2011.

Censky, Annalyn. "How the Middle Class Became the Underclass," *CNN Money*, February 16, 2011.

Chen, Baizhu. "The Real Reason the U.S. Doesn't Make iPhones: We Wouldn't Want To," Opinion, *Forbes*, January 25, 2012.

"China Warns Against Further Pollution Protests." Associated Press/CBC News, July 23, 2012.

Chu, Ben. "Get Your Fiscal House in Order: China Warns U.S. As Asia Expresses Concern for $1.3 (trillion) of Investments," *The Independent*, October 8, 2013.

Demick, Barbara. "Bo Xilai's Wealth on Trial in China," *Los Angeles Times*, August 11, 2013.

Demick, Barbara. "U.S. Ambassador to China Gary Locke to Resign," *Los Angeles Times*, November 19, 2013.

Duhigg, Charles and David Barboza. "In China, Human Costs Are Built Into an iPad," *The New York Times*, January 25, 2012.

Duhigg, Charles and Keith Bradsher. "How the U.S. Lost Out on iPhone Work," *The New York Times*, January 21, 2012.

"Embassy Air Quality Tweets Said to 'Confuse' Chinese Public." US Diplomatic Cables Sent July 10, 2009, Wikileaks.org.

"Extreme Air Pollution Events in Beijing, China 2010 & 2013." Report Edited by David L. Alles, Western Washington University, April 24, 2013.

Fenby, Jonathan. *Tiger Head Snake Tails.*

Flanagan, Ed. "Chinese Mining Tycoon Liu Han Sentenced to Death for Running Gangs," NBC News, May 23, 2014

Forsythe, Michael, "As China's Leader Fights Graft, His Relatives Shed Assets," *The New York Times*, June 17, 2014

FlorCruz, Jaime A. "Beijing's New Year Surprise: PM 2.5 Readings," CNN, January 27, 2012.

Goldman, Adam. "CIA Hatched Plan to Make Demon Toy to Counter Osama Bin Laden's Influence," *The Washington Post*, June 19, 2014.

Guevara, Marina Walker, Gerard Ryle, Alexa Olesen, Mar Cabra, Michael Hudson and Christoph Giesen. "Leaked Records Reveal Offshore Holdings of China's Elite," The International Consortium of Investigative Journalists, January 21, 2014.

Irwin, Neil. "The Typical American Family Makes Less Than It Did In 1989," *The Washington Post*—Wonkblog, September 17, 2013.

Jacobs, Andrew. "Protests Over Chemical Plant Force Chinese Officials to Back Down," *The New York Times*, October 28, 2012.

Jacobs, Andrew. "The Privileges of China's Elite Include Purified Air," *The New York Times*, November 4, 2011.

Jacobs, Chip and Kelly. William J., *Smogtown*.

Jun, Ma. Interview with Ma Jun, executive director of the Institute of Public & Environmental Affairs in Beijing, August 30, 2013.

Kan, Michael. "Apple Suppliers Accused of Environmental Damage," IDG News Service/PCWorld, August 31, 2011.

Kaplan, Ken. "Will You Choose a Conflict-Free Microprocessor?" The Daily Beast, January 7, 2014.

Mong, Adrienne. "Beijing Residents Call Foul Over the Air," NBC News—*Behind the Wall* blog, November 9, 2011.

Larson, Christina. "Protests in China Get a Boost From Social Media," *Bloomberg Businessweek*," October 29, 2012.

"Lawmakers Furious Over China-Made Olympic Uniform." Associated Press/ ESPN, July 12, 2012.

"Netizen Voices: Clearing the Air." *China Digital Times*, June 6, 2012.

Olsen, Robert. "To Reduce Poverty And Pollution, China Needs More Billionaires Like This," *Forbes*, July 9, 2012.

The Other Side of Apple, IT Industry Investigative Report (Phase IV), Special Edition: Apple Inc. Report, Friends of Nature, Institute of Investigative & Environmental Affairs and Green Beagle, January 20, 2011.

The Other Side of Apple II, Pollution Spreads Through Apple's Supply Chain. Friends of Nature, Institute of Public & Environmental Affairs, Green Beagle, Envirofriends and Green Stone Environmental Network, Fall 2011.

Phillips, Tom. "Communist Party Congress: Inside the Chinese Village 'Shrouded in the Shadow of Cancer,'" *The Telegraph*, November 13, 2012.

"Primer on Short-Lived Climate Pollutants." Institute for Governance & Sustainable Development," Report, November 2012.

"Prodding China to Confront its Urban Air Pollution Problems." *The Washington Post*/The Partnership for Public Service, October 22, 2013.

Ramzy, Austin. "Twittering Bad Air Particles in Beijing, *TIME*, June 19, 2009.

Schmitz, Rob. "In China, the Polluter 'That-Must-Not-Be Named," *Marketplace*, July 15, 2014.

Sparkes, Matthew. "Apple Bans Two Dangerous Toxins Used in Your iPhone," The Telegraph, August. 14, 2014.

Shuang, Yan. "Masking the Pollution," *Global Times*, October 12, 2011.

Silva, Mark. "Al Gore is Romney-Rich," Bloomberg News—Political Capital blog, May 6, 2013.

Tatlow, Didi Kirsten, "How Climate Change Could Foil China's Smog-Fighting Efforts," *The New York Times*, July 3, 2014.

"Toxic Threads: Putting Pollution on Parade." Report, Greenpeace International, December 4, 2012.

Vincent, Roger and Julie Makinen. "Chinese Developer Buys Major Lot in Downtown L.A.," *Los Angeles Times*, January 31, 2014.

Wang, YueSi, Li Yao, LiLi Wang, ZiRui Liu, DongSheng Ji, GuiQian Tang, JunKe Zhang, Yang Sun, Bo Hu and JinYuan Xin. "Mechanism for the Formation of the January 2013 Heavy Haze Pollution Episode Over Central and Eastern China," Science China Earth Sciences/Springer Link, Report, January 2014.

Watt, Louise. "Chinese Group Launches App to Shame Heavily Polluting Companies in Step Toward Transparency," Associated Press, June 9, 2014.

Watt, Louise. "Hospital in Southwest China Opens Smog Clinic," Associated Press/ Yahoo! News, December 18, 2013.

Wee, Sui-Lee. "China Says Will Shut Plant As Thousands Protest," Reuters, August 14, 2011.

Wong, Gillian. "China Seeks to Stem Environmental Protests," Associated Press, November 12, 2012.

Woody, Todd. "How China Will Dominate the U.S. Electric-Bus Market," The Atlantic Cities, April 2014.

Zhang, Chi-Chi. "U.S. Embassy: Beijing Air Quality is 'Crazy Bad,'" Associated Press/*The Huffington Post,* November 19, 2010.

CHAPTER 13

"Air Pollution Linked to 500,000 Premature Deaths in China." ECNS.cn (official English-translated website of China New Service), January 7, 2014.

Anderlini, Jamil. "Beijing Confronts Pollution Dilemma," *Financial Times,* January 14, 2013.

"Around China: Villagers Win Fight Helping Build a 'Beautiful China.'" Xinhua/ China.org.cn, December 23, 2012.

Atkin, Emily. "As the Planet Warms, Scientists Say More People Will Go Without Food and Water," ThinkProgress, July 28, 2014.

"Beijing Air Akin to Living in Smoking Lounge: Chart of the Day." Bloomberg News, January 30, 2013.

"Beijing Air Quality Improves for 14th Consecutive Year." Xinhua, December 31, 2012.

"Big Bang Measures to Fight Air Pollution." Deutsche Bank Asset & Wealth Management.

Bishop, Bill. "Questions About China's Growth, Censorship and Air Pollution," *The New York Times*—Dealbook blog, January 14, 2013.

Bruno, Debra. "China Pollution: Airpocalypse and the Expat Parenting Dilemma," *Christian Science Monitor/Modern Parenthood,* January 17, 2013.

Buckley, Chris. "Novel Tactics for Dealing with Pollution," *The New York Times*—Sinosphere Blog, December 10, 2013.

Caldwell, Carla. "Report: Coke Paying Employees More to Work in China Due to Pollution," *Atlanta Business Chronicle*, July 10, 2014.

Cha, Frances and Hiufu Wong, "Chinese Residents Line Up for Bags of Fresh Mountain Air," CNN, April 3, 2014.

Chen, Stephen. "Agriculture Feels the Choke as China Smog Starts to Foster Disastrous Conditions," *South China Morning Post*, February 25, 2014.

"China Career Comes with Health Worries." Australian Associated Press/Yahoo! Finance, May 8, 2013.

"China's Smog Splits Expatriate Families As Companies Pay for Fresh Air," Bloomberg BusinessWeek, May 7, 2014.

"Chinese Man Seeks Divorce After Smog Drive Family Apart," Reuters, May 1, 2014.

"China Suffers Smoggiest March in 52 Years." Xinhua, April 2, 2013.

"China Tells Pilots to Improve Landing Skills to Deal with Beijing Smog." Reuters/Australia News Network, December 12, 2013.

"China to Release Real-Time Air Quality Data." Xinhua, December 28, 2012.

"China to Tackle Air Pollution." *United Press International*, January 15, 2013.

"Chinese Anger Over Pollution Becomes Main Cause of Social Unrest." Bloomberg News, March 6, 2013.

"Chinese Cities to Build "Wind Corridor" to Disperse Smog," Crienglish.com, May 19, 2004.

Davies, Paul J. "Hong Kong Fails on Pollution Targets," *Financial Times*, November 14, 2012.

Davison, Nicola. "China Loves Pork Too Much," *The Guardian*, March 23, 2013.

Davison, Nicola. "Rivers of Blood: the Dead Pigs Rotting in China's Water Supply," *The Guardian*, March 29, 2013.

Demick, Barbara. "China Entrepreneurs Cash in on Air Pollution," *Los Angeles Times*, February 2, 2013.

Demick, Barbara. "China Hit by Extreme Air Pollution," *Los Angeles Times*, January 13, 2013.

Demick, Barbara. "Lung cancer: A Cloud on China's Polluted Horizon," *Los Angeles Times*, December 24, 2013.

Demick, Barbara. "U.S. Ambassador to China Gary Locke to Resign," *Los Angeles Times*.

Denyer, Simon. "China's Rise and Asian Tensions Send U.S. Relations into a Downward Spiral," *The Washington Post*, July 7, 2014.

"The East is Grey." *The Economist*.

"The Economics of China's Pollution Problem." Knowledge @ Wharton blog, University of Pennsylvania, May 1, 2013.

"Environment: Act Now or Face Costly Consequences, Warns OECD." *The Newsroom*, The Organisation for Economic Co-Operation and Development, March 15, 2012.

Ernst, Sieren. "Media Coverage of Pollution in China and the U.S." *The Energy Collective*—blog post, June 8, 2013.

"Every Smog Cloud Has Six Silver Linings." *China Digital Times*, December 9, 2013.

"Extreme Air Pollution Events in Beijing, China 2010 & 2013." Western Washington University.

Flanagan, Ed. "Can China Really Stop 350 Million People from Smoking?" MSN News/NBC News, January 18, 2014.

Flanagan, Ed. "Sandstorm Pushes Beijing Pollution Levels off the Charts," NBC News—Behind the Wall blog, February 28, 2013.

Flora, Liz. "Dior Beauty Campaign Exploits China's Urban Pollution Numbers," Jingdaily.com, June 17, 2013.

Ford, Peter. "Beijing is Booming, But Talent is Leaving Due to Bad Air," *The Christian Science Monitor*, April 4, 2013.

Hsu, Jeremy. "Kite Flying Measures Air Pollution in China," *Mother Nature Network*, October 15, 2012.

Jacobs, Chip and William J. Kelly. *Smogtown*.

Jinran, Zheng. "Traffic Police Ask to Wear Face Masks," *China Daily USA*, January 31, 2013.

Kaiman, Jonathan. "China's Toxic Air Pollution Resembles Nuclear Winter, Say Scientists," *The Guardian*, February 25, 2014.

Kaiman, Jonathan. "Suck It and See: Dutch Artist's Vacuum Cleaner Could Clear China Smog," *The Guardian*, October 24, 2013.

Kan, Michael. "IBM Tries to Forecast and Control Beijing's Air Pollution," PC World, July 7, 2014.

Khan, Natasha, "Masses of Mercedes Thicken Hong Kong Air-Pollution Mess," Bloomberg Businessweek, April 15, 2014.

Li, Le. "China's State Media Finally Admits to Air Pollution Crisis," NBC News— *Behind the Wall* blog, January 15, 2013.

Luo, Chris. "Smog? It Bolsters Military Defence, Says Chinese Nationalist Newspaper," *South China Morning Post*, December 9, 2013.

MacLeod, Calum. "In China, Air Pollution Report Brings Despair, Humor," *USA Today*, July 9, 2013.

MacLeod, Calum. "Typhoon Batters Southeast China As Smog Chokes North," *USA Today*, October 6, 2013.

Makinen, Julie. "Artists Finding Inspiration in China's Bad Air," *Los Angeles Times*, May 7, 2014.

Masuda, Yoko. "New Japan-China Air Tensions: Smog," *The Wall Street Journal*— China Realtime, February 8, 2013.

Minter, Adam. "In China, Golf Has a New Hazard: Killer Smog," Bloomberg News, Opinion, October 6, 2013.

Mosbergen, Dominique. "Chen Guangbiao, Chinese Millionaire, Sells Canned Fresh Air To Combat Pollution," *The Huffington Post*, January 29, 2013.

Nye, James. "China Starts Televising the Sunrise on Giant TV Screens Because Beijing Is So Clouded in Smog," *The Daily Mail*, January 17, 2014.

O'Hanlon, Larry. "China's Urban Air Kills Rural Plants," *Discovery News*, January 18, 2013.

Park, Madison and Wei Yuan Men Min. "Report: More Chinese Cities Need to Come Clean on Air Pollution," CNN, October 25, 2012.

Pierson, David. "China's Smog Taints Economy, Health," *Los Angeles Times*, January 26, 2013.

Qian, Wang. "Ministry Calls Air Pollution Study 'Unconvincing,'" *China Daily*, July 10, 2013.

Riggs, Mike. "Intense Smog Is Making Beijing's Massive Surveillance Network Practically Useless," *The Atlantic*, November 5, 2013.

"Smoking, Air Pollution Major Health Threats in China." Xinhua, April 15, 2013.

Solon, Olivia. "Pollution-Detecting Kites to Monitor Beijing's Air Quality," *Wired*, July 23, 2012.

Stamp, Jimmy. "How to Survive China's Pollution Problem: Masks and Bubbles," *Smithsonian* magazine, February 26, 2013.

Sutter, John D. "China Needs Smog-Free Air in a Can," CNN, Opinion, March 1, 2013.

Tatlow, Didi Kirsten. "Gallows Humor, and Smog, Engulf China," *The New York Times*—IHT Rendezvous blog, January 29, 2013.

"Things May Be Bad, But at Least We Can't Chew Our Air." *The Daily Show with Jon Stewart*, January 24, 2013.

"The Top 10 Causes of Death." World Health Organization, last updated July 2013.

Thornhill, Ted. "Chinese to Spray Water 2,000 Feet Into the Air to Dispel Smog," *The Daily Mail*, May 8, 2014.

"Untrustworthy comment" appeared in story no longer public accessible. *China File*, July 16, 2013.

Wan, William. "China's Air Pollution Prompts Creative, Sometimes Wacky, Solutions," *The Washington Post,* January 25, 2014.

Wan, William. "Thousands of Dead Pigs Surfacing in Shanghai's Rivers," *The Washington Post*, March 13, 2013.

Wang, Jeanette. "Skyscraper Sprinkler System Seen As Way to Reduce China's Air Pollution," *South China Morning Post*, January 20, 2014.

Wong, Edward. "Air Pollution Linked to 1.2 Million Premature Deaths in China," *The New York Times*, April 1, 2013.

Wong, Edward. "As Pollution Worsens in China, Solutions Succumb to Infighting," *The New York Times*, March 21, 2013.

Wong, Edward. "Cost of Environmental Damage in China Growing Rapidly Amid Industrialization," *The New York Times*, March 29, 2013.

Wong, Edward. "In China, Breathing Becomes a Childhood Risk," *The New York Times*.

Wong, Edward. "Pollution Leads to Drop in Life Span in Northern China, Research Finds," *The New York Times*, July 8, 2013.

Wong, Edward. "Urbanites Flee China's Smog for Blue Skies," *The New York Times*, November 22, 2013.

Zhang, Junfeng (Jim), Denise L Mauzerall, Tong Zhu, Song Liang, Majid Ezzati and Justin V Remais. "Environmental Health in China," *The Lancet*.

CHAPTER 14

Andrews, Steven Q. Phone interview.

"Big Bang Measures to Fight Air Pollution." Deutsche Bank Asset & Wealth Management.

Bradsher, Keith. "Trucks at Heart of China's Diesel Problems," *The New York Times* December 8, 2007.

Chapman, Justin. Email Interview.

"Chinese Prefer Gas-Guzzling Vehicles?" *United Press International*, April 23, 2013.

Cliff, Steven. Phone Interview.

"Country Comparison—Oil—Consumption." CIA World Factbook/Indexmundi. com, January 1, 2012.

Eisenstein, Paul A. "China on Track to Become Globe's Top Luxury Car Market," NBC News—The Detroit Bureau, March 7, 2013.

Eisenstein, Paul A. "China to Limit Car Sales in Fight Against Air Pollution," NBC News—Business, July 11, 2013.

Eisenstein, Paul A. "With Help from Chinese Auto Plan, Volvo Hopes to Thrive," NBC News—Business, June 18, 2013.

Eells-Adams, Jesse, "China Leveling Mountains, Creating New Environmental Issues," *The Guardian*, June 6, 2014.

Fenby, Jonathan. *Tiger Head Snake Tails*.

Galuszka, Peter. "With China and India Ravenous for Energy, Coal's Future Seems Assured," *The New York Times*, November 12, 2012.

Gates, Sara. "China's 'Mountain-Moving Project' Near Lanzhou Aims To Flatten Territory For Development," *The Huffington Post*, December 7, 2012.

Hamlin, Kevin. "China's Soviet-Style Suburbia Risks Environmental Disaster," Bloomberg News, November 7, 2013.

Jacobs, Andrew and Ian Johnson, "Pollution Killed 7 Million People Worldwide in 2012, Report Finds," *The New York Times*.

Jin, Bruce. Personal meeting with Jin and tour of his factory, Ample International, Inc., in Changzhou, China, August 24, 2013.

Kennedy, Bruce. "China Breaks World Record for Car Sales in 2013," CBS News Moneywatch, January 31, 2014.

Langfitt, Frank. "China's Air Pollution: Is The Government Willing To Act?" NPR, May 24, 2013.

Liu, Lee. "Made in China: Cancer Villages," *Environment*.

Minter, Adam. "Chinese Drivers Pollute Without Guilt," Bloomberg News, January 13, 2014.

Rush, James. "Russian Passenger Arrested Trying to Smuggle Two Exotic Birds Out of China," *The Daily Mail*, June 9, 2014.

"Scary Statistic: China May Have 1 Billion Drivers," Bloomberg News, May 29, 2014.

Shen, Samuel and Kazunori Takada, "Global Auto Component Makes Gear Up for China's Tough Emission Rules," Reuters, June 8, 2014.

Spegele, Brian and Wayne Ma. "China Clean-Air Bid Faces Resistance," *The Wall Street Journal*, January 22, 2013.

Szczesny, Joseph. "China New GM's Biggest Market," NBC News—The Detroit Bureau, July 8, 2013.

Watt, Louise. "China Pollution: Cars Cause Major Air Problems in Chinese Cities," Associated Press/ *The Huffington Post*, January 31, 2013.

Watts, Jonathan. "China's Love Affair with the Car Shuns Green Vehicles," *The Guardian*, August 24, 2011.

Wolfe, Sarah. "These New Cars in China Have Filters So You Can Breathe Fresh Air While You Drive," Globalpost.com, May 7, 2014.

CHAPTER 15

Aden, Nate, James Bradbury and Forbes Tompkins. "Energy Efficiency in Manufacturing: The Case of Midwest Pulp and Paper Mills," World Resources Institute, 2013.

Asanova-Taylor, Saodat. "China Second Largest Source of Great Lakes Mercury Pollution," *Great Lakes Echo*, June 7, 2012.

"Asian Air Pollution Affecting World's Weather." *TAMUtimes*, Texas A&M University, January 21, 2014.

Barboza, Tony. "Climate Change Could Worsen Ozone Levels Across the U.S., Study Says," *Los Angeles Times*, May 6, 2014.

Beachy, Ben. Interview with Ben Beachy, Research Director for Public Citizen's Global Trade Watch, 2013.

Block, Ben. "Exports Account for One-Third of China's Emissions," World Resources Institute, 2013.

Bradsher, Keith and David Barboza. "Pollution From Chinese Coal Casts a Global Shadow." *The New York Times*.

Boxall, Bettina. "Sahara Desert Dust Affects California Water Supply, Study Finds," *Los Angeles Times*, February 28, 2013.

Edgar, Tricia. "Up In the Atmosphere: Mercury From the Sky," *Decoded Science*, December 20, 2011.

Chea, Terence. "Pollution from China Drifting East," Associated Press/ *Honolulu Advertiser*, July 30, 2006.

Dilbeck, Steve. "Frank McCourt Gets Offer: The Reds Are Coming?" *Los Angeles Times*—Dodgers Now blog, September 1, 2011.

"Global Mercury Assessment 2013." United Nations Environment Programme, January 2013.

"Global Sources of Local Pollution." The National Academy of Sciences.

Haley, Usha. "No Paper Tiger: Subsidies to China's Paper Industry From 2002-09," Economic Policy Institute, June 2010.

Haley, Usha. Interview, February 27, 2014.

Irwin, Neil. "The Typical American Family Makes Less Than It Did in 1989," *The Washington Post*—Wonkblog," September 17, 2013.

Jaffe, Dan. Phone Interview.

Kroll, Andy. "The Truth About Mike Daisey—and Walmart," *Mother Jones*, March 21, 2012.

Leslie, Jacques. "The Last Empire: China's Pollution Problem Goes Global," *Mother Jones*, December 10, 2007.

Logan, Tim. "Chinese Drive Surge in Foreign Home-Buying in U.S., Southern California, *Los Angeles Times*, July 8, 2014.

Martín, Hugo. "Chinese Tourists' Spending in the U.S. Takes Off," *Los Angeles Times*, May 24, 2013.

McLeod, Judi. "Made-in-China Massive Air Pollution Ignored by Global Warming Gurus Al Gore & Maurice Strong," *Canada Free Press*, July 27. 2007.

Minard, Anne. "Asia Pollution Changing World's Weather, Scientists Say," *National Geographic News*, March 6, 2007.

Mohan, Geoffrey. "Mercury Fingerprint of Pacific Fish Points to Asia Coal Power Plants," *Los Angeles Times*, August 28, 2013.

Monastersky, R. "Asian Pollution Drifts Over North America," *Science News*.

"NRDC Fights to Stop Mercury Pollution in China." Report, Natural Resources Defense Council International, April 2007.

Plumer, Brad. "Is U.S. Manufacturing Making a Comeback—Or Is It Just Hype?" *The Washington Post*—Wonkblog, May 1, 2013.

Reckard, E. Scott. "Chinese Investors Buying Up U.S. Golf Courses," *Los Angeles Times*, June 14, 2014.

"Reforming the Paper Industry." Natural Resources Defense Council, September 19, 2006.

Scott, Robert. "Unfair China Trade Costs Local Jobs," Economic Policy Institute, March 23, 2010.

Simons, Craig. "China's Rise Creates Clouds of U.S. Pollution," Stories, The Alicia Patterson Foundation, June 6, 2013.

Simpson, Bob. "Pollution Not an Issue for Samoa Pulp Mill," *The Humboldt Herald*, April 4, 2010.

Sims, Hank. "Samoa Pulp Mill Officially Dead," *The North Coast Journal*, Sept. 28, 2010.

Spegele, Brian. "U.S. Consumers Contribute, Not a Little, to Chinese Air Pollution," *The Wall Street Journal* China Realtime," January 21, 2014.

"The Pacific Dust Express." NASA—Science News, May 17, 2001.

"TRI Report for Samoa Mill, EPA, 2007," the Environmental Protection Agency.

Watson, Traci. "Air Pollution From Other Countries Drifts into USA," *USA Today*, March 13, 2005.

Weisskopf, Michael. "30 Years After Mercury Poisoning at Minamata: Ecological Disaster at Japan Village Leaves Legacy of Suffering," *The Washington Post/Los Angeles Times*, May 10, 1987.

Wood, Shelby. "China's Mercury Flushes into Oregon's Rivers," *The Oregonian*, November 24, 2006.

CHAPTER 16

"3.33 (Million) Hectares of Land Too Contaminated to Grow Food." *Shanghai Daily*," December 31, 2013.

"Beijing Destroys Barbecue Grills to Battle Air Pollution." Xinhua, November 26, 2013.

Chin, Josh. "Beijing's Next Target in Pollution Fight Is…. Barbecue?" *The Wall Street Journal*—China Realtime, May 14, 2013.

Chin, Josh. "Why China's State Soil Secrets Matter," *The Wall Street Journal*—China Realtime," February 28, 2013.

"China Air Quality Standards: Two-Thirds Of Cities Failing." Associated Press/*The Huffington Post*, March 2, 2012.

"China Making Biggest Moves In Global Nuclear Power Market in 2014, says GlobalData Analyst." GlobalData, August 20, 2014.

"China Media: New Year Haze." BBC News—China, February 11, 2013.

"China Targets Polluters with Judicial Action." Xinhua/People's Daily Online, June 18, 2013.

"China to 'Declare War' on Pollution, Premier Says," Reuters, March 5, 2014.

"China to Impose Limits on Six Industries to Tackle Air Pollution." Bloomberg News, February 19, 2013.

"China to Scrap Millions of Cars to Improve Air Quality," BBC News, May 26, 2014.

"China's Cement Industry to Face Tougher Emission Rules." Xinhua, May 24, 2013.

"Chinese Capital to Ban Coal Use to Curb Pollution," Reuters, August 4, 2014.

"Chinese Local Gov'ts to be Graded on Pollution Reduction," Xinhua, August 1, 2014.

Denyer, Simon. "In China's War on Bad Air, Government Decision to Release Data Gives Fresh Hope," *The Washington Post*, February 2, 2014.

Duggan, Jennifer. "China Deploys Drones to Spy on Polluting Industries," *The Guardian*, March 19, 2014.

Flanagan, Ed. "'Get Out': Over 1,000 Take to the Streets in China to Protest Oil Refinery," NBC News—*Behind the Wall* blog," May 16, 2013.

Gillis, Justin. "Heat-Trapping Gas Passes Milestone, Raising Fears," *The New York Times*, May 10, 2013.

"Hebei Tears Down 19 Steel Furnaces to Curb Air Pollution." CCTV.com English, February 24, 2014.

"Hundreds of Barbecues Destroyed in China's New Anti-Pollution Drive." Thestar.com (Toronto), November 27, 2013.

Hvistendahl, Mara. "China Rethinks the Death Penalty," *The New York Times*, July 8, 2014.

Koronowski, Ryan. "We're Number One: US Installed Most Wind Power in 2012, US Company GE Wind #1 Supplier," *Climate Progress*, March 27, 2013.

Kuo, Lily. "China Has a Spectacularly Silly New Plan to Fix its Pollution Problem," *Quartz*, February 21, 2013.

Lam, Sue Tip and Jing Jing Liu. Interview with Sue Tip Lam and Jing Jing Liu, Vermont Law School professors, March 27, 2013.

Linshi, Jack. "China Is Using Drones to Fight Pollution," *TIME*, July 2, 2014.

Ma, Wayne. "In Air Pollution Fight, Beijing Replaces BBQ with Burning Buses," The Wall Street Journal – China Realtime, May 7, 2014.

Ma, Wayne. "U.S. Firm Targeted Twice in Pollution Push," *The Wall Street Journal* – China Realtime, July 7, 2014.

Makinen, Julie. "Toxic Smog Hangs Over Large Swath of China But Many Ignore Threat," *Los Angeles Times*, February 25, 2014.

Moore, Scott M. "Pollution Without Revolution," *Foreign Affairs*, June 10, 2014.

Mufson, Steve. "China Wrestles with Stubborn Air Polluters," *The Washington Post*, May 10, 2013.

Phillips, Ari. "China Will Install More Soalr This Year Than The US Ever Has," *Climate Progress*, August 8, 2014.

Phillips, Tom. "Linfen: How China's Chernobyl Turned the Corner," *The Telegraph*, October 24, 2012.

"Polluting to Death: China Introduces Execution for Environmental Offenders." RT.com (formerly *Russia Today*), June 20, 2013.

"Protest Against Waste Plant in Hangzhou Turns Violent," Bloomberg News, May 10, 2014.

Qi, Liyan "China Vows Fresh Measures to Fight Air Pollution," *The Wall Street Journal*, June 14, 2013.

Ramzy, Austin. "Will Chinese New Year Fireworks Make Beijing's 'Crazy Bad' Air Worse?" *TIME*, February 8, 2013.

Shen, Samuel and Adam Jourdan. "Beijing Slashes Car Sales Quota in Anti-Pollution Drive," Reuters, November 5, 2013.

Sojung, Yoon. "Korea, China, Japan Make Joint Effort on Air Pollution," Korea.net, May 7, 2014.

Standaert, Michael. "China Supreme Court Established Special Environmental Tribunal to Combat Pollution," Bloomberg, July 10, 2014.

"The East is Grey." *The Economist.*

Wang, Feng, Cai Yong and Gu Baochang. "Population, Policy and Politics: How Will History Judge China's One Child Policy?" *Population and Development Review*, The Population Council, 2013.

Wee, Sui-Lee. "Man Becomes First to Sue Chinese Government Over Severe Smog," Reuters/*Chicago Tribune*, February 25, 2014

Wertime, David. "Chinese State Media Shares Powerful Map of 'Cancer Villages' Creeping Inland," *Tea Leaf Nation*, February 22, 2013.

Wong, Edward. "As Pollution Worsens in China, Solutions Succumb to Infighting," *The New York Times*, March 21, 2013.

Wong, Edward. "China Sees Long Road to Cleaning up Pollution," *The New York Times*, July 2, 2014.

Wong, Edward. "Most Chinese Cities Fail Pollution Standard, China Says," *The New York Times*, March 27, 2014.

Xin, Zheng. "Beijing Cracking Down on Illegal Barbecues," *China Daily USA*, May 14, 2013.

CHAPTER 17

"Air Pollution in China." Factsanddetails.com.

Anishchuk, Alexi. "As Putin looks east, China and Russia sign $400 billion gas deal," Reuters, May 21, 2014.

Chi-Jen, Yang. Interview with Chi-Jen Yang, Duke University Center on Global Change research scientist, November 25, 2013.

Chi-Jen, Yang and Robert B. Jackson. "China's Synthetic Natural Gas Revolution," *Nature Climate Change*, October 2013.

"China." Energy Information Agency, April 23, 2013.

"China Consumes Nearly as Much Coal as the Rest of the World Combined." Energy Information Agency, January 29, 2013.

"Coal Chemicals." Shenhua Group Corp., Ltd.,

"China Mongol Herders' Protest March Blocked." *World War 4 Report*, March 30, 2013.

Collins, D. "The Chinese Coal Boss Who Paid the 'Price of Cabbage'," *The China Money Report*, March 29, 2012.

Deng, Ping. Interview with Deng Ping, Greenpeace climate and energy campaigner in Beijing, August 30, 2013.

"Energy Market Recap." PIRA Energy Group, August 17, 2014.

Finamore, Barbara. Interview with Barbara Finamore, Natural Resources Defense Council senior attorney and Asia director, 2013.

Freese, Barbara. Interview with Barbara Freese, attorney and author of *Coal: A Human History*, 2013.

Fridley, David, Nina Zheng, Nan Zhou, Jing Ke, Ali Hasanbeigi, Bill Morrow and Lynn Price. *China Energy and Emissions Paths to 2030*, Lawrence Berkeley National Laboratory, August 2012.

Fuquiang, Yang. Interview with Fuqiang Yang, Natural Resources Defense Council senior advisor on energy, environment, and climate change in Beijing, August 30, 2013.

Hatton, Laura. "XGC88000 Breaks Another Record," *International Cranes & Specialized Transport*, November 14, 2013.

"International Energy Statistics." Energy Information Agency.

"Key developments since Thirsty Coal 2: Shenhua's Water Grab." Greenpeace, April 8, 2014.

Kolker, Allan, Mark Engle, Glenn Stracher, James Hower, Anupma Prakesh, Lawrence Radkey, Amoutter Schure and Ed Heffren. "Emissions from Coal Fires & Their Impact on the Environment," US Geological Survey, September 2009.

Krajick, Kevin. "Fire in the Hole: Raging in Mines from Pennsylvania to China, Coal fires Threaten Towns, Poison Air and Water, and Add to Global Warming," *Smithsonian Magazine*, May 5, 2005.

Lipes, Joshua. "Herders Blocked from Protest Marches to Beijing," Radio Free Asia, March 7, 2013.

Luo, Tianyi, Betsy Otto, and Andrew Maddocks. "Majority of China's Proposed Coal-Fired Power Plants Located in Water Stressed Regions," World Resources Institute, August 26, 2013.

Markey, Edward. Letter by Rep. Edward Markey to the US Government Accountability Office, April 24, 2012.

Martin, Richard. "China's Great Coal Migration," *Fortune*, July 11, 2014.

Northam, Jackie. "Russia-China Natural Gas Deal Likely To Reshape Energy Markets," NPR, May 29, 2014.

"One More Mongolian Herder Killed by the Chinese Defending His Grazing Land." Southern Mongolian Human Rights Information Center, August 20, 2013.

"Point of No Return: The Massive Climate Threats We Must Avoid." Greenpeace 2013.

Rui, Huaichuan, Richard K.,Morse and Gang He. "Remaking the World's Largest Coal Market: The Quest to Develop Large Coal-Power Bases in China," Stanford Program on Energy & Sustainable Development, December 2010.

Sexton, John and Li Pang. "Shenhua Coal-Chemical Base Takes Shape in Ningxia," China.org.cn, July 21, 2008.

"Shanxi Coal Boss Spends 70 Million on Daughter's Wedding." *China Daily*, March 29, 2012.

"Shenning Profile." Shenhua Ningxia Coal Industry Group.

"The End of China's Coal Boom." Greenpeace, April 2014.

"The True Cost of Coal: Coal Dust Storms: Toxic Wind." Greenpeace 2011.

"Thirsty Coal: A Water Crisis Exacerbated By China's New Mega Coal Power Bases." Greenpeace, August 2012.

"Thirsty Coal 2: Shenhua's Water Grab." Greenpeace, 2013.

Togochog, Enghebatu. Interview with Enghebatu Togochog, Southern Mongolian Human Rights Information Center, September 2, 2013.

"Total Primary Energy Supply: People's Republic of China." International Energy Agency, 2011.

"25% of U.S. Coal Exports Go to Asia, But Remain a Small Share of Asia's Total Coal Imports." Energy Information Agency, June 21, 2013.

"Update to the Murder of Bayanbaatar: Control Government Involved, Family Rejects." Southern Mongolian Human Rights Information Center, August 22, 2013.

Uzra Zeya. Acting Assistant Secretary, Bureau of Democracy, Human Rights, and Labor, Remarks, US State Department, US Embassy, Beijing, August 2, 2013.

EPILOGUE

"Summary for Policymakers." Intergovernmental Panel on Climate Change, 2013.

"12th Session of Working Group I Contribution to the IPCC Fifth Assessment Report Climate Change 2013: The Physical Science Basis, Summary for Policymakers." Intergovernmental Panel on Climate Change, September 27, 2013.

Blanchard, Ben. "Profile: Xi Jinping," BBC News, last updated June 5, 2013.

"Final Draft: IPCC WGII AR5 Summary for Policymakers: Climate Change 2014-Impacts, Adaptation, and Vulnerability." Intergovernmental Panel on Climate Change, October 28, 2013.

Fridley, David. Interview with David Fridley, Lawrence Berkeley Laboratory scientist, 2013.

Gore, Al. *An Inconvenient Truth.*

Hoffman, David E. *The Dead Hand: The Untold Story of the Cold War Arms Race and its Dangerous Legacy*, Anchor Books, 2009.

Kantor, Mickey. Interview.

Palmer, Martin. "Can Confucianism save China's environment?," *South China Morning Post*, August 6, 2013.

"Profile: China's President Xi Jinping," Reuters, July 2, 2013.

ACKNOWLEDGEMENTS

First off, we thank the Society of Environmental Journalists for a travel grant to China, and Michael and Annie Cacciotti for arranging meetings there that provided us insight into the nation's environmental crisis, as well as its culture, grassroots attitudes and policies. Among the many others deserving our gratitude are: Steven Q. Andrews, Sam Atwood, Jim Birakos, Barbara Briggs, Christie Baxter, Ben Beachy, Justin Chapman, Steven Cliff, David Coates, Steven Davis, Lifeng Fang, Barbara Finamore, Barbara Freese, David Fridley, Paul Goldberg, Usha Haley, Aaron Heifetz, Lauren Jacobs, Dan Jaffe, Bruce Jin, Barry Jones, Ma Jun, Mickey Kantor, Sue Tip-Lam, Haiquan Liu, Jing Jing Liu, Dan Mabe, J.R. McNeill, Karen Magliano, Asher Miller, David Petit, Deng Ping, Li Ping, Cecily Qu, Chen Quiliang, Enghebatu Togochog, Peter Ueberroth, Kevin Ummel, Zen Vuong, Morey Wolfson, Chi-Jen Yang, Fuqiang Yang, Chong Yu, Junfeng ("Jim") Zhang, and Zhu Zhiping. Our everlasting gratitude also extends closer to home, specifically to the gifted, hard-working folks at Rare Bird Books—the wondrous Tyson Cornell, Alice Marsh-Elmer, and Julia Callahan. Through thick and thin, their faith in us was our literary epoxy. Conceptual editor Seth Fischer, who continually reminded us to knit human struggle into the chemical narrative, was a Godsend unto himself.

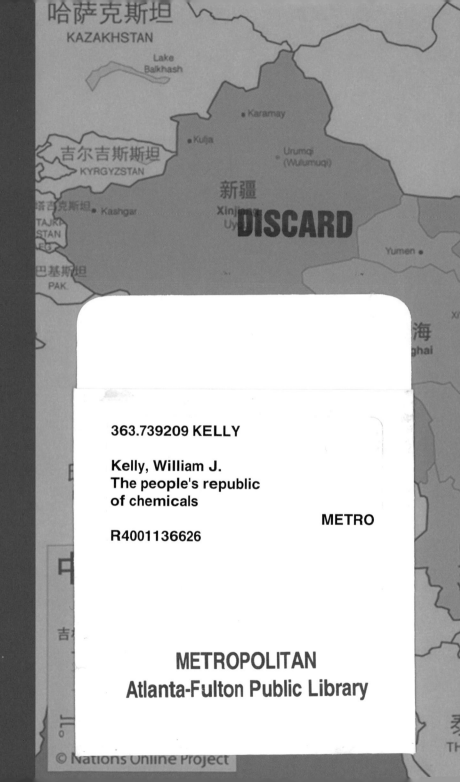